NATURAL SCIENCES
LIBRARY

UNIVERSITY OF WALES
SWANSEA

Outdoor Recreation and Resource Management

John Pigram

CROOM HELM London & Canberra
ST. MARTIN'S PRESS New York

© 1983 J. Pigram
Croom Helm Ltd, Provident House, Burrell Row,
Beckenham, Kent BR3 1AT

British Library Cataloguing in Publication Data
Pigram, John J
   Outdoor recreation and resources management.
   1. Outdoor recreation – Management
   I. Title
   796.068   GV191.66

ISBN 0-7099-2017-2

© 1983 J. Pigram
All rights reserved. For information write:
St. Martin's Press, Inc., 175 Fifth Avenue, New York, N.Y. 10010

First published in the United States of America in 1983

Library of Congress Cataloging in Publication Data

Pigram, John J.
   Outdoor recreation and resource management.
   1. Outdoor recreation – Management. 2. Outdoor
recreation. 3. Leisure. I. Title.
GV191.66.P53 1983   790'.06'9   83-2989
ISBN 0-312-59135-7

Printed and bound in Great Britain by
Biddles Ltd, Guildford and King's Lynn

CONTENTS

Contents

FIGURES

TABLES

PREFACE

The industrialised world is entering an important new era in which the dominant role traditionally given to work is being challenged by an altogether different human experience; the reality of leisure. Those fortunate enough to remain in the workforce continue to strive for and achieve more time off the job, while millions of others face redundancy as microelectronic technology eliminates the routine and repetitive tasks of the office and the factory floor. For both, an abundance of 'free time', whether voluntarily acquired or enforced, is becoming the norm and with it the opportunity and even the necessity to adjust to a way of life in which the emphasis has switched from work to leisure.

In most circumstances the availability of more time free from work might be considered a significant advance. Instead, for large sections of society, the acquisition of greater amounts of leisure is emerging as a major social problem. The work-habit has become so ingrained that coping with a jobless existence or with long periods of unobligated time can be a difficult process. It is this conditioning which makes employment so critical and which, in its absence, stimulates the search for some functional alternative to fill the void. One such alternative is recreation.

This book concerns itself with the implications of the 'leisure revolution' and in particular, with the potential of recreation to contribute to pleasurable, satisfying use of leisure time. Outdoor recreation is recognised as an important form of resource use and particular attention is given to the adequacy of the resource base to provide a quality environment for sustained recreational use. An underlying theme in the book is choice and the various influences and constraints which impinge upon informed choice of leisure activities. It is the expansion of choice through a diversity of leisure opportunities in which recreation planning and resource management are seen to play an essential part.

Material for the book has been drawn from North America, Britain, Europe and Australia to indicate the many resource issues involved in the allocation and use of extensive areas of land and water for outdoor recreation. Individual chapters are devoted to urban and rural recreation and national parks and tourism to illustrate the range of conflict situations which arise in specific settings, and the scope for application of recreation resource management in the minimisation of conflict.

Preface

The book aims to present a comprehensive, non-specialised introduction to the subject of outdoor recreation as an area both of academic study and real world relevance. Particular care has been taken to put forward a balanced, rational approach and to support this with an extensive list of references to recent work and publications in the field.

Much appreciated assistance in the preparation of the manuscript was given by Karoly Lockwood and with the cartography by Rudi Boskovic and other members of the cartographic unit at the University of New England.

1 PERSPECTIVES ON LEISURE AND OUTDOOR RECREATION

Leisure and Recreation

The term leisure means different things to different people. For some, leisure equates with the enjoyment and satisfaction associated with free-time activities and the word stirs up happy thoughts of the beach, the ball game or the bar. To others, leisure represents almost a spiritual condition or state of mind with the emphasis on self-expression and subjectively perceived freedom (Neulinger, 1982). For the latter, 'leisure lack' or the inability, for whatever reason, to experience this positive, highly desirable state is seen as an impairment of the meaning and quality of life.

Aristotle is said to have viewed leisure as 'the state of being free from the necessity to labour' (Farina, 1980: 27). Yet, the concept clearly implies more than the antithesis of work. The opposite to work is unemployment and lack of employment is not necessarily true leisure, as many of those currently laid off, unfortunately will agree. Such 'leisure-stricken' groups have effectively been denied the right to choose between work and leisure. For them, an abundance of unsought leisure is the norm. Frustration and anti-social behaviour can occur because of the difficulty of occupying this time with any meaningful activity. Enforced idleness as a result of unemployment, underemployment, redundancy or early retirement is rapidly becoming a fact of life in many countries; so much so that the work ethic which has typified society for generations may no longer be relevant to a changing world. However, imposing a leisure ethic in its place can only be appropriate if this new found leisure is acquired free of guilt, discomfort and anxiety about survival (Bannon, 1976).

Freedom is generally considered the hallmark of leisure and many commonly accepted definitions link the notion of leisure with free time; periods which are relatively free of economic, social or physical constraints. In these terms, leisure is a residual component comprising discretionary time over and beyond that needed for existence (Clawson and Knetsch, 1966). The problem with this point of view is that leisure may well be experienced *within* the context of primary role obligations. At least for a few fortunate people leisure and work can become indistinguishable. On the other hand, parents' leisure for example, may

1

be eroded if they feel *obliged* to use it for their children's amusement. The differentiating factors are freedom of choice and freedom from necessity to fulfil occupational and family duties and expectations (Farina, 1980).

Thus, perception of leisure depends very much on subjective, individual circumstances and the sharp distinction implied between discretionary time and time needed for existence is becoming blurred as leisure is seen to overlap with other uses of time (Figure 1.1). Despite

Figure 1.1: The Diffusion of Leisure Time

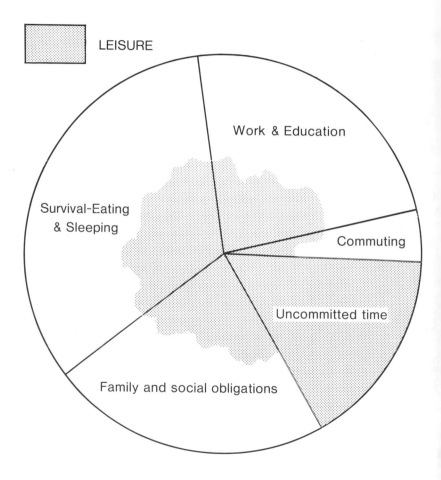

Source: Department of Environment, Housing and Community Development, 1977: 1.

these qualifications, it is probably true to say that for most people leisure remains closely associated with uncommitted time and this is the sense in which the concept generally will be applied in this discussion.

Further confusion can arise over the indiscriminate use of the terms 'leisure' and 'recreation'. The two are closely related and are often used interchangeably, but are not synonymous. The simplest distinction identifies recreation with *activity* and leisure with *time*. Recreation is considered to be activity voluntarily undertaken, primarily for pleasure and satisfaction, during leisure time. Whereas it is possible to conceive some jobs as also being recreative, the definition normally requires that no obligation, compulsion or economic incentive be attached to the activity. Recreation, therefore, contrasts with work, the mechanics of life and other activities to which people are normally highly committed. Certain activities are often thought of as inherently recreational. However, the distinguishing characteristic is not the activity or experience itself, but the attitude with which it is undertaken. To the professional, golf is an occupation; for the weekend golfer, presumably it is looked upon as recreation and sport, even though at times it can involve much physical effort and frustration.

Recreational pursuits are as diversified as the interests of man and because the concept is personal and subjective, value judgements as to the worth or 'moral soundness' of a particular activity are inappropriate (Godbey, 1981). However, for the majority, recreation implies revitalisation of the individual. Indeed, purists would argue that *recreation* is, or should be, the culmination of recreational activity – 'the activity is the medium: it is not the message' (Gray and Pelegrino, 1973: 6). If this were to be accepted, recreation could only be defined in terms of end-results and potentially recreative activities which, for whatever reason, fail to 'revitalise' the participant, would be excluded. Rather than attempt to split ends from means, it would seem more rational to identify recreation with *both* process and response and this is the interpretation adopted here.

Trends in Leisure

In past times leisure was the privilege of the elite, but today it has become the prerogative of the masses. Man's historical preoccupation with work as a means of livelihood appears to have been replaced by a new set of priorities geared towards the acquisition of more leisure.

Developed countries increasingly are faced with the situation of adjusting to and providing for a society orientated towards leisure rather than labour.

The origins of this social revolution can be traced primarily to the operation of socioeconomic and institutional forces and technological progress in reducing the necessity to work long hours for the maintenance of living standards. Progressive reductions in the working week, provision of more substantial periods of paid annual leave, and earlier retirement have meant that workers are now provided with lengthy segments of free time. The working week has been reduced from an estimated 70-hour, six-day week in the mid-nineteenth century to around 40 hours or less, spread over as little as four days. The right to generous periods of paid annual leave has been established with the addition, at least in countries such as Australia, of an additional holiday pay loading to enable workers to take better advantage of their vacations. Not only have work periods been reduced, but various peripheral activities such as travel time and lunch breaks may be incorporated into the paid working day, so that non-obligated time is increased. The age of retirement, too, has receded to the point where 60 is the accepted norm and even earlier retirement is commonplace.

In most circumstances it might be assumed that the availability of more hours free from work would be regarded as a significant social advance. Yet, for large sections of society the acquisition of greater amounts of leisure is emerging instead as a major social problem.

Leisure first became recognised as a cause for concern during the Great Depression of the 1930s. The concern continues and conferences on the subject of leisure and recreation have proliferated around the world. In 1981, for example, at least six major international meetings were scheduled around the leisure theme. These gatherings were sponsored by a diverse set of organisations ranging from academic bodies to professional administrators and marketing groups. Although most of the venues were in North America and Europe, one meeting took place in Brazil concerned with 'Leisure Prospects in Latin America' and a further congress devoted to the 'Sociology of Leisure' was scheduled for Mexico City in August, 1982.

Despite this, the problem of leisure remains essentially one for the developed world. Dower recognised the dimensions of the problem in 1965 when he described the leisure phenomenon as a 'fourth wave' comparable with the advent of industrialisation, the railway age, and urban sprawl. In the United States for example, calculations show that so far this century, American workers have gained about 800 hours of additional leisure time and should experience further substantial increases in leisure by the year 2000 (Dunn, 1976). A similar trend has been experienced in other parts of the developed world. For Britain, the Report of the Cobham Committee (1974) suggests an absolute rise in leisure time of one-fifth by the turn of the century, with consequent implications for the leisure industries and government in the provision of recreation opportunities. In France, leisure is increasingly recognised, both by providers and users, as a central life interest and the newly-elected Mitterand Government has gone so far as to establish a Ministry for Leisure (Hantrais, 1982). In Australia too, liberal working conditions are pervasive and Australians now work 31 days fewer than they did in 1947, an increase of 26 per cent in leisure time or an extra month off work each year. Current moves for a 35-hour week and three-day weekends will bring about even more fundamental changes and learning to live with this amount of leisure is predicted to become '*the* problem of the 1980s' for Australians (Whitlam, 1972).

Nor is concern necessarily confined to western societies. In the Soviet Union the working week had progressively declined to less than 40 hours by 1980. Leisure is now playing an increasingly important role in Soviet society despite some political manipulation (Riordan, 1982). Yet even in the closely-structured social order of the USSR, some misgivings have been expressed about the implications of this most recent 'revolution'.

Now that the most urgent material needs have been satisfied, an ever-widening section of Soviet society is displaying new and qualitatively different material and spiritual needs, among which one of the most important is the need for full-fledged and diversified use of leisure (Gerasimov *et al.*, 1971: 220).

The disadvantages of a leisured existence were foreseen by George Bernard Shaw who is reputed to have described a perpetual holiday as 'a good working definition of hell' (Gray and Pelegrino, 1973: 3). Shaw's assertion reflects the apparent psychological inability of modern man to cope with the monotony and burden of a non-structured existence. The fact that many people attempt to occupy their extra leisure with additional employment gives some substance to the notion that, for whatever reason, a life of leisure may not be the source of gratification it should be.

Work satisfaction does fulfil many human needs and undoubtedly, a minority of the workforce might be considered the reluctant victims of an abundance of leisure. However, for the majority, a reduction in work commitments must seem a highly desirable goal. At the same time, it is being realised that the overall amount of increased leisure gained is not the fundamental consideration, so much as the distribution of disposable time. Of practical importance in determining the recreational response is whether this time is concentrated or dispersed. Rodgers (1969) predicted that in Britain the workshift will replace the workday and the distinction between weekday and weekend will disappear as workers strive for more 'leisure-bunching' rather than a shorter working day. In Australia, for example, progressive reductions in working hours are being introduced by means of a 19-day month or a nine-day fortnight to maximise recreation opportunities. Although the compression of leisure into standard packages probably suits the convenience of both employers and employees, concentrated periods of use place great pressure on the recreation environment (Chapter 4). Therefore it would seem desirable, in the interests of recreation resource management, to devise a system of more flexible work patterns incorporating extended, but staggered blocks of disposable time.

Constraints on Leisure

Not all sections of society, even in the developed world, enjoy greater access to leisure. A broad group on whom increased leisure appears to have had considerably less impact is the female component of the population. The 'gender liberation' movement would claim that women experience unequal access to and participation in leisure as an inevitable consequence of 'sexist' policies in society.

> It is not that men's leisure is untramelled by any constraints . . . but rather that women's leisure carries greater constraints than men's leisure does. In addition, women's participation in leisure activities, especially those outside the home, is frequently dependent on their social and power relationships with men, especially whether men are willing to 'allow' women to engage in particular leisure pursuits (Deem, 1982: 32).

More generally, the problem appears to relate to an unequal incidence of leisure time. This contention is supported by a Canadian study which suggests that, although males have only a slight advantage in the total amount of leisure available, their free time tends to fall in larger blocks and during prime time such as evenings and at weekends (Heit and Malpass, 1975). As well, the burdens of household chores fall inequitably on married women who, rightly or wrongly, make up an increasing percentage of the workforce in western countries. In the United States in 1980, for example, the ratio of housewives to working women was 41 per cent to 59 per cent (Bartos, 1982). However, their leisure time is subject to considerable inroads from domestic commitments to the point where there may be no unobligated time left for personal pursuits. 'Weekends therefore become more a matter of overtime work for married women and more a matter of recreation for men' (Rapoport and Rapoport, 1975: 13).

For the workforce in general, the same technological progress and social advances which have permitted reductions in working hours have imposed pressures on the way this additional leisure is used. Lapage (1970) suggests that non-work discretionary time, ostensibly available for recreation, is constantly eroded by the time necessarily spent in commuting to work and in travel to and from sites for social purposes. More than 20 years ago, Wilensky (1961: 136) deplored the fact that leisure was spent '. . . commuting and waiting — hanging on the phone, standing in line, cruising for parking space'. Since then the picture has been further complicated by the effect of evolving social mores and changing life-styles, particularly of urban dwellers. Couples where both partners are working, for instance, require more ancillary time in the home for necessary chores and maintenance, so that hours set free from work are taken up with domestic tasks.

Moreover, in a materialistic and sophisticated society, leisure without affluence seems of little relevance. Preoccupation with material possessions can distort values away from the acceptance and simple enjoyment of leisure and the benefits of improved working conditions are often translated into money terms. Economic circumstances or personal inclination force a trade off between more free time and increased disposable income and can lead to the filling up of leisure hours with overtime or a second job. This in turn curtails the opportunity for recreative use of leisure

One of the paradoxes of leisure is that while time and money are *complementary* in the production of leisure activities, they are *competitive* in terms of the resources available to the individual. Some leisure time and some money to buy leisure goods and services are *both* needed before most leisure activities can be pursued (Martin and Mason, 1976: 62).

Bearing in mind the continuing emphasis on material possessions in a consumer-based society, there is little reason to expect an early reversal of this trend towards acquisition of leisure durables at the expense of leisure time. However, the pursuit of affluence is self-limiting to the extent that ultimately time is needed to make use of the possessions acquired, and that beyond a certain level, marginal tax rates usually ensure that additional income becomes an 'inferior good' compared with disposable time.

Sociocultural factors too can have a bearing on the appreciation of leisure and its use for recreation. Contrasting attitudes and value systems mean that some individuals and societies continue to equate leisure with frivolity and wasted time. For others, a hedonistic orientation which clearly ranks free time more highly than work appears to welcome the emergence of a leisured society without any sense of guilt.

In Australia, for example, at least one state (New South Wales) has its own Ministry for Leisure, Sport and Tourism and the pursuit of leisure is considered by some observers to be an enduring interest. Pearson (1977) relates this tendency to institutional arrangements biased towards greater amounts of disposable time and an environment with significant leisure potential. Certainly, the efforts of labour unions and enlightened social reformers and legislators have contributed to a relatively leisured existence for the great bulk of the population. Yet even in Australia, there is evidence of the persistence of a puritan work ethic, especially on the part of those new settlers who have migrated to the country since World War II from a different cultural background.

Such anti-leisure sentiment displayed by apparently compulsive workers is, of course, not restricted to Australia. Indeed, it could arise in any situation as a function of deficiencies in the leisure environment, rather than from a conviction of the necessity and desirability of work. These same deficiencies can inhibit recreative use of leisure time. The individual slumped in front of the television set may be there in part because of socioeconomic circumstances and inclination, but also because of the lack of a more constructive outlet for leisure. The physical and mental demands of work in an automated society emphasise the necessity for challenging and satisfying leisure pursuits. At the same time, the existence and apparent acceptance of a persistent core of permanently unemployed must be acknowledged, for whom the provision of satisfying recreational outlets is even a more urgent task. Yet the leisure environment very often cannot provide the opportunities needed for more positive use of disposable time, whether voluntarily acquired or enforced. Identification and remedy of such deficiencies are necessary for a fuller realisation of what this new-found leisure has to offer.

Patterns of Recreation

Despite contrasts noted earlier in the availability and appreciation of leisure, there is abundant evidence to demonstrate that, at least in developed countries, participation in outdoor recreation has spiralled in the postwar era. In Britain, the Cobham Committee reported that in 1973, active outdoor recreation activities took up about 19 per cent of leisure time and that this level was expected to grow by at least 25 per cent by the end of the century. Some growth estimates quoted in the report for particular activities are impressive, e.g. camping, + 64%; golf, +74%; motor sports, +42%; and 'something like a 10 to 15 per cent compound increase in the rate of recreational activity in the country- side' (Cobham Committee, 1974: xxi). Spectacular increases have also been noted in many European countries in swimming, angling and other water sports and in casual family activities such as picnicking and pleasure motoring (Hookway and Davidson, 1970).

In the United States, earlier predictions of recreation growth by the Outdoor Recreation Resources Review Commission are considered too low. Total participation in outdoor recreation is now expected to triple by the year 2000 (Figure 1.2). Trends in individual activities reveal some interesting adjustments in ranking from earlier estimates with greater emphasis on self-reliant, self-mobile, physical activities. Some activities with low *total* participation rates are not shown on the diagram, but are predicted to show even more marked increases. Wilder- ness recreation, for example, is estimated to rise by over 800 per cent by the year 2000 (Jubenville, 1976).

Recreation in Australia reflects similar trends with some interesting changes in specific types of leisure activities. Although recreation devel- opment probably lags behind the United States, statistics suggest an annual rate of expansion in recent years of some 12 per cent in areas such as water-based and wilderness recreation, camping, picknicking and tourism (Department of Environment, Housing and Community Development, 1977). Australia has long had an image as a sporting nation and there is some evidence to suggest that active participation in individualised sports is replacing passive spectator roles at team games. At the same time Australians are demonstrating an increase of interest in artistic, cultural and intellectual pursuits. However, much leisure

Figure 1.2: Participation in Outdoor Summer Recreation Activities, USA

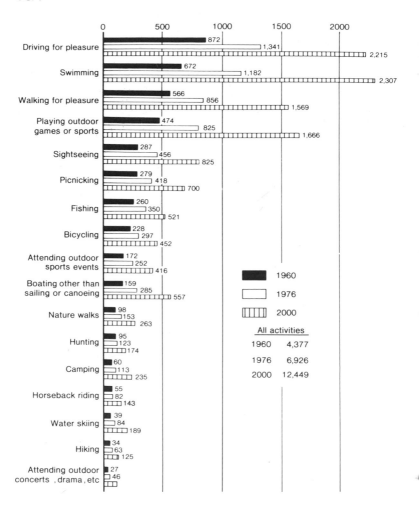

Source: Gold, 1980a: 164.

activity remains home-centred, perhaps also television-centred, a feature which may well be reinforced in the immediate future.

Clearly, the 'leisure explosion' which has occurred in the developed world has been parallelled by a striking upsurge in all levels of recreation activity. Institutional forces responsible for the redistribution of time already noted between work and leisure must account for some of this growth. However, technological and socioeconomic factors have also been influential.

Improved levels of mobility and awareness coupled with technological advances in equipment and infrastructure have expanded opportunities for recreation participation. At the same time, serious questions must be asked as to the continuation of these trends in the light of energy shortages and widespread inflation. Any reduction in discretionary income must have an effect on mobility and the manner and spatial pattern of recreation activity, if not total recreation participation (Table 1.1).

Table 1.1: Potential Effect of Fuel Prices on Mode of Vacation Travel in USA

	1979 Pricing	$1.00/ gallon	$1.25/ gallon	$1.50/ gallon	$2.00/ gallon
Automobile	60.7%	48.6%	31.8%	21.4%	17.1%
Pickup camper	5.4	5.0	2.1	1.1	1.1
Motor home	4.6	4.3	1.4	1.1	1.1
Travel trailer	5.7	5.0	2.9	1.4	1.4
Motorcycle	1.1	2.1	2.1	2.5	2.5
Plane	19.6	18.2	21.8	22.9	24.6
Bus	2.1	1.4	2.5	2.9	2.5
Train	2.1	2.5	3.2	3.2	3.2
No travel	0.0	14.3	33.6	45.0	47.9

Source: Williams *et al.*, 1979: 6.

Participation in recreation activity is also influenced by socioeconomic factors. Income and education, which are often reflected in occupation and correlate highly with car ownership, probably have the greatest impact on recreation. Demographic variables too, such as age, sex, family structure and diversity are of obvious importance in explaining recreation patterns. Participation tends to decline progressively with age and types of leisure pursuits change through the life cycle. An important demographic aspect is the general ageing of western societies, so that provision must be made for a less active, but growing segment of the population with excess leisure time (Table 1.2).

Thus institutional, technological and socioeconomic forces, together and separately, have had a significant influence on the emergence of recreation patterns in the developed world. Figure 1.3 indicates the probable position in relation to some of these factors during the period

Table 1.2: Projections on the Aged in Australia

	Total aged	Inc. on 1981 (%)	Proportion of population (%)
1981	1 759,238	—	11.8
1986	2,019,575	15	12.6
1991	2,290,990	30	13.3
1996	2,519,147	43	13.6
2001	2,745,233	56	13.8

Note: Aged population defined as females 60 years and over and males 65 years and over.
Source: Australian Bureau of Statistics, 1982.

1960-1985. However, it is difficult to generalise regarding their overall effect. The use of leisure varies spatially and temporally and participation in specific recreation activities fluctuates unpredictably with taste and fashion. More importantly, the concept of life-style might provide 'the essential key', as Rodgers (1969: 371) puts it, to an understanding of recreation behaviour.

Life-style is a phenomenon which subsumes demographic and socio-economic variables, race, personality, values, attitudes, religious beliefs and cultural heritage. So pervasive is life-style as a social indicator for determining leisure interests that Murphy (1974) recommends it as a basis for the structuring of services provided by recreation and leisure agencies. Edwards (1974) shares this point of view and suggests that 'leisure counselling' may even become necessary for the selection of appropriate leisure activities for particular life-styles. Such initiatives would have still greater relevance for those individuals and groups whose recreation outlets are limited by circumstances not experienced by the population at large. Minority groups, the handicapped, the unemployed, the elderly, even the so-called deviants, all have their own special leisure requirements.

A society that does not tolerate the minority or is intolerant of victimless deviant behavior is in danger of curbing creativity and the realization of mass leisure (Gold, 1974: 20).

For many in these categories, lack of status, money, mobility, ability and agility, access or awareness can all inhibit the purposeful use of leisure.

Figure 1.3: Factors Affecting Growth of Outdoor Recreation, 1960-85

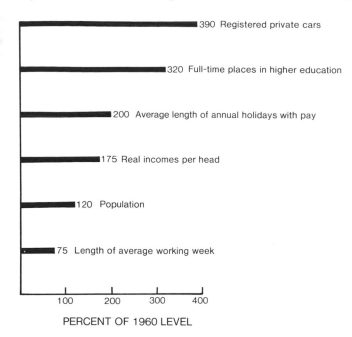

PERCENT OF 1960 LEVEL

Source: Seeley, 1973: 9

Outdoor Recreation and Space

The general upsurge in recreation which has accompanied the increased availability of disposable time throws into relief the various influences and constraints which impinge upon choice of leisure activities. Figure 1.4 presents a schematic presentation of the interrelationships between the characteristics of participants and the providers of recreation opportunities within the particular constraints of time, money and space. The authors make the point that some forms of recreation are *time* intensive, some are *money* intensive and some are *space* intensive; so that even where the necessary resources of *time and money* are adequate, certain activities will be inhibited if the *space* requirement is not met (Martin and Mason, 1976). It is this latter kind of situation for which most concern has been expressed (Coppock and Duffield, 1975; Jubenville, 1976; 1978).

For the resource manager in particular, the focus of interest is on

Figure 1.4: A Schematic Model of Leisure Choice

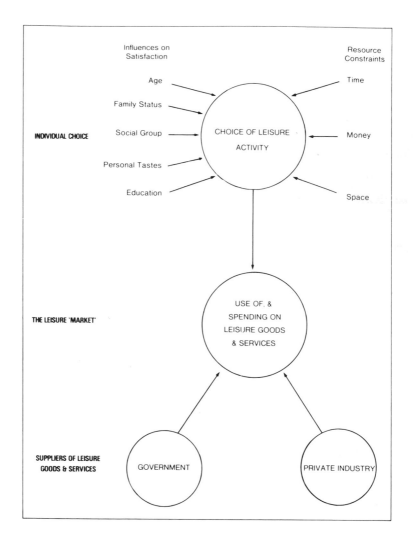

Source: Martin and Mason, 1976: 61.

active, informal, outdoor recreation; those activities carried on beyond the confines of a building or home. This is not meant to denigrate the use of free time for individual indoor pursuits such as reading and hobbies, or for formal, structured and institutionalised activities such as

organised sports. It simply recognises that the really important resource
issues arise with the allocation and use of extensive areas of land and
water for outdoor recreation. This is where space consumption and
spatial competition and conflict are most likely to occur; ' . . . it is in
this context that spatial organisation and spatial concerns become para-
mount' (Patmore, 1973: 225). By considering outdoor recreation as a
process in spatial organisation and interaction, the resource manager
can focus on those aspects with spatial implications, in particular,
imbalance or discordance between population-related demand and
environmentally-related supply of recreation opportunities and facilities
(Wolfe, 1964; Toyne, 1974). Obviously too, this is where the opportunities and the need for recreation resource management are greatest.

For too long, the subject of leisure has lacked the gloss of academic
respectability and acceptance (Murphy, 1963; Mercer, 1970). However,
increasingly, social scientists have come to realise the need for greater
professional involvement in matters of social relevance. The recognition of outdoor recreation as an important form of resource use in a
changing world has opened up challenging new fields for research.
Planning and management of physical and human resources to achieve
designed and desirable goals in the recreational use of leisure should
form an essential part of this initiative. To paraphrase Cosgrove and
Jackson (1972): If people spend as much time at leisure as they do at
work then the management of recreation resources and the study of
recreation behaviour are just as important as the study of mineral
resources and coalmining.

2 OUTDOOR RECREATION AND PEOPLE

The process of recreation resource management begins with people; they are at the heart of any recreation system. The demographic features, socioeconomic status and geographic distribution of community groups are fundamental inputs to the success of recreation development programmes. Insights into population characteristics are the key to understanding of trends in leisure behaviour and to ensuring that the planning of recreation opportunities is sensitive to the desires and aspirations of the recreation clientele. However, as with other aspects of human social behaviour, explanation of leisure behaviour is complex. Part of this complexity comes from confusion concerning the nature of recreation demand.

Recreation Demand

Miles and Seabrook (1977) point to the general lack of clarity in the application of the term 'demand' in recreational writing. In particular, there is an apparent inability to distinguish between the concept of demand in the broad, generic sense and its use to refer to the existing level of recreation activity. The latter, as indicated by numbers of participants and visitation rates, is not a true measure of demand, but relates to actual observed behaviour which may be only a component of overall aggregate demand.

Used generically, the term recreation demand is equated with an individual's preferences or desires, whether or not the individual has the economic and other resources necessary for their satisfaction (Driver and Brown, 1975). Recreation demand, so defined, is at the preference — aspiration — desire level, before it is expressed in overt, observable behaviour or participation. In this sense it is a propensity concept, reflecting potential or behavioural tendencies and is detached from subsequent recreation activity. As one authority puts it:

> Recreation demand is a conditional statement of the participation that would result . . . under a specific set of conditions and assumptions about an individual . . . and the availability of recreation resources . . . (US Bureau of Outdoor Recreation, 1975b: 10-22).

In particular, this broad notion of demand is supply — independent, assuming no constraints on recreation opportunities or access to them. In these terms, recreation demand depends only on the specific characteristics of the population, such as age, income, family structure, occupation and psychological parameters and not on the relative location of user groups, or the quality and capacity of facilities, or the ease of access (Kates, Peat, Marwick and Co, 1970).

However, actual consumption or participation in recreation activities is very much a function of the *supply* of those opportunities. Observed levels of leisure behaviour may conceal frustrated demand which can only be satisfied by the creation of new recreation opportunities or by increasing the capacity of existing facilities. If opportunities are less than ideal, people will actually participate less in recreation than their theoretical level of demand would indicate.

In the real world, therefore, recreation demand rarely equals participation. The difference between aggregate demand and actual participation (or effective, observed, revealed demand) is referred to as *latent* demand or latent participation — the unsatisfied component of demand that would be converted to participation if conditions of supply of recreation opportunities were brought to ideal levels (Figure 2.1).

Figure 2.1: Recreation Demand and Participation

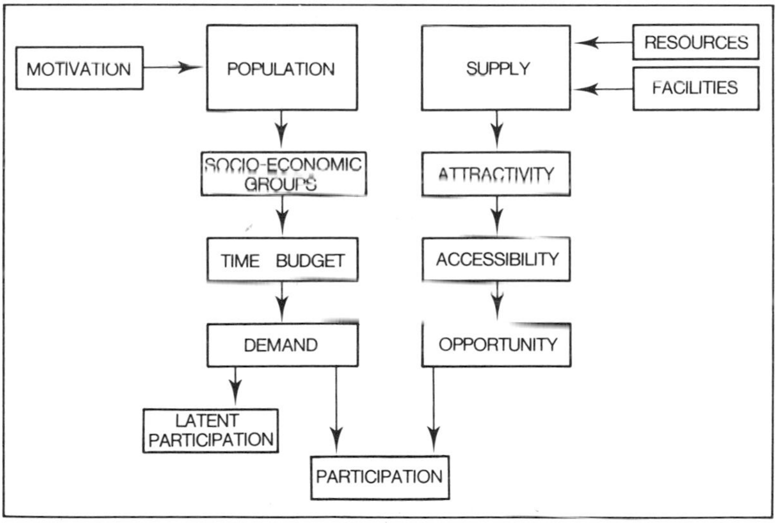

Source: Adapted from Kates, Peat, Marwick and Co, 1970: 1.1.

Knetsch (1972, 1974) has written at length on the confusion between recreation demand and participation, and the implications of such misinterpretation. It is not enough simply to look at what people *do* and interpret this as reflecting what they *want to do*; it also reflects what they are *able* to do. Participation data are important, but they must be interpreted in terms of both supply and demand variables. Knetsch (1972) points out, for example, that if the participation rate in swimming in a given area is found to be very large relative to that in some other area, it may be almost entirely due to greater availability of swimming opportunities. Adoption of attendance figures as a measure of demand confuses manifest behaviour with recreation propensities and preferences.

Nor is the problem merely one of semantics; the planning implications are clear for adjusting the supply of recreation opportunities and estimating the probable effect of alternative programmes and policies. It is important for planners to have answers to questions such as how much, what type and where, in regard to the introduction of new recreation facilities. Equating demand with existing consumption, i.e. participation rates, can lead to the assumption that people will want only increasing quantities of what they now have, ' . . . perpetuating the kind of facilities already existing in the areas already best served and further impoverishing already disadvantaged groups' (Knetsch, 1974: 20).

Another problem in relying upon past participation to guide future decisions is that observed activity patterns reveal little regarding satisfaction or the quality of the recreation experience.

> . . . when opportunities are available, particularly at little or no cost, they will be used. But use should not lead us to automatically assume people are satisfied with existing opportunities or that alternative opportunities might not have been even more sought after (Stankey, 1977a: 156).

A deeper understanding of the true nature of recreation demand would throw light on the reasons for non-participation or under-participation in specific areas and activities and reduce mis-allocation of resources. It should ensure also that any induced demand as a result of additional recreation investment is directed towards remedying these deficiencies. Not only can the supply of opportunities release latent participation and translate it into effective demand, but can be used to manipulate and redirect demand from one area or activity to another.

Mercer (1980a) gives several examples of induced, substitute, or diverted demand as the result of creation of new resources and improvements in access and technology. It should be noted, of course, that heightened levels of participation can just as readily be achieved by improvements in awareness and by education and training and similar 'triggers' (see below).

Awareness of the factors generating recreation demand and the relationships between its various components are important in recreation planning and resource management. That said, it is obvious that most attention in the social sciences has been devoted to recreation behaviour *per se*, i.e. to actual participation or *effective* demand. It is in the spatial and temporal expression of demand and the use made of specific sites and facilities where most of the resource problems exist. Whereas these patterns of use are derived in part from underlying preferences, they reflect also the availability, quality and effective location of recreation opportunities. Explanation of revealed recreation behaviour, therefore, must be sought in terms of the interaction between recreationists and the resource base.

Recreation Participation

A simplified representation of the factors which influence the decision to participate in recreation is set out in Figure 2.2. Once again a broad distinction can be made between the potential demand or propensity for recreation and the supply of opportunities to realise these preferences or desires. The variables can be grouped into the demographic, socioeconomic and situational characteristics which generate a propensity to recreate and those external factors which facilitate or constrain the decision and the choice of activities and site.

Demographic Characteristics

The size, distribution and structure of the population are of crucial significance in explaining recreation patterns. Age and sex, marital status and family composition or diversity, have all been recognised as affecting recreation preference.

At the aggregate level, important demographic considerations are the overall size and distribution of the population. Although population growth rates in Western countries remain low, significant shifts of population are taking place internally. The most widely publicised of these is migration from the Frost Belt to the Sun Belt States of North

Figure 2.2: The Decision Process in Outdoor Recreation

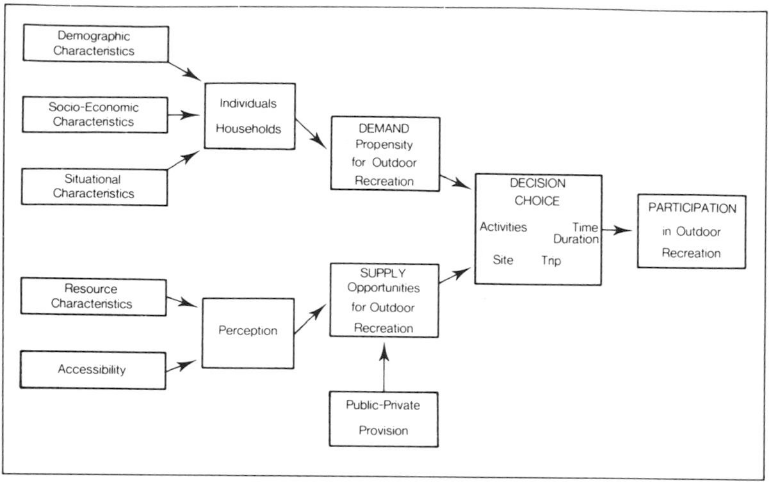

America. Whereas part of the attraction of the Sun Belt can be found in the outdoor recreation opportunities available, too rapid, unplanned growth in these areas may destroy the very qualities the newcomers are seeking (Heritage Conservation and Recreation Service, 1979).

At the disaggregated, individual, or family level, a good deal has been written on the effect of age and the progression of life from one phase to another through what is known as the life cycle. It has been suggested that although sharp lines of division cannot be drawn, certain preoccupations and interests predominate at specific stages in the life cycle. With regard to recreation, not only are preferences influenced by age, but also an individual's physical, mental and social ability to participate are affected.

It is clear that the recreational importance of each phase is closely related to the family framework and to other 'life event' phases in an individual's 'life career' (Mercer, 1981). Apart from the family setting, these include the broader cultural background, government policies and the mass media. Mercer emphasises that the average life span subsumes and obscures major traumas such as illness, divorce, bankruptcy and the so-called 'mid-life crisis'. Moreover, during any life episode recreation opportunities may be constrained by relative poverty, immobility and lack of time.

The implications of the family life cycle approach are that recreation requirements can be expected to vary from individual to individual and between different people at different stages of the cycle with important consequences for the planning and management of recreation space and resources. What is perhaps more important for current policy considerations is that significant demographic changes are even now taking place within the family life cycle and these, in turn, will generate altered priorities in the area of recreation provision.

In several countries of the Western world the most dramatic demographic changes are shifts in age structure, as the result, first, of the post-war 'baby boom' and subsequent 'baby bust' (Heritage Conservation and Recreation Service, 1979). As these ripples move into maturity and beyond, so their influence is reflected in recreation patterns and resource managers need to be alert if a rapid and appropriate response is to be made. The changing status (some would say demise) of the family in modern society is another factor affecting individual and community participation in recreation. The prevalence of working couples and the freeing of women (noted in Chapter 1) from many pre-existing constraints are gradually blurring sex-related differences in recreation participation. Earlier marriage, childless couples, ummarried couples living together and elderly people living alone, all contribute to the growing complexity of 'family' life to which recreation planning must adapt.

Finally, there is the emergence of a significant elderly and retired component in the population, for whom greater longevity, improved health care and better financial provision generate a new set of leisure opportunities and requirements. This takes on greater significance because of the high concentrations of older people in particular areas. Mercer (1980a) identifies several localities in Australia, in particular the Gold Coast of southern Queensland, as geriatric colonies, with above average numbers of retired people. However, retirement migration in Australia is not yet as pronounced in its regional effects as on the south coast of England, known as *Costa Geriatrica* nor as in Florida where the aged make up 16 per cent of the populaton (Howe, 1980). As Mercer (1980a) points out, such ageing of the population can occur very rapidly and when accompanied by departure of the youth in search of employment or excitement, can give rise to a succession of strains and imbalances in the community.

Socioeconomic Characteristics

Among the factors which influence the desires or inclinations of individuals for recreation are social relationships and social structure, education, occupation and income.

Recreation is a form of social interaction and the way in which a society is organised affects recreation behaviour. Interaction among families, peer groups and ethnic communities helps mould many facets of human behaviour including goals and motivations for use of leisure.

Levels of education too, whether considered in formal, structured terms or as incidental improvements in awareness and knowledge, must have a pronounced influence on actual recreation behaviour. Indeed, the emphasis on advertising and marketing in the leisure industries reflects this relationship and the efforts made by commercial enterprises to convince patrons of the quality of their attractions are themselves a form of education.

However, Mercer (1977) questions whether this correlation is causal when it comes to determining underlying propensities for recreation. The fact that the more highly educated person is likely to be more recreationally active may only reflect further correlation with a higher status occupation and reinforce already present income and class differences. As with so many of the factors impinging upon recreation *demand* there is a degree of overlap, both with other influential factors and with the process of expression of demand through participation. Education contributes to knowledge, awareness and the development of attitudes and values, which in turn may generate aspirations and desires for recreation. At the same time, the acquisition of recreational skills through education can enhance opportunities for participation and for gaining satisfaction from recreation.

A similar problem occurs with income and occupation, each already highly correlated with the other. Undoubtedly, the amount of discretionary income available to an individual or family is a major factor affecting recreation participation, but does it help structure underlying recreation preferences? Do well-to-do people really prefer active outdoor recreation activities or does their wealth and associated possessions merely open doors closed to the less affluent? Again, the former sharp distinction in attitudes to work and leisure between high status occupations and manual workers is becoming blurred. No longer can it be said with certainty that upper class occupational groups show a preference for a more serious range of leisure pursuits or view with disdain the thought of more mundane forms of recreation.

Situational Characteristics

The third group of factors which impinge upon recreational choice is linked to some of those previously discussed and shows similar ambivalence. Under the category of situational or environmental factors could be placed:

Residence — which incorporates such aspects as location, type, lot size and existence of a garden and which, to some extent, are again a function of income and occupation. At a larger scale the place of residence can influence recreation patterns. Obvious examples are coastal locations, winter sports areas and large urban centres.

Time — which also frequently reflects occupation, although this is changing with innovations in working conditions and the high incidence of unemployment. It is not merely the amount of time but its incidence in terms of usable 'blocks' at convenient periods, e.g. weekends. In general, self-employed persons have greater control over their time budgets and are, or should be, in a position to allocate more time to leisure. This, in turn, has the potential to widen the dimensions of recreation demand.

Mobility — which, for most people, freely translates to car ownership or access to a motor vehicle. If a vehicle is not available a person's recreation action space is obviously limited, in terms of choice of site, journey, timing and duration of trip. Presumably, too, possession of a car generates a desire, or at least permits a propensity for, forms of recreation which otherwise could not be considered.

External Factors

As noted above, some of the variables which are considered important in determining an underlying proclivity for recreation, can also be influential in the actual decision to participate. Several of the socio-economic and situational factors, for example, appear to operate at several stages of the decision-making process. In addition, the role of resource-related characteristics is indicated in Figure 2.2 and these have direct relevance to choice of recreation site, activities and travel.

These factors are concerned with the *opportunity* to recreate; to *activate* latent participation. Opportunity depends upon the inter-related features of availability and accessibility of recreation resources or sites. The nature of recreation resources is discussed in the following chapter, but their availability in functional terms depends upon such things as quality, degree of development, carrying capacity, ownership, distribution and access.These, in turn, reflect economic, behavioural and political factors which help shape public and private decision making about recreation provision.

Accessibility to recreation opportunities is a key influence on participation and its several facets are examined in ensuing chapters. Its importance as the final deciding factor in determining the 'what' and 'where' of recreation participation is stressed by Chubb and Chubb:

If all other external and personal factors favor people taking part in an activity but problems with access to the necessary recreation resources make participation impossible, the favorable external and personal factors are of no consequence (Chubb and Chubb, 1981: 153).

Gateway National Recreation Area at the entrance of New York Harbour is a good example. The only effective access to the area is by automobile and many would-be-users must share the view of one frustrated New Yorker quoted as saying: 'What good is a $300 million park to that half of the people who can't get out to it?' (Howard and Crompton, 1980: 364).

It is the interaction of such environmentally-related *supply* factors with demographic, socioeconomic and situational variables, or population-related *demand* factors, which generates *opportunities* to *participate* in recreation. However, recreation decisions depend not on actual objective opportunities but on individual perception of those opportunities, which in turn depends greatly on formal and informal social and information networks and on the personal characteristics of potential recreationists (US Bureau of Outdoor Recreation, 1975b).

Perception of Recreation Opportunity

Predictions regarding recreation behaviour would be of greater reliability if more was known about attitudes, motivations and perceptions which affect recreation decision making. This kind of information would help explain why certain activities, sites and routeways are favoured; why some attractions are failures while others provide satisfaction and even draw excess patronage; how and why alternative recreation opportunities are ranked and so on. The process of choice of recreation activities and location is influenced by an individual's perception of what opportunities are perceived as being available. In other words, a predisposition for recreation is translated into actual participation through a choice mechanism heavily dependent upon perception of the recreation opportunity and experience on offer (Elson, 1973).

Perceptions (or personal mental constructs) are a function of the perceiver's past experience, present values, motivation and needs. Information levels, as well as other factors which have a bearing upon the ability to use that information (including personality characteristics, e.g. shyness or aversion to risk) also help structure evaluative beliefs and mental images concerning the nature and quality of anticipated recreation sites, trips and activities. Perception operates over several dimensions and various scales in recreation decision making and initial mental constructs may be confirmed or revised as a result of further spatial search and learning.

Outdoor recreation by definition is resource-related and increasing attention is being given to the 'setting' in which action takes place as a prime influence on perception and on the pleasure gained from the ensuing recreation experience. Environmental psychologists (Barker, 1968; Ittelson, *et al.*, 1976; Levy, 1979) suggest that all human behaviour should be interpreted with reference to the ecological environment or behaviour setting in which it occurs. Given a knowledge of the behaviour setting for a specific recreation experience, such as a park visit, it should be possible to identify the human values and expectations associated with the experience. Examination of the human and non-human attributes of the behaviour setting should indicate those contributing to and detracting from social satisfaction. It is, of course, the interaction of the environment with users which is fundamental; which 'turns people on'. All recreation environments affect recreation behaviour in some way and with insight into recreation preferences, can be structured to facilitate expression of demand through participation (Hecock, 1970).

The Recreation Opportunity Spectrum

Allied to behaviour setting analysis is the concept of the Recreation Opportunity Spectrum (Clark and Stankey, 1979; Wood, 1980). Once again, the focus is on the setting in which recreation occurs. The recreation opportunity spectrum describes the range of recreational experiences which could be demanded by a potential user clientele if a full array of recreation opportunity settings was available through time. Clark and Stankey (1979) define a recreation opportunity setting as:

> . . . the combination of physical, biological, social and managerial conditions that give value to a place (for recreation purposes). Thus, a recreation opportunity setting includes those qualities provided by nature (vegetation, landscape, topography, scenery), qualities associated with recreational use (levels and types of use) and conditions provided by management (roads, developments, regulations). By combining variations of these qualities and conditions, management can provide a variety of opportunities for recreationists (Clark

and Stankey, 1979: 1).

The basic premiss underlying the concept of the recreation opportunity spectrum is that a range of such settings is required to provide
for the many tastes and preferences that motivate people to participate
in outdoor recreation. Quality recreation experiences can be best
assured by providing a diverse set of recreation opportunities. Failure to
provide diversity and flexibility ignores consideration of equity and
social welfare and invites charges of discrimination and elitism (Clark
and Stankey, 1979). A sufficiently broad recreation opportunity
spectrum should be capable of handling changes or disturbances in the
recreation system stemming from such factors as social change, e.g. in
demographic characteristics, or technological innovations, e.g. all-
terrain recreation vehicles (Stankey, 1982).

The recreation opportunity spectrum offers a framework within
which to examine the effect of manipulating environmental and situational attributes or factors to produce different recreation opportunity
settings. Clark and Stankey (1979) suggest that the most important of
these 'opportunity factors' are: access; other non-recreational resource
uses; on-site management; social interaction; acceptability of visitor
impacts; and acceptable regimentation. Some of these factors are discussed in greater detail in later chapters. In particular, it should be
noted that the weight or importance given to each will vary with individual circumstances.

The range of conditions to which an opportunity factor can be subjected and the way each can be managed to achieve desired objectives
are shown in Figure 2.3. By packaging a recreation opportunity setting
in some combination of the six factors described, a variety of recreation
opportunities or options can be generated and the recreation opportunity spectrum materially enlarged. In their scenario the authors
present only four generic opportunity types arrayed along a 'modern
to primitive opportunity continuum'. However, within each there is
scope for many complex combinations thus providing even more
diversity.

The recreation opportunity spectrum also allows an examination of
opportunity settings with respect to the capability of potential users
to avail themselves of the opportunities presented. Limited resources
and perhaps lack of awareness or imagination mean that, generally
speaking, the established recreation system caters for the majority, on
the premiss apparently that everyone is young, healthy, ambulant,
educated, equal and possesses the means to participate. The reality, of

Figure 2.3: Management Factors Defining Recreation Opportunity Settings

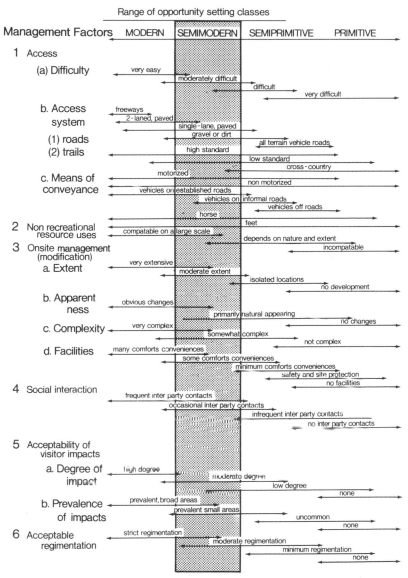

ACCEPTABLE COMBINATIONS FOR SEMIMODERN OPPORTUNITIES

Source: Clark and Stankey, 1979: 15.

course, is very different. Reference has already been made to constraints on recreation because of age and lack of income or other possessions. Racial and ethnic origins likewise can be a disadvantage, particularly in inner cities where these minorities are often concentrated. Increasing efforts have lately been directed especially towards improving recreation opportunities for the mentally and physically disabled.

Recreation and the Disabled

In the past few years public attention has been drawn to the problems facing disabled and handicapped people in society and changing attitudes are gradually emerging in the areas of health, transportation, education, employment, architecture and now, recreation. This culminated in 1981 in the United Nations International Year of Disabled Persons.

A handicapped person has been defined as one 'whose physical, mental and/or social well-being is temporarily or permanently impaired . . . ' (Calder, 1974: 7.3). It is perhaps proper to distinguish between functional *disability* as a result of primary impairment and *handicap* which is determined by individual and societal reaction to limitations on social roles and relationships. However, for simplicity, the two terms will be used interchangeably in this discussion. In terms of the above definition, nearly ten per cent of the population of Australia, for example, suffer from handicaps which restrict their activities and mobility, i.e. about 1.5 million people. In the United States it is estimated that approximately 36 million disabled persons do not enjoy equal access to recreation facilities and programmes (Heritage Conservation and Recreation Service, 1979). These figures are likely to increase in similar Western countries as advances in medical care prolong the lives of many who, in earlier times, may not have survived accidents or sickness.

Chubb and Chubb (1981) present a useful summary of the effects of disabilities on participation in recreation. The conditions and characteristics listed range from left-handedness, allergies and aberrations of body size, through impaired manual dexterity and mental retardation, to physical disabilities including sensory impairment. In the area of outdoor recreation most emphasis has been given to this last category, especially to those affected by constraints on mobility and access and impaired sight and hearing. Recreation assumes great importance in the lives of such people who often have a greater proportion of leisure time then most other people. Yet opportunities to participate, restricted in the first place by disability, are often worsened by building and design standards and regulations and requirements drawn up only with able-bodied people in mind.

The dimensions of the recreation opportunity spectrum for handicapped persons are limited by what have been termed 'environmental barriers', which are taken to include architectural barriers, transportation problems and societal attitudes (Calder, 1974). Recreation participation and spectator opportunities for the handicapped are seriously impaired by almost insurmountable barriers of one kind or another built in to the design and construction of public and private buildings, national parks and playgrounds and other recreation sites and facilities. For a person in a wheelchair, a six-inch (approx. 15 cm) kerb on a footpath is as great an obstacle as a six-foot (approx. 1.8 m) wall would be for others. Steps, escalators and narrow entrances all effectively deny access for many classes of handicapped persons. Transportation, likewise, is often inaccessible to the handicapped because of unsuitable design, inadequate services or lack of appropriate facilities, especially space.

In many circumstances relatively simple and cheap adjustments may be all that is necessary to change the access situation for the better. Interesting developments are taking place in several countries in making recreation more readily available to the disabled. In USA the Third Nationwide Outdoor Recreation Plan (Heritage Conservation and Recreation Service, 1979) included a Task Force Report on the recreation needs of the handicapped and this led to the preparation of a comprehensive 'Guide to Designing Accessible Outdoor Recreation Facilities', including picnic sites, campgrounds, trails, swimming and fishing sites, playgrounds and historic sites (Heritage Conservation and Recreation Service, 1980). The US National Park Service has also recognised the problem and has adopted guidelines to improve accessibility for the blind and those in wheelchairs (Goldthorpe, 1980). Existing structures have been converted where feasible and most new facilities and services, including interpretative material, are designed to cater for the handicapped.

In Britain, an ambitious project, yet involving only a modest outlay, demonstrated how an outdoor nature trail could be used effectively and enjoyably by the blind, as well as by sighted people (Countryside Commission, 1973a). Features along the trail were identified using embossed lettering, a variety of firm walking surfaces was constructed, taped commentaries were provided to aid in interpretation of bird calls and scented shrubs and a small museum were installed housing exhibits displayed with blind people in mind. The exhibits largely comprised items which could readily be handled, such as distinctive rock specimens, small stuffed animals, birds' nests and eggs and sections of tree trunks, bark, leaves and pine cones. It is a matter for regret that this trail has since closed because of relative inaccessibility and consequent lack of use. However, a great deal of effort is being devoted to providing similar facilities for handicapped people in Britain (Countryside Recreation Management Association, 1979).

Technical and mechanistic approaches are only part of the solution. Attitudinal barriers within the community also have a marked influence on the ease with which the disabled can participate in recreation. In general, society discriminates against the handicapped as a minority group and because of misinformation and misconceptions, stereotypes the disabled as being incapable, unproductive and in need of protection (Calder, 1974). The attitude of the disabled also has a bearing on their ability to make good use of what opportunities do exist. Problems of adaptation, education and retraining, especially where the onset of the handicapped condition is sudden, can reinforce already difficult circumstances which tend to exclude these people from the normal leisure experiences enjoyed by the wider community.

The discussion of the recreation opportunities for a particular disadvantaged group — the disabled — helps illustrate the broad application of the recreation opportunity spectrum concept as a technique in recreation resource planning and management. However, as will be stressed repeatedly throughout these pages, interaction of people with resources is two-way. Understanding of recreation behaviour and participation patterns certainly calls for examination of recreation opportunity settings and the remedying of deficiencies therein. It also demands appreciation of the characteristics of potential user groups and, especially, awareness of any particular human conditions or requirements which may detract from the recreation experience.

Recreation Travel Behaviour

Recreation travel may be depicted as a process in spatial interaction. This implies that space and distance separate recreationists from the sites and activities to which they wish to relate. Spatial interaction is stimulated as efforts are made to reduce spatial deterrents and offset spatial imbalance in recreational opportunities. The ease and difficulty of movement and communications are basic to the explanation of spatial interaction. Mobility and information diffusion thus become key elements in the spatial relationship between recreationists at the origin, e.g. place of residence and the destination, i.e. the recreation site.

The 'friction of distance' is important in all forms of recreation travel and for most movements a 'distance-decay effect' can be recognised so that the strength of interaction declines as distance increases. Put simply, this means that recreation sites at a greater distance, or for which the journey is *perceived* as involving more time, effort or cost, are patronised less. However, the effect of the friction of distance varies spatially and with modes of movement and types of recreation activity. It can also change dramatically over time and space with technological advances in transportation.

Wolfe (1972) points out that for some forms of recreation travel, distance itself affects perception of distance. The distance-decay effect may be heightened, which manifests itself in *inertia* or the reluctance to move at all. Alternatively, the reaction to distance may be in marginal terms. In most cases, the effect of distance will be negative, in that beyond some point, further travel becomes less desirable; each kilometre offers more resistance or impedance than the last. Conversely, the effect may be *positive*, where the friction of distance is reversed; for some people and some occasions, e.g. ocean cruises, travel becomes so stimulating as an integral part of the recreation experience, that the further the distance, the greater the desire to prolong it.

The movement linking residence or workplace to the recreation site has been aptly described as 'the journey to play' (Patmore, 1974). Whereas the trip itself can be a recreation event in its own right, it also forms an important part of the overall recreation experience. Recreation travel comprises an integral component of Clawson's depiction of the recreation experience (Figure 2.4) and his model provides a useful framework for reviewing the role of perception and choice during each phase of that experience (Mercer, 1971a).

In the anticipation phase various options are canvassed in the light of motivations, goals, previous experience, information levels and constraints especially of time, income and mobility. Perception of the type of people, the trip and the activities associated with a particular recreation site obviously influence decision making during this stage.

Of the travel phases, Clawson wrote: 'we know very little about travel either way and still less about differences according to the

Figure 2.4: The Clawson 5-Phase Model of the Recreation Experience

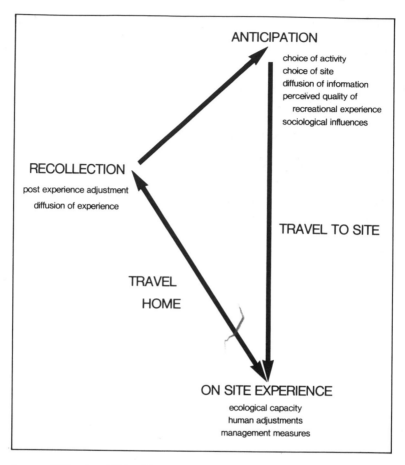

ANTICIPATION

choice of activity
choice of site
diffusion of information
perceived quality of
      recreational experience
sociological influences

RECOLLECTION

post experience adjustment
diffusion of experience

TRAVEL TO SITE

TRAVEL
HOME

ON SITE EXPERIENCE

ecological capacity
human adjustments
management measures

Source: O'Riordan, 1970: 152.

direction of travel' (Clawson, 1963: 42). As has been noted above, the problem rests with the conflicting ways in which distance may be perceived — positively or negatively — and the influence of perception on the aspects of travel open to choice e.g. mode, route, duration, cost, group, etc. Reaction to distance is again fundamental. In some circumstances it can be seen as a utility with intervening opportunities viewed as stepping stones rather than barriers (Mercer, 1971a). Perception varies also with the direction of travel. Different motivations and states of mind operate during travel to and travel from the site. Familiarity of the route, the road and traffic conditions, likewise, can be important.

A major aspect of the on-site phase is the attractiveness of the setting and the capacity of its attributes and facilities to promote satisfaction. Once again, generalisation becomes difficult because the same set of environmental features are perceived differently by different users. In this phase, too, aspects of environmental capacity impinge upon perception. However, whether the recreational experience is enhanced or impaired as a result, depends upon the subjective, personal reaction of individuals.

The recollection phase is marked by a review of the extent to which the several phases of the recreation experience contributed to overall satisfaction. Perception is important at this stage because of its influence on future choice. As Mercer (1971: 271) points out: 'recreation behaviour can be viewed as a continual temporal and spatial learning or adjustment process . . . ' and recollected pleasant and unpleasant episodes may well influence the perception and choice of others as well.

Consideration of Clawson's model brings out the effect of travel on recreation behaviour and its key role in the satisfaction gained from total recreation experience. The journey can 'make or break' the outing and it is often the individual's perception of what is involved in the travel phases which is the crucial factor in the decision to participate or stay at home.

Recreation travel, in common with all aspects of recreation, is discretionary in nature in that it lacks the orderliness and monotony of, for instance, the journey to work. Yet, certain regularities can be discerned in recreation movement patterns in response to time-distance, direction, connection and network bias (Cox, 1972).

Time-distance bias, where the intensity of movement is an inverse function of travel time and distance, reveals itself in the distance-decay effect referred to earlier. Despite aberrations concerning the role of distance in recreation travel, day and half-day excursions involving journeys of between five and 50 miles (approx. 8 km to 80 km), are the most popular form of outdoor recreation especially for city and suburban dwellers with access to cars (Patmore, 1972). Distance is constrained (or 'biased') by the time available and the type of recreation envisaged (Figure 2.5).

Distance is also the basis for determining the extent of urban recreation hinterlands (Campbell, 1966). In terms of travel distance it is possible to conceptualise recreation traffic movements by a series of concentric rings progressively distant from the city to distinguish between day-trips, weekend trips and vacations (Mercer, 1970b). This

Figure 2.5: Recreation Travel by Toronto Residents

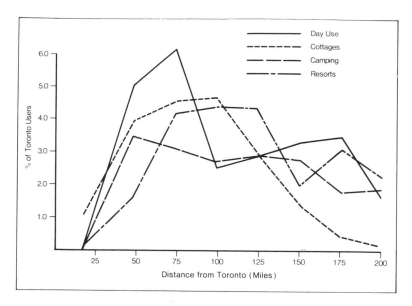

Source: Greer and Wall, 1979: 243.

structure corresponds to Rajotte's (1975) model of peri-urban recreation zones in which intensity of recreation is related to travel time-distance from the centre (Figure 2.6). There is clearly scope for overlap between zones and such an arrangement may represent an oversimplification in an era of more sophisticated and efficient transportation systems.

Direction or orientation bias can also occur in recreation travel when movement or the intensity of movement is related to direction. In the first place, because interaction for economic purposes or with other population groups is normally not the primary goal of trip-makers, recreational travel is unidirectional. Traffic is generated at the origin, usually an urbanised area and drawn to the recreation site by dissimilar and perceivedly attractive physical circumstances. There is no reverse movement, apart from return trips after the recreation outing (Dent, 1974).

Mercer (1971b) also detected directional bias in a study of recreational trips centred on the city of Melbourne, Australia. It was found that desire-lines for day-trips out of the city were orientated or biased according to the individual's awareness of a particular wedge of the

Figure 2.6: Relationship between Peri-urban Recreational Zones and
Travel-Time Distance

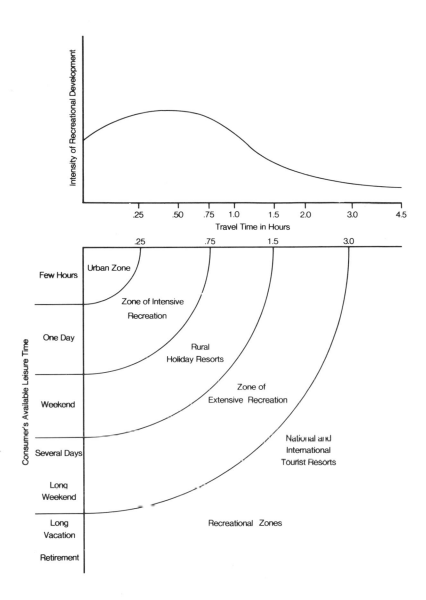

Source: Adapted from Rajotte, 1975: 44.

urban area and hinterland. Recreational travel was orientated away from the downtown area, which was perceived as a barrier by all except central city residents and towards the relative proximity of the rural environment. Recreationists' mental maps became progressively more narrowly defined towards the periphery and assumed a wedge-like form associated with a few familiar outlet arteries and static recreation resources such as beaches.

Connectivity, and conversely barriers to movement, is another important aspect of transferability affecting the means or ease of spatial interaction. The presence or absence of interaction and the intensity of recreation travel, are related to the existence and capacity of connecting channels of traffic flow. Recreational trip making will respond positively or negatively to alterations in connectivity between origin and destination. An additional traffic facility, such as a motor bypass, a bridge or a tunnel, can transform locational relationships by providing new or improved connections between places. Removal of linkages (such as destruction of a bridge) or impairment of capacity will lead to drastic alteration in patterns of recreation movement and the resulting redistribution of traffic pressure can generate severe adjustments in dependent services and enterprises. Any number of examples exist where new communities and recreation facilities have sprung up and established sites have gone into decline because of alterations to pre-existing routes and modes of movement. Closure of railway lines, relocation of river crossings, construction of highway-motorway bypasses, even the conversion of streets to one-way traffic, can all have dramatic effects on recreation travel behaviour.

Finally, part of the explanation for regularities in recreation movements can be found in the characteristics of existing communications networks. Acording to Cox (1972), spatial interaction is more likely between places belonging to the same network than if they belong to different networks. Presumably, this holds for recreational travel where networks can relate to shared information channels, a common transport system or the same sociocultural, national, political or even religious grouping. The huge volume of tourist flows based on group tours is but one example of the influence of network bias in promoting recreation travel on a large scale. The network effect, too, can be heightened by constraints on expansion of links within or between systems, such as occurs with national boundaries or language barriers.

Despite the regularities noted above, the essentially discretionary nature of recreation movements and the element of unpredictability present put some difficulties in the way of developing an efficient and economic system of management for the special characteristics of recreation travel. Particular problems are the incidence of peaking and variability in participation and the heavy reliance placed on the motor vehicle. Patterns of recreation movement display daily, periodic and seasonal peaks and troughs, associated with time of day, weekends, vacations and suitable weather especially in the summer season. Some of these peaks are cyclical and to that extent predictable. However, the problem remains of providing a transport system which can cope with short periods of saturation set against longer periods of under-utilisation.

The situation is worsened by the pervasive reliance on the automobile as the primary means of recreation travel. The motor vehicle ranks with television as the most powerful influence, positively and negatively, on recreation participation and the reasons are not hard to find. Use of the car allows for the unstructured nature of recreation trips and provides for flexibility in timing and duration of the outing and choice of route and destination. The car is readily available and gives a good means of access to most sites without the necessity for change of travel mode. It combines the function of moving people, food and equipment with shelter, privacy, a degree of comfort and even in these days of inflationary fuel prices, a relatively inexpensive means of transport.

Preoccupation with the car as a recreation vehicle should not obscure the part played by the many specialised alternative forms of transport in use (Countryside Commission, 1973b), some of which have great potential for environmental degradation (see Chapter 4). However, the expectation of car ownership and its dominant role in outdoor recreation affect more than travel behaviour. It is a fundamental influence on recreation landscapes and on the type and location of recreation facilities. As is noted in Chapter 8, the fact of the car has changed the morphology and function of tourist resorts and given rise to a completely new series of leisure activities and support industries.

In considering this close attachment of the recreationist and the motor vehicle, it would be wrong to assume that car ownership is universal. There will always be a social need to provide for the non-motorist in the community, if recreation opportunities for the less mobile are not to be severely restricted. Indeed, if concern for fuel shortages, inflation and pollution continues to increase, the luxury, or privilege as Wall (1974) calls it, of individually-structured recreation behaviour based on the family car may be at an end. More and more motorists will then be joining the ranks of those who now rely on less convenient means of recreation transport.

Prediction of Recreation Travel Behaviour

Given that recreational trip making is largely unstructured and discretionary in nature, some effort has been made by researchers to isolate common variables influencing decision making and to use these to explain and predict recreation behaviour and associated patterns of movement.

Studies of trip generation are increasing, using models incorporating a variety of predictive variables to attempt to answer questions as to why particular forms of outdoor recreation are selected by different individuals and groups, why certain sites are patronised and others neglected, the expected frequency and duration of recreational trips and the degree of substitutability between recreation activities and recreation sites.

One of the most popular and frequently applied techniques is some version of the gravity model, which has been used with success in the forecasting of flows of visitors to recreation sites. Essentially, gravity models are based on the premiss that some specific and measurable relationship exists between the number of visitors arriving at a given destination from specific origins or markets and a series of independent variables, in particular, population and travel distance.

If these variables can be quantified with reasonable accuracy, predictions can be made as to the likely attendance at selected recreation sites from designated points or areas of origin, e.g. visitation rates to parks from surrounding counties or cities. If the actual, measured levels of attendance match the expected, then the model can be used to predict visits to proposed new parks, to indicate the need for greater efforts in publicity and advertising, or to assess the impact of improved accessibility on the propensity to travel.

The technique can also be applied to delineate the extent of the hinterland of a particular site or attraction. Here, the term hinterland is used in the sense of range or impact zone from which a site could be expected to attract visitors. This tributary area, or sphere of influence, is much like the retail trade area of a city in character. In theory, if the hinterland was merely a function of the friction of distance, it would consist of a series of concentric zones surrounding the site with numbers of visitors progressively declining outwards from the centre (Deasy and Griess, 1966). However, distortion of the size and shape of the area is to be expected because of the kind of factors noted above. Variations in demographic characteristics, in conditions of accessibility and in the orientation and impact of promotional advertising within the hinterland, as well as competition from peripheral attractions, all help to explain why actual patterns of patronage depart from the theoretical. Models of outdoor recreation participation can be developed at various levels of sophistication, but all must involve compromise and rest on certain assumptions because of the complex nature of recreation behaviour. Caution is necessary then, in the use of models and in the application of the results. In particular, difficulties arise in aggregating data derived from individual studies or small groups such as households. In such an unstructured field of choice making as recreation, where decisions are often more intuitive than rational and more impulsive than considered, norms are not appropriate. It is inadvisable, therefore, to make broad behavioural inferences with confidence from aggregate data and different levels of aggregation may produce contradictory results (Smith and Young, 1977). Qualified conclusions could perhaps be drawn from in-depth surveys of specific occupational, sex, or age groups or other relatively homogeneous populations at particular locations.

A further cause for concern in modelling recreation behaviour is the assumption that relationships between the several sets of variables remain constant. Actually, life-styles and social mores change progressively, as do economic and technological circumstances, making prediction difficult. The dynamic nature of much of the inputs into recreation decision making can be both a source of miscalculation in planning and a useful means of encouraging broader patterns of participation without the need to provide additional facilities. New trends and fashions, changing values, charismatic leaders and different policies by governments or other institutions, can all act as 'triggers' to release more *latent* participation and bring *effective* demand more into line with overall demand.

Finally, the underlying element of choice in recreation means that individual participants or particular recreation pursuits should not be studied in isolation:

Rather, the entire spectrum of leisure activities must be examined as a series of substitutes and complements that are capable of providing a variety of satisfactions and that act as potential trade-offs for one another (Phillips, 1977: 1).

Substitutability and interchangeability are a response to the relationship between the satisfactions sought in outdoor recreation and the geographic, social, psychological, economic or physiological barriers which prevent those satisfactions from being realised. The effect of these barriers is to stimulate replication of satisfactions by resort to some other activity. In short, the concept of substitutability implies that recreation preferences and propensities are much more elastic and open to manipulation than is generally accepted. If this is so, the implications are far-reaching and information as to which activities constitute alternatives will be vital to planners (Park, 1981).

If individuals can be satisfied in similar ways and to similar degrees by a range of recreation activities with a high degree of substitutability, then the allocation of recreation resources has wide flexibility and many alternatives. On the other hand, where certain activities deliver high levels of satisfaction, but are shown to have a low level of substitutability, these pursuits will need to receive greater emphasis and protection in future policy-making (Phillips, 1977: 5-6).

The concept of recreation resources and the role of recreation resource management are taken up in following chapters.

3 THE RESOURCE BASE FOR OUTDOOR RECREA-
TION

For many people, the concept of resources is commonly taken to refer only to tangible objects in nature which are considered of economic value for productive purposes. Thus, environmental elements such as mineral deposits, water bodies, forests or agricultural soils, are regarded as 'natural resources' necessary for human existence. An alternative view is to see resources not so much as material substances, but as *functions* which such substances are capable of performing. In this sense, resource functions are created by man through selection and manipulation of certain attributes of the environment. The mere fact of the physical existence of coal, iron ore or fertile soils does not constitute a resource; such elements *become* resources as a result of society's subjective evaluation of their potential to satisfy human wants relative to human capabilities.

This functional approach to resource phenomena was set out formally many years ago by Zimmerman (1951) and restated by O'Riordan (1971) who defined a resource as:

An attribute of the environment appraised by man to be of value over time within constraints imposed by his social, political, economic and institutional framework (O'Riordan, 1971: 4).

In these terms, resource materials of themselves are inert, passive and permissive, rather than mandatory, prescriptive and deterministic. Creative use of resource potential requires the existence of a cultural and socioeconomic frame of reference in which elements of the environment acquire a function as a means of production, or for the attainment of certain socially valued goals.

Recreation Resources

The process of creation, use and depletion of resources for outdoor recreation differs little from that in other areas of human activity such as agriculture, forestry or mining. As Clawson and Knetsch (1966) put it:

There is nothing in the physical landscape or features of any particular piece of land or body of water that makes it a recreation
resource; it is the combination of the natural qualities and the ability
and desire of man to use them that makes a resource out of what
might otherwise be a more or less meaningless combination of rocks,
soil and trees (Clawson and Knetsch, 1966: 7).

At the same time, recreation resources are not static or constant, but
take on a dynamic character varying in time and space. Presently
valued resources can become redundant and changing economic, social
and technological conditions can reveal new recreation potential in
previously neglected areas. Natural resources are indeed cultural
appraisals and what is recognised as a recreation resource by one group
of people at one period in time may be of no conceivable use or value
to them or others in different circumstances. The renowned surfing
beaches which fringe the Australian coastline, for instance, have really
only achieved prominence for outdoor recreation in the past half-
century with the relaxation of attitudes to public bathing. To the
Aboriginal inhabitants of the continent they were little more than a
source of food, whereas the early European colonists found the surf a
formidable hazard in coping with the isolation of coastal settlements.
Moreover, the gleaming sand itself, which to most Australians is an
integral and attractive component of the recreation resource base,
represents a very different kind of resource function for the rutile
miner or the building contractor. Contrasting perceptions of environment help explain conflicts which arise over recreation resource utilisation. Forest and wild land recreation, for example, is largely a product
of the conservation movement of the twentieth century and claims on
countryside and water resources can conflict with more traditional uses
of rural land (Chapter 6).

Hart (1966) uses the term 'recreation resource base' to describe the
total natural values of a particular landscape or countryside. He
includes in his definition, such attractions as the view of a quiet agricultural scene, along with more tangible phenomena such as sites for
picnicking, camping and boating. In fact, given the appropriate circumstances, most landscapes are in some sense recreational and therefore
resources for outdoor recreation embrace a wide spectrum of environmental attributes. These can range over space itself, taking in airspace
and even subterranean and submarine features; topographical phenomena, including tracts of land, water bodies, vegetation and distinctive
ecological, cultural or historical sites; and as well, the often neglected

climatic characteristics of an area.

Space, Location and Accessibility

Outdoor recreation necessarily has its focus in space consuming activities. Certainly, it is in the spatial distribution and frequent locational imbalance of leisure opportunities where much of the resource manager's interest and emphasis are found. Space, then, is a critical resource for outdoor recreation and certain kinds of activities may require space with specific attributes, dimensions and qualities.

As recreationists increase in number and mobility, pressure on space grows; not only space in which to recreate, but service-space for ancillary facilities and access-space in the form of parking areas, routeways, etc. These latter considerations can have a marked bearing on the effectiveness of recreation resource space. Pressure on capacity too may stimulate multiple use of space over time for varied activities, day *and* evening, week *and* weekend and year-round rather than seasonal.

Conditions of location and access are basic to the definition of certain types of recreation space. Indeed, these aspects are a major part of the rationale supporting some methods of classification for recreation resources (see below). For some outdoor recreation activities, isolation from the masses is vital to maintain the individual experience sought. On the other hand, valuation of the spatial element for user-orientated recreation resources depends very much on their location and conditions of access relative to population concentrations. For example, in the state of Nebraska in the midwest of the United States, more than 70 per cent of the population is located in the three eastern regions, but 87 per cent of the recreational resources are in the west of the state. The problem is how to get the recreationists from the east to the recreation opportunities in the west (Nebraska Game and Parks Commission, 1979).

The question of what constitutes a recreation resource and what factors add to or detract from the quality of the leisure environment can best be answered by a systematic assessment of resource potential. The task begins with identification and classification of elements of the recreation resource base.

Classification of Recreation Resources

An important initial stage in the resource creation process is the establishment of some estimate of the quantity and quality of resource materials available; those presently valued as resources and those which may function as recreation resources in different socioeconomic and technological circumstances. Such stocktaking is necessary before the significance of stocks can be evaluated.

However, of themselves, inventories are of doubtful value; more than simple reporting of what is there is required. The resource elements must be described and classified according to some recognised and agreed system in order to determine categories of resource deficiency and surplus as an input to recreation planning.

Classification of recreation resources can be approached from several angles. One of the earliest systems was devised by Clawson *et al.* (1960) and distinguishes between recreation areas and opportunity on the basis of location and other characteristics such as size, major use and degree of artificial development. Under this system, recreation areas are arranged on a continuum of recreational opportunities from user-orientated through intermediate to resource-based (Table 3.1).

User-orientated Areas are characterised by ready access to users (after work or after school) with small space demands and often a number of artificial features. City parks, pools and playgrounds fall into this category. They are the focus of considerable user pressure with supervised activities dominating and basic landscape elements less important.

Resource-based Areas are at the other end of the continuum with the primary focus on resource quality and less emphasis on the activities undertaken. Very large units are usually involved, with remoteness (and hence substantial travel time and cost involved) a basic ingredient. National parks, forests and wilderness areas are typical of this group where artificial development is minimal and visitor usage confined largely to vacations.

Intermediate Areas fall between the two extremes, both spatially and in terms of use. Accessibility is relatively important with most sites within one to two hours drive from potential users. Many water-based recreation sites and smaller state and countryside parks would be classed as intermediate.

The Clawson system of classification has been widely applied although the terminology can be confusing. All recreation areas must be user-orientated to some extent if they are to satisfy the functional concept of resources. At the same time, exclusion from the resource-based category of urban and near-urban recreation sites reflects a narrow interpretation of the term resources. Obviously there is scope

Table 3.1: General Classification of Outdoor Recreational Uses and Resources

	User-orientated	Type of Recreation Area Resource-based	Intermediate
1. General location	Close to users; on whatever resources are available	Where outstanding resources can be found; may be distant from most users	Must not be too remote from users; on best resources available within distance limitation
2. Major types of activity	Games, such as golf and tennis; swimming; picnicking; walks and horseback riding; zoos, etc; playing by children	Major sightseeing scientific and historical interest; hiking and mountain climbing; camping, fishing and hunting	Camping, picnicking, hiking, swimming, hunting, fishing
3. When major use occurs	After hours (school or work)	Vacations	Day outings and weekends
4. Typical sizes of areas	One to a hundred, or at most, a few hundred acres	Usually some thousands of acres, perhaps many thousands	A hundred to several thousand acres
5. Common types of agency responsibility	City, county, or other local government; private	National parks and national forests primarily; state parks in some cases; private, especially for seashore and major lakes	Federal reservoirs; state parks; private

Source: Clawson, Held and Stoddard, 1960: 136.

for considerable overlap and city parklands can be just as much 'resource-based' as remote wilderness. Moreover, large national parks, such as those which ring the city of Sydney, Australia (see Chapter 7) and are close enough for casual day visits, actually qualify as user-orientated recreation areas. Obviously too, there can be interchange-ability over time, as resource-based areas, for example, come within the recreation opportunity spectrum of an increasingly mobile and affluent user population.

Another broad classification system which has had mixed success in application is that proposed by the Outdoor Recreation Resources Review Commission (1962a) and developed by the US Bureau of Outdoor Recreation. The system classifies recreation areas according to physical resource characteristics, level of development and manage-ment, intensity of use and anticipated behavioural patterns. The six classes are; High Density Recreation Areas; General Outdoor Recrea-tion Areas; Natural Environment Areas; Unique Natural Areas; Primitive Areas; and Historic and Cultural Sites.

The Bureau of Outdoor Recreation system was devised in the hope that it would provide a common framework for planning and an effective aid for recreation management. Overlap between classes is reduced by selecting the classification which promises the optimum combination of recreation values for an area. The system also acknowledges that, in most cases, a recreation unit such as a park or forest, would incorporate recreation areas of two or more classes.

Different areas and different types of recreation call for alterna-tive approaches to classification. On a national scale, Vedenin and Miroschnichenko (1971) undertook a resource-based classification of recreation potential for the whole of the Soviet Union. They classified the country into broad zones according to suitability for summer and winter recreation and for tourism on the basis of selected climatic and physiographic factors which favour or inhibit outdoor recreation. The classification and associated maps indicate large areas of USSR which are suitable for extended periods of recreation across both seasons.

One of the most ambitious and exhaustive schemes for classifica-tion of recreation potential has been carried out in Canada as part of the Canada Land Inventory. This was a comprehensive project to assess land capability for four major purposes — agriculture, forestry, wild-life and recreation. The inventory has been applied to settled parts of rural Canada (urbanised areas are excluded) and is designed for comput-erised data storage and retrieval as a basis for resource and land use planning at local, provincial and national levels.

A total of 48 'presently popular' outdoor recreation activities was considered and the basis of the capability classification was the *quantity* of recreation which may be generated and sustained per unit area of land per year, given certain assumptions regarding sound management, uniform demand and accessibility and with no allowance for modifications or improvements. Quantity was expressed in terms of total visitor days or hours. A seven-class capability rating scale was used ranging from Class 1 (very high), Class 2 (high), Class 3 (moderately high), Class 4 (moderate), Class 5 (moderately low), Class 6 (low) to Class 7 (very low).

The system uses 25 sub-classes to denote recreational features or aspects of land units providing opportunities for outdoor recreation. For example, *Sub-class A – Angling*, refers to land providing access to water with natural capability for production, harvesting and/or viewing of sport fish. The classification into which an area is placed depends upon the total quantity of recreation which the particular association of features within the land unit is considered capable of generating on an annual basis. Mapping limitations required that a maximum of three recreational features or sub-classes be recorded for each land unit and the sequence in which they are listed, vertically or horizontally, indicates the order of recreational significance. Typical of annotations on the larger scale (1:50000) capability maps would be:

$$\begin{array}{c} B \\ 2\ S\ K \\ A \end{array}$$ or 2SBKA, indicating a Class 2 shoreland unit with a bathing beach (B), terrain suited to camping (K), and accessible to adjoining angling water (A), in that order of importance (Department of Regional Economic Expansion, 1970: 100).

Despite its apparent complexity, the system permits inter- and intra-sectoral comparisons to delineate suitable locations for recreational development and to define priority areas between competing uses, as well as opportunities for compatible multiple resource use. However, the methodology does have some deficiencies. Although the classification is designed to accommodate a wide range of (then) popular outdoor recreation activities, inevitably it excludes certain pursuits, e.g. hang gliding, which have emerged since the 1960s as a result of technological advances and increasing levels of specialisation in recreation activities. Nor does the scheme have much to say about the *quality* of a recreation experience. Recreation resource capability is equated with the *quantity* or level of use, which does not always coincide with satisfaction. Moreover, the Canada Land Inventory is essentially a reconnaissance type survey, valuable in identifying basic resource potentials, but not intended to provide input for detailed recreational planning for a region or site (Cressman and Hoffman, 1979). On a regional level, attempts have been made to identify recreation environments for selected categories of outdoor recreation. Among the techniques being developed is Potential Surface Analysis.

Potential Surface Analysis

Recent recreation research in England and Wales has employed potential surface analysis to develop a strategy for informal recreation in the countryside (Countryside Commission, 1974). In recreation studies potential surface analysis represents a technique for making a comparative evaluation of the spatial distribution of recreation potential according to the capability of the resource base to meet certain predetermined objectives. How well each unit area satisfies the objectives specified is quantified and weighted and the scores aggregated to produce a 'potential surface' of high and low capability or potential (comparable in some ways to a contour relief map).

In simple terms the steps involved in the technique, as a method of recreation resource evaluation, consist of:

*Establishment of goals and objectives for provision of outdoor recreation opportunities.
*Identification of ideal factors, conditions or requirements which should be met if the area is to satisfy these goals and objectives.
*Measurement and mapping of the occurrence of these conditions as a potential surface.

The broad generalised goal adopted for a study in South Wales was to ensure that there were sufficient and suitable areas available for informal countryside recreation. Five objectives relating to this goal were then defined, representing accessibility, attraction and capacity. Although capacity was considered basic to recreation potential and ranked first in importance by a group of planning experts, it was decided to exclude it from subsequent consideration because of difficulties of assessment. Indices were then derived for the four remaining objectives to measure the extent to which they were achieved in the survey area and thereby contributed towards potential for countryside recreation (Countryside Commission, 1974).

Potential surface analysis represents a versatile, flexible and economical technique for systematic assessment of recreation resource capability. Although it inevitably involves an element of subjectivity in the evaluation and comparison of resource attributes, it can provide valuable input to strategic planning at the regional scale, especially where alternative forms of development and multiple resource use are being considered.

A refinement of the potential surface analysis technique has been developed in Scotland by way of application of the Tourism and Recreation Information Package (TRIP) devised by the Tourism and Recreation Research Unit at Edinburgh (Owen *et al.*, 1974). The computer-based TRIP system is designed to delineate and depict areas of tourism and recreation potential in Scotland according to the presence and capacity of relevant resources and constraints on their use and development. Many such resources can be located in space and have characteristics and interrelationships which can be spatially defined. The system is ideally suited for the construction and manipulation of potential surfaces. Information on each of the objectives used in the South Wales study, for example, could be assembled and mapped under this system and then combined to form a countryside recreation surface identifying areas of greatest potential for development. An important feature of the TRIP system is its flexibility and unlimited scope for experimentation, so that weighting factors may be applied to individual resource attributes and fresh data on demand or supply factors incorporated as they become available.

Evaluation of Recreation Environments

Measurement of the suitability of the resource base to support various different forms of outdoor recreation is a more difficult undertaking than if the task is confined to classification or assessment for a single purpose, as with potential surface analysis. Yet, an area seldom provides for only one kind of recreation and it is more realistic to consider activities not singly, but in groups, with due regard also for the complex relationships between outdoor recreation and other resource uses (Coppock and Duffield, 1975). The complexity of the task is typified by an investigation undertaken in central Scotland to identify and evaluate recreation environments on the basis of functional connections between different recreational activities, resources and users

(Duffield and Owen, 1970; Coppock, Duffield and Sewell, 1974).

The approach adopted was to make four separate, independent assessments of the components of resource capability for outdoor recreation and then combine these into one single assessment. The components used were suitability for land-based recreation; suitability for water-based recreation, scenic quality and ecological significance. The basic spatial unit was a two kilometre (approx. 1.25 miles) square grid overlay involving 607 survey units covering the study area. Rather than evaluating for a single type of recreation activity, sets of six land-based activities and five water-based activities were grouped. After consultation with experts, minimal criteria were then established for each activity within each group, to indicate levels at which recreational development would be warranted. For example, the criterion for rock climbing was that all cliff faces be over 30 metres (approx. 100 feet) in height, while angling on inland water required unpolluted rivers, streams and canals over eight metres (approx. 26 feet) in width and enclosed waterbodies over five hectares (approx. 12.4 acres) in area. If such criteria were satisfied within a grid square, a point was scored, so that a theoretical maximum of six points for land-based recreation activities and five points for water-based recreation activities could be recorded for any one square. An interesting outcome was that the highest scores for water-based recreation potential were recorded in grid squares containing reservoirs, from which it is generally the current policy in Scotland to exclude most water sports (see Chapter 6).

An adaptation of Linton's (1968) technique for landscape evaluation (see below) was used to assess scenic quality, with an allocation of up to five points for landform and for land use. Ecological significance was ranked according to diversity of habitats or biological richness with four points being the maximum possible grid score.

Data on the four components were obtained from existing maps, aerial photographs and other published sources and each grid square was evaluated separately for each category. Grid scores were then weighted with 100 representing the highest possible score for each component. Thus, the maximum theoretical score for the four components combined was 400 for each grid square. The investigators revealed that this was nowhere approached and any grid score exceeding 250 was considered an area with a high capacity to support outdoor recreation. Areas with a combined score of less than 100 were judged to have only a very limited recreational capacity. The combined grid scores were then graded into six classes and mapped to indicate composite recreation environments (Figure 3.1).

Figure 3.1: An Assessment of the Recreation Resources of Lanarkshire

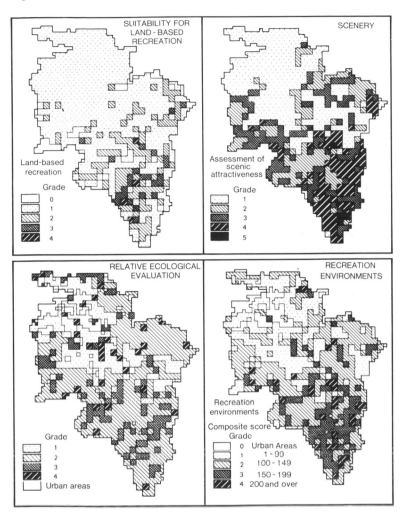

Source: Duffield and Owen, 1970, Appendix 2.1.

The technique is experimental and subject to criticism. The authors concede that the assessment might be altered if other forms of outdoor recreation and other features which attract visitors had been considered. The somewhat arbitrary choice of the four components and the decision to give them equal weight, can also be challenged. Moreover, questions as to whether high ecological significance should be treated as a constraint, along with other negative factors such as lack of access or the attitudes of management authorities, need to be examined at a subsequent stage of resource assessment and development.

Implicit in this discussion of recreation resource classification and evaluation has been the existence and even acceptance of a strong element of subjectivity in the assessment process. One of the most difficult areas to contend with from the point of view of subjectivity is that of landscape evaluation.

Landscape as a Recreational Resource

Until relatively recently, landscape has been largely ignored as part of the recreation environment. However, growing concern for environmental quality has led to recognition of the scenic quality of landscape as a major recreational resource in its own right, rather than merely the visual backdrop for other recreation pursuits (Dearden, 1980). This, in turn, has generated an upsurge of interest in systematic attempts to evaluate scenic beauty and to examine the features of landscapes which contribute to their attractiveness and to their resource value in outdoor recreation (Robinson *et al.*, 1976).

That said, difficulties remain with assessment procedures because of the intangible and multi-faceted nature of landscape which does not permit precise measurement. The resource function can take on several dimensions depending upon which senses are being satisfied and the characteristics of the population involved. These difficulties are compounded with assessment of recreational values. Whereas most landscapes probably have some recreation potential, this is not easy to establish with any agreement because of the personal nature of recreation and the subjective manner in which it is experienced. Generalisation and interpersonal comparisons are of doubtful validity and the multiple characteristics of landscape make dissection and evaluation a risky undertaking.

Despite the essentially subjective nature of the variables involved, efforts are being made towards identification and measurement of scenic landscape values in response to competing resource uses. In the ensuing discussion it is useful to distinguish between landscape *character* and landscape *quality*.

Analysis of landscape character is essentially descriptive and concerned with the attributes or components of landscape which constitute it as a visual entity — landform, water, vegetation, buildings and the like. The US Forest Service has been concerned for some time with the characteristics of landscape and which of these impinge upon human assessment and use and lend themselves to forest landscape conservation and management. Litton (1968) considered that landscape as a visual, scenic resource was derived from six variable factors — form, spatial definition and light (inherent to the landscape and capable of indirect manipulation) and distance, observer position and sequence (peculiar to the individual and open to direct manipulation). Litton goes on to explain how each of these can affect what he terms the 'visual harvesting of scenic resources'. The US Forest Service (1973) has applied these concepts to forest landscapes and developed a sophisticated system for forest landscape character analysis and management. The principles involved have also been applied to non-forested landscapes such as the Great Plains (Litton and Tetlow, 1978) and have been adapted for visual assessment of recreation sites near Sydney, Australia (New South Wales Department of Lands, 1980).

In contrast to landscape character, landscape quality is essentially a comparative, evaluative concept, subsequent to determination of landscape characteristics. Assessment of landscape quality is a three-phase process (Unwin, 1975):

Landscape Description — relatively objective inventory of landscape elements or characteristics (above) and classification of landscape types, without any scoring, ranking, or reference to quality.

Landscape Preference — establishment of visual preference ratings or indices for landscape characteristics or types based on personal value judgements, or the opinions of panels of experts or representative populations.

Landscape Evaluation — assessment of the quality of the particular landscapes under study in terms of the values or preferences expressed.

A variety of methods and procedures has been suggested to manipulate and rank landscape attributes in order to establish visual preferences. Criticism has been directed at particular approaches which claim to present an *objective* measurement of landscape quality. Such refinement is impossible with such an inherently subjective process, despite all manner of devices, e.g. photographic and even 'cineramic', to portray or simulate landscapes realistically, and no matter what sophisticated analytical methods are used. As Gans (1968, 7) puts it: 'an *objective* environment *must* be perceived *subjectively* before it affects behaviour'. Landscape evaluation can never be divorced entirely from subjective interpretations and the best that can be achieved is some appropriate balance between operational utility and scientific elegance (Jacobs, 1975).

Some simple, but effective evaluation methods rest on the assumption that it is possible to disaggregate landscape into a number of significant elements and allocate values according to the quantity and quality present of these elements. Robinson *et al.* (1976) and Kane (1981) give a listing of possible landscape components and alternative measures for these which might be applied. This was the approach adopted by Tandy (1971) who included seven landscape elements for measurement. Quantity was scored from O (none), through 1 (some), to 2 (all), with quality ranked on a five-point scale from -2 (intolerable), -1 (undesirable), 0 (acceptable), +1 (desirable), to +2 (highly desirable). Table 3.2 gives an example of Tandy's system applied to a one square kilometre

Table 3.2: Landscape Evaluation Technique

	Landscape		Element	Quantity		Quality		
a)	Surface cover	:	partly poor grassland	1	x	-1	=	-1
b)	Undulation	:	flat	2	x	-1	=	-2
c)	Trees in mass	:	none	0			=	0
d)	Trees singly	:	none	0			=	0
e)	Water	:	river	1	x	+1	=	+1
f)	Artifacts	:	mineral workings	1	x	-2	=	-2
g)	Views out	:	none	0			=	0
						Total		-4

Source: Robinson *et al*, 1976; 289.

(approx. 0.4 square miles) landscape unit with the quantity and quality scores multiplied and the scores for all seven elements totalled to give an overall landscape index. However, it needs to be recognised that the whole of any landscape is greater than the sum of its component parts.

The questions of subjectivity and disaggregation have been canvassed in other approaches to landscape evaluation. Fines (1968) set out to assess landscapes in their *totality* in his research in Sussex and attempted to reduce subjectivity and personal bias by asking a small panel of specialist observers to rank, in terms of beauty, carefully chosen colour photographs of selected landscapes. The values derived from these test views were placed in six descriptive categories ranging from 'unsightly' to 'spectacular'. Fines then evaluated real views in the field against the test scale and assigned numerical values to each scene or landscape.

Fines's system has been criticised also; first because of the use of two-dimensional visual stimuli (photographs) as a surrogate for actual landscapes in establishing a scale of visual peference and because of the assumed relationship between *global* parameters and local scale views. Even his reference to collective opinions of specialists has brought the charge of 'elitism' (Dunn, 1976) and Brancher (1969: 92) goes so far as to label Fines's work as 'subjectivism dressed up as science!'

Linton (1968) also criticised Fines's method on the grounds of the values attached to the various landscape categories and the labour, time and cost involved. He favoured a measure of disaggregation and in a study of landscape quality in Scotland, considered the two basic contributory elements to be, *landform* and *land use*. Linton identified and gave a subjective numerical value to six landform landscapes, ranging from 8 (mountains) to 0 (lowlands) and seven land use landscapes, from +6 (wild landscapes) to -5 (urbanised/industrialised landscapes). He obtained a composite assessment by combining and mapping these two evaluations into a total score which he claimed represented a 'cartographic statement' of Scotland's scenic resources (Figure 3.2).

Once again, the technique has been criticised (Crofts, 1975) because of imprecise definitions of the components being evaluated and because of the assumptions underlying the rating scale, e.g. that landscape appeal increases with boldness of relief and that all urban landscapes are unattractive. Reservations have also been expressed about the general applicability of Linton's technique outside Scotland without substantial modification (Gilg, 1975).

The TRIP system, referred to earlier, has also been adapted to classify and evaluate landscape in Scotland (Duffield and Coppock, 1975). Using a similar methodological approach to that for potential surface analysis, individual resources contributing to landscape quality were assessed and progressively aggregated to define a succession of 'resource surfaces'. These were then related to certain planning constraints (e.g. access and population pressure) to identify areas of 'environmental worth'. This approach was considered of more practical relevance to planning and conservation than the definition of inherent landscape quality. The TRIP system places emphasis not merely on isolated pockets of high quality landscape, but on the equally important tract of surrounding countryside and the spatial setting or perspective. The technique was developed in response to doubts

Figure 3.2: Scotland Scenic Resources: A Composite Assessment

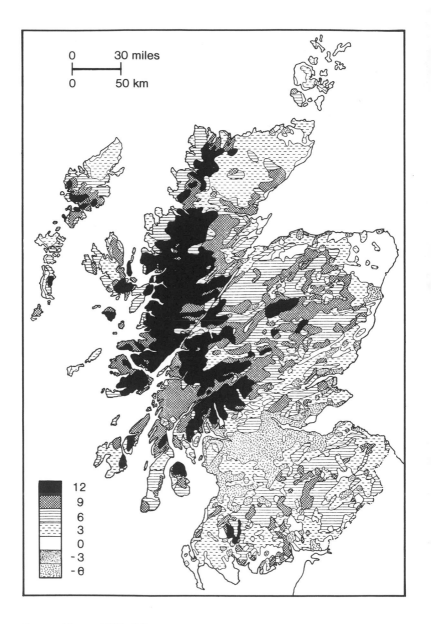

Source: Linton, 1968: 235.

concerning the synthetic landscapes which various assessors previously had put together. The authors consider that:

> The *process* of amalgamating (landscape) resources is as important as the final product and the (TRIP) information system provides insights into this process and thereby allows syntheses to be continually refined by varying the contribution of individual resources (Duffield and Coppock, 1975: 143).

Apart from problems of subjectivity and the appropriate mix of landscape attributes, assessment procedures are unable to cope, as yet, with the internal visible arrangement and spatial composition of landscape, as opposed to its resource content. With all the difficulties and reservations regarding methodology, the question may be asked, why evaluate landscape at all?

The answer can be found in the four broad objectives designated for landscape management by Penning-Rowsell (1975):

Landscape preservation — identification of areas of landscape worthy of preservation and deserving of priority for conservation.
Landscape protection — as a basis for development control decisions, to guide the direction of development, monitor environmental impact and provide for planned landscape change.
Recreation policy — aimed at enjoyment of the landscape and realisation of its long-term potential for appropriate forms of outdoor recreation.
Landscape improvement — identification of visual features which detract from landscape quality so that such 'eyesores' can be removed or modified.

To these could be added the requirement to satisfy a growing body of environmental law in many countries. Kane (1981) points out that in the United States, for example, all government agencies must ensure that 'environmental amenities' are given appropriate consideration in planning decisions. In Australia, too, there is a growing commitment to landscape conservation in both the natural and built environment (Williamson, 1979). Several urban renewal projects have been delayed or abandoned because of 'green bans' imposed by trade unions anxious to preserve parts of the national heritage and landscape. The Australian Conservation Foundation sponsored a conference on landscape in 1975 and from this emerged a stronger appreciation of Australian landscape values, along with increasing readiness to provide for visual assessment of landscape in public and private developmental projects (Colleran and Geering, 1980).

Evaluation of Recreation Sites

At a finer scale, attention needs to be directed towards evaluation of the potential of the resource base to support a specific recreation activity or experience at a specific *site*. Evaluation at this level calls for a different approach from that used in broad regional assessment, where questions of land tenure, access and management can often be disregarded.

Site evaluation assumes knowledge and understanding of the detailed resource requirements for each type of recreation involved. Hogg (1977) indicates the kind of questions which might need to be answered:

> *What kind of topography is most suitable for bushwalking, for horseriding, or for trail bike riding?
> *What river conditions are ideal for white water canoeing, for trout fishing, or for bathing?
> *What types of vegetation are preferred for orienteering or for children's adventure play?
> *What snow conditions are best for snow climbing, for cross-country skiing, or for snowshoe walking?
> *What characteristics make a rockface good for mechanical climbing, or a pool suitable for fly-casting? (Hogg,1977: 102).

As Hogg points out, answers to such questions are not easy to come by. Short of becoming an expert by participation in an activity, or acquiring knowledge through systematic observation, the most efficient and readily applicable method of obtaining information on user requirements is the approach adopted by Hockin *et al.* (1977) who interviewed experts and representatives of organisations concerned, to assemble a detailed list of specifications for a wide range of recreational pursuits.

For certain activities, conditions are necessarily more specific and closely defined than others which are more flexible. Competitive activities, for example, are more demanding than less formal recreational use of countryside. Physical and natural circumstances will be most important for some forms of recreation, whereas for others social factors may need to be taken into account and man-made facilities and infrastructure may be mandatory for effective functioning of the recreation resource base.

Recognition of recreation site potential really involves synthesis of an 'identikit' specification (incorporating all the relevant site factors) which conforms most closely to the ideal (Miles and Seabrooke, 1977). However, in the evaluation process, it is important to distinguish between *minimum* and *optimum* site requirements. Hockin *et al.* (1977) point out that the former represent a threshold or entry zone concept, in that they describe the set of obligatory conditions within a narrow range of acceptability which is critical for the activity to take place at all. Unless such bare minimum standards are satisfied, the type of recreation envisaged will be unable to make use of the site. Optimum requirements imply a preferred situation such as might be demanded or experienced at a site of national or international repute. Such standards are obviously much more demanding and precise and are applicable only to exceptional situations.

Hockin *et al.* (1977) describe in detail the process of establishing site requirements for specific types of recreation. For each specified activity, information should be compiled on:

Physical site requirements — space, including area, dimensions and configuration; ground surface texture, soil conditions and need for artificial surfaces; terrain dissection or undulation; range of slope tolerance; and dependence on presence of water.

Mantle requirements — relevance of presence or absence of wooded environments and advantages of seclusion, screening and noise reduction.

Man-made facilities, including local access — need for parking space, signposting, specialised buildings, facilities and utilities for both participants and spectators.

Constraints — seasonal, climatic, or capacity limitations, compatibility problems and legal or institutional restrictions.

The authors go on to identify the site requirements for each of a wide range of outdoor recreation activities from orienteering to pheasant shooting. A similar approach to recreation site evaluation is canvassed by Jubenville (1976) who lists the physical and socioeconomic factors to be considered in evaluating forest campground sites, together with a relatively simple rating system for use in choosing between sites. Part of this system is reproduced in Table 3.3. Jubenville also describes the criteria applied by the US Forest Service in evaluating occupancy and observation sites, potential waterfront sites and winter sports sites.

Once the necessary minimum site conditions have been established, a method of ranking or rating is needed which reflects the relative importance of each requirement and indicates whether it is considered an asset or a constraint. Jubenville suggests an ordinal scoring method (good, better, best) as being most appropriate with highest values being assigned to the most favourable conditions. Thus, in evaluating a stream's suitability for 'scenic floating', as a recreation experience, a basic requirement to be taken into account is stream velocity, in that the rate of flow should be neither too fast, nor too slow. Jubenville allots three points for what he considers an optimum velocity of four to seven miles per hour (approx. 6.4 − 11.2 kph); two points for a velocity less than four miles per hour; and one point for a site (stream) with a velocity greater than seven miles per hour.

A similar system has been devised by Hogg (1977) in Australia who uses the term 'recreational unit' as the basic resource component for evaluation. In many ways, this term is preferable to site, because it can be used to refer to a block or area over which recreationists are dispersed, for example, for boating; for a linear routeway such as a river or trail; or for a specific resource feature such as a cliff used for rock climbing (Figure 3.3).

By way of illustration, Hogg lists the natural and cultural factors he considers important for overnight bushwalking or hiking (Table 3.4). Unless *all* site (route) requirements are held to be *equally* fundamental, the points allotted and rating scales used need to be adjusted to reflect their greater or lesser importance. Without some weighting of this kind, serious deficiencies in more critical factors can be largely overcome by high ratings for more trivial aspects. Moreover, a zero rating given to indicate *total* unsuitability on the basis of a single vital factor can be swamped in the additive process by high ratings for more mundane requirements.

Thus, in Hogg's example, presence of quality campsites is assigned the highest maximum positive points value (25), whereas refuge huts are apparently considered of passing importance to bushwalkers and are lowly rated (5). On the other hand, the presence of hazards is judged to be a most serious constraint (-50), and some factors, such as restrictions on access, are considered so critical as to be allotted the most negative value of -00. A recreational unit in which any *single* factor is rated -00 will also have a *total* rating of -00 and therefore, is judged

Table 3.3: Evaluating Forest Campground Sites

Part 1: PHYSICAL FACTORS

Factor	Condition and Point Value				Sites	
					A	B
WATER						
A Size	20 Lake, over 200 acres	15 Lake 50-200 acres	10 Large pond or stream	5 Small pond or stream	☐	☐
B Quality	20 Clear	15 Semi-clear	10 Turbid	5 Very turbid	☐	☐
C Shoreline	20 Sand or gravel level	15 Sand or gravel slight slope	10 Rocky or muddy moderate slope	5 Rocky or muddy steep slope	☐	☐
D Water depth fluctuation	20 Under 1 foot	15 1-2 feet	10 2.5-4.0 feet	5 Over 4 feet	☐	☐
E Frontage owned	20 Over 1,000 feet	15 500-1,000 feet	10 100-490 feet	5 Under 100 feet	☐	☐
F Av. dist from tent sites	20 Under 400 feet	15 400-600 feet	10 610-800 feet	5 Over 800 feet	☐	☐
RATING	120 EXCELLENT	90 GOOD	60 FAIR	30 POOR	☐	☐
TOPOGRAPHY						
A Slope	20 Under 10%	15 10-15%	10 16-20%	5 Over 20%	☐	☐
B Size of area	20 Over 50 acres	15 30-50 acres	10 15-29 acres	5 Under 15 acres	☐	☐
C Soil conditions	20 Smooth well-drained	15 Small rocks, moderately drained	10 Rocky, moderately drained	5 Boulders, ledge, poorly drained	☐	☐
RATING	60 EXCELLENT	45 GOOD	30 FAIR	15 POOR	☐	☐

Source: Jubenville, 1976: 144.

Figure 3.3: Hypothetical Recreational Unit Patterns

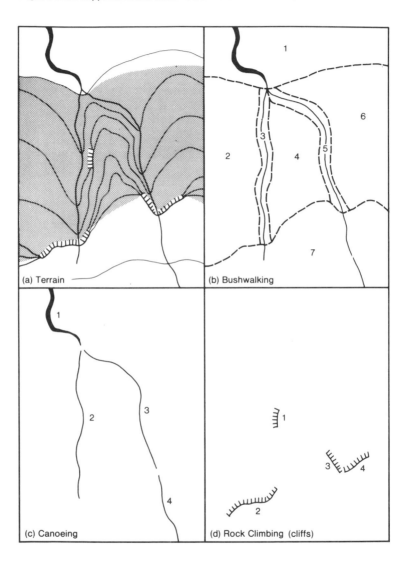

(a) Terrain

(b) Bushwalking

(c) Canoeing

(d) Rock Climbing (cliffs)

Source: Adapted from Hogg, 1977: 105.

totally unsuitable on the basis of that one factor, no matter how favourable other factors may be. Table 3.5 sets out some examples of rating scales devised by Hogg for certain factors affecting overnight

Table 3.4: Factors Affecting Suitability for Overnight Bushwalking

Factor	Maximum Value	Minimum Value
Natural factors		
1. Topography (steepness and variability of terrain, length of uphill climbs)	15	-00
2. Rockiness of terrain for walking	0	-5
3. Weather characteristics during walking season	15	-15
4. Ease of negotiation of vegetation (denseness of scrub, fallen timber, blackberries, nettles etc.)	0	-30
5. Presence and quality of campsites (ground suitable for pitching tents, firewood and drinking water, general environment)	25	-00
6. Extent of area	15	-00
7. Proximity to users	15	-5
8. Scenic quality (general attractiveness, variety, special features)	10	-5
9. Availability of drinking water between campsites	5	-8
10. Miscellaneous attractions (wildlife, swimming holes, historical features etc.)	10	0
11. Undesirable features (snakes, leeches, mosquitoes, bushflies etc.)	0	-00
Cultural factors		
12. Access to suitable starting points	20	-10
13. Tracks suitable for walking (related to 5)	15	0
14. Unnecessary to undesirable tracks and roads	0	-00
15. Refuge huts	5	0
16. Unnecessary or undesirable buildings	0	-00
17. Adequate track marking and signposting (incl. snowpoles)	8	0
18. Escape routes for emergency use	8	0
19. Hazards (e.g. mineshafts)	0	-50
20. Presence of conflicting recreational activities	0	-00
21. Presence of other conflicting land uses (e.g. logging, mining, grazing)	0	-00
22. Restrictions on access or certain activities (e.g. camping, fires)	0	-00

Source: Hogg, 1977: 106.

bushwalking. Note that with negative constraints, e.g. ease of negotiation of vegetation, a rating of *zero* is the *most favourable* in that it indicates that the constraint is considered insignificant.

Table 3.5: Examples of Ratings for Factors Affecting Overnight Bushwalking

---

Ease of negotiation of vegetation
0   Open walking, typical walking speed 5 km/hr
-5   Mostly open with patches or dense scrub   )
                                    or   ) average walking speed
        Light scrub   )   3 km/hr
-15   Consistent scrub, very slow progress, 1 km/hr
-30   Virtually impenetrable, need to cut path through, 0.2 km/hr or less

Proximity to users
15   Less than 30 km
10   100 km
5   200 km
0   300 km (maximum acceptable travel distance for weekend trips)
-5   More than 500 km (restricted to extended trips).

Scenic quality
10   Excellent scenery, variation in views along route
5   Views pleasant but not spectacular, limited variety
0   Views rather uninteresting, do not add to enjoyment of walk
-5   Undesirable views (e.g. clear felling operations)

        The presence of special desirable or undesirable features raises or lowers
        the rating otherwise obtained by 1 or 2 points.

Refuge huts
5   Small attractive bush huts at ½ to 1 day intervals along route
3   Attractive huts at 2 to 3 day intervals
                                    or
        Huts at ½ to 1 days intervals but aesthetically unattractive (e.g.
        aluminium construction) or in mediocre condition.
1   Occasional huts in poor condition
0   No huts in serviceable condition

Source: Hogg, 1977: 107.

Actual evaluation of a specific site or recreational unit involves scoring the resource endowment according to the degree to which it satisfies each of the user requirements identified and how it matches up to the conditions stipulated. This gives an indication of the potential of a site for a specified form of recreation in terms of the presence or absence and quality of certain features. The evaluation, therefore, provides a kind of inventory and appraisal of the site's latent potential to supply particular recreation resource functions, although this does not mean that development of this potential will necessarily occur. Evaluation is not always a straightforward field checking procedure, and suitability scores should not be accepted without qualification. Some conditions need to be sustained over time and others may only be ephemeral or present intermittently, e.g. wave conditions for surfboard riding. It is important for the assessor to be able to recognise in a low scoring site, latent potential which can be realised if certain shortcomings can be remedied, and with provision of additional features and sound management. Conversely, such insight is just as vital in the detection of inherent disadvantages, e.g. ground cover with low tolerance to trampling, or an unreliable water supply, which may become obvious with use and create a problem for subsequent management (see Chapter 4).

Overall evaluation scores can be used directly to compare the suitability of *different* sites for the *same* recreation activity, thus providing a basis for ranking and selection of the most suitable site. However, because different activities have different user requirements and therefore different rating procedures, no direct comparison of total evaluation scores for *different* activities is possible, even within the one recreational unit. Hogg points out that to make such a comparison, the totals must first be converted to standardised suitability indices using predetermined calibration curves or conversion tables.

Any evaluation procedure is subjective to some degree, in the user requirements established, the weightings assigned, the rating scales adopted and their application to the assessment of actual site conditions. Again, the assumption that conditions within any site or unit area are constant, inevitably involves a good deal of generalisation. This can be reduced by using a more complex grid pattern to break up the site, but with an associated increase in detail and field research. Mercer (1980a) notes that evaluation studies at too fine a level of precision have been criticised. Different groups or recreationists have varying levels of tolerance to relatively minor site requirements and evaluation techniques developed in one region are not necessarily applicable in another. A more pragmatic approach might assume that many areas are more or less equally suitable for a range of recreational activities and leave the finely tuned ranking of sites to the intimate knowledge and perception of experienced recreationists familiar with the particular environment concerned.

Evaluation of Streams and Routeways

Linear recreation resources such as streams and scenic routeways frequently call for specialised application of evaluation techniques. In a wide-ranging symposium on river recreation management sponsored by the US Forest Service in 1977, the various methods in use for classifying and evaluating river recreation potential were reviewed (Leatherberry, 1977). These schemes seek to identify and measure or rank the physical, cultural and aesthetic attributes of the river and its environment which are considered significant in assessing its recreational value. Typically, the schemes divide the river into manageable segments for analysis from maps, air photographs and on-site inspection. An element of subjectivity again is inevitable in judgements made concerning the features to be assessed, the recreation activities envisaged and the scoring and weighting procedures adopted. Most of the methods reviewed focus on relatively remote river resources, although some attempts have been made to develop and apply criteria for evaluating urban river settings for recreational use (Gunn *et al.*, 1974; Chubb and Bauman, 1976).

The symposium advocated more research on assessment of the recreation potential of urban rivers and other general purpose streams 'close to the centre of the river recreation opportunity spectrum'. It was considered that efforts should also be made to incorporate the concept of carrying capacity (Chapter 4) into evaluation and classification schemes and to provide for user perception and public participation in the process. It is clear that despite recent attention given to the refining of assessment procedures, there is still some way to go before development of an effective technique which will allow for the dynamic nature of the river resource and the potential users and is capable of being replicated in many different river situations.

A systematic attempt to identify and assess scenic routeways was made by Priddle (1975) in southern Ontario. Priddle's approach also was to break each selected routeway into segments, based on intersections or major changes in landscape. Each segment was then traversed and evaluated in terms of the distance that could be seen, the alignment of the road and the scenic features and variety present. Whereas some of these parameters might be clarified and additional aspects considered, evaluation of linear recreation resources such as routeways and streams, can provide valuable input to decision making.

Classification and evaluation of resource potential is a critical element in recreation planning and management. Yet it is important to stress that, although significant in its own right, it is only one phase in the formulation of a rational strategy for recreational development (Coppock and Duffield, 1975). Comparative evaluation of resources provides valuable input to the process of informed, effective choice and decision making. However, strict adherence to evaluation procedures and too rigid application of the findings may obscure opportunities for substitution between sites of recreation activities with more flexible user requirements and hence higher spatial elasticity (Hockin *et al.*, 1977). Scope should always be retained for interpretation and sound judgement by management in the incorporation of assessment data into recreation resource development programmes. The role of management in the implementation of such programmes is taken up in the following chapter.

4 OUTDOOR RECREATION AND THE ENVIRONMENT

Identification, classification and evaluation of recreation resource potential is a very necessary first step in the process of creating recreational opportunities. However, the real problems for environmental management arise from actual use of the recreation resource base. In the final analysis concern is for the quality of the recreational experience or the degree to which that experience contributes to the physical and mental well-being of participants. Quality recreational experiences are a function of the environment in which they take place but the relationship is a reciprocal one. The environment impacts on users, who in turn, have an impact on the environment. For satisfaction to be sustained environmental values must not be used up faster than they are produced. The capability of the resource base to continue to provide for recreational use raises the concept of carrying capacity.

Recreational Carrying Capacity

Like many concepts in outdoor recreation the term 'carrying capacity' is bedevilled by varying and sometimes conflicting interpretations. Definitions abound, and most attempt to combine the notion of protection of the resource base from overuse, with at the same time assurance of enjoyment and satisfaction for the participant. Thus, in broad terms, recreational carrying capacity involves the bio-physical attributes of the site as well as the attitudes and behaviour of the users. One authority defines the concept as follows: 'The level of recreation use an area can sustain without an unacceptable degree of deterioration of the character and quality of the resource or of the recreation experience' (Countryside Commission, 1970: 2). The Commission goes on to define four separate types of carrying capacity: physical capacity, economic capacity, ecological capacity and perceptual or social carrying capacity.

The first aspect, physical carrying capacity, is concerned with the maximum number of people (or activities, cars, boats, etc.) which can be accommodated or handled by a site. In many ways it is a design concept, as when referring to the capacity of a carpark, a spectator stand, or a restaurant. In other circumstances it relates to safety limits, e.g. for ski-slopes, or specific numbers for participation in sports. As will be seen later, restriction of the physical capacity of ancillary facilities can be a useful management tool for applying indirect control over visitor numbers. It is easier to limit boating activity on a lake, for instance, by deliberately reducing the physical capacity of on-shore facilities such as access points, boat-ramps and trailer parks, than to regulate boats on the water surface.

Economic carrying capacity relates to situations of multiple use of resources where outdoor recreation is combined with some other enterprise. Economic compatibility might be a better description because the term is concerned with getting the right mix of resource uses so that recreation does not reach a point at which interference with the non-recreational activity becomes economically unacceptable from the management viewpoint. This could happen, for example, at a domestic water supply reservoir where recreation is permitted but where the consequent costs of supervision, or of water treatment, cannot be justified. Similarly, with a farm or a forest, the demands and depredations of recreationists may push the costs of efficient production too high for economic management.

The final two components of carrying capacity — ecological and social — are of greatest relevance to outdoor recreation management and receive the most emphasis in the ensuing discussion.

Ecological Carrying Capacity

Ecological carrying capacity (sometimes confusedly referred to also as physical, biophysical, or environmental capacity) is concerned with the maximum level of recreational use, in terms of numbers and activities, that can be accommodated by an area or an ecosystem before an unacceptable or irreversible decline in ecological values occurs. The concept has been the subject of controversy especially regarding the subjective judgement of what is unacceptable, or irreversible decline. *Any* use of an ecosystem will result in some change and over-restrictive management could negate the recreation resource function altogether.

It could be argued that an area's ecological capacity is reached when further recreational use will impact the site beyond its ability to restore itself by *natural* means. However, such a viewpoint ignores the essential plasticity of the carrying capacity concept and the scope for, and even the presumption of, sound management practices to stretch carrying capacity beyond so-called natural limits. Technological and financial considerations are obviously also relevant to the question of irreversibility.

> Any estimate of ecological carrying capacity must take account of:
> The nature of the plant and animal communities upon which the recreation activity impinges . . .
> The nature of the recreation activity and its distribution in space and time . . . (Brotherton, 1973: 6-7).

Several writers have warned against the misconception that capacity levels are somehow inherent or site-specific (Wagar, 1968; Lime and Stankey, 1971; Brotherton, 1973; Ohmann, 1974; Bury, 1976). Bury is especially critical of the notion of a fixed, uniquely correct recreational carrying capacity for a site and suggests that the concept may be hypothetical in terms of managerial usefulness. He demonstrates the various components of biological and ecological carrying capacity and the interrelationships between them which inhibit generalisation. Bury gives the example of Big Bend National Park in southern Texas which has about reached its *hydrologic* carrying capacity under 'existing standards of water use'. Lower standards, or elimination of certain forms of water use, could increase the hydrologic carrying capacity of the park. Similarly, capacity for sewage and waste disposal is, to some degree, a function of whatever mandatory regulation is adopted.

With all the contrasting physical characteristics possible within any particular site, development of precise measures of ecological carrying capacity capable of general application appears pointless. Geological and edaphic conditions vary, as do hydrology, terrain, fauna and flora. The capacity of a site can also be materially altered by ephemeral or transitory aberrations in weather and climate. The simplest illustration of this is the difference in effect of the same volume and type of recreational activity in summer and winter (Mitchell, 1979). Ability of a site to recover over time also varies with the season and the weather.

A second group of factors which has a bearing on the ecological carrying capacity of the resource base is related to the nature of the recreation activity and the characteristics of users. A site may well be able to withstand the impact of any number of sedate picnic groups, but would quickly deteriorate if subjected to a Rugby football match. Not only is the latter activity inherently harder on the ground surface and soil cover, but its concentrated nature has greater potential for damage than the normally dispersed pattern of picnicking. Some activities, too, rely on certain kinds of equipment, e.g. trail bikes and power boats which add to site degradation and adversely affect the chances of recuperation.

Characteristics of participants likewise influence the ecological carrying capacity, although as will be seen subsequently, this is more important with social capacity. Popularity and the attraction of large numbers of visitor to a site as well as the manner in which they distribute themselves within the site are obviously important. However, severity of impact does not necessarily correlate with absolute numbers, as was revealed in research on campsites along the Colorado River in Grand Canyon National Park (US Heritage Conservation and Recreation Service, 1979). Some recreationists act responsibly and leave a site in the same condition they find it; others are not so conservation-conscious and make unreasonable demands on the resource base.

Despite sophisticated attempts to estimate ecological carrying capacity and to monitor environmental degradation (see below), the final test of whether a site measures up rests with the minds of the visitors and their perception of and reaction to the state of the recreational environment (Barkham, 1973). Another component of carrying capacity where perception also plays an important part is social carrying capacity.

Social Carrying Capacity

Outdoor recreation involves people, and the social environment in which recreation takes place has a good deal to do with the level of satisfaction experienced. Social carrying capacity (also referred to as perceptual, psychological, or even behavioural capacity) relates to the visitors' perception of the presence (or absence) of others at the same time and the effect of crowding (or in some cases, solitude) on their enjoyment and appreciation of the site. Social carrying capacity may be defined as the maximum level of recreational use, in terms of numbers and activities, above which there is a decline in the quality of the recreation experience from the point of view of the recreation participant (Countryside Commission, 1970a).

The concept has much to do with tolerance levels and sensitivity to others and as such is a personal, subjective notion linked to human psychological and behavioural characteristics. Put simply, social carrying capacity represents 'the number of people (a site) can absorb before the latest arrivals perceive the area to be "full" and seek satisfaction elsewhere' (Patmore, 1973: 241). It is the least tangible aspect of recreational carrying capacity and the most difficult to measure. Not only does it vary between individuals, but also for the same person at different times and for different situations.

Bury (1976) suggests that visitor satisfaction is linked to the notion of 'territory'and 'living space', so that social carrying capacity is derived from the number and type of encounters with other humans in the recreation area. Bury makes the interesting point that it is not merely the *actual* number of times an individual meets other recreationists, but the *potential* number and type of such encounters which are important.

. . . recreation satisfactions may be impaired even before any encounters occur if the number and density of people *seem* higher than the visitor would prefer, or if the potential encounters seem likely to be more intense, or closer, than the visitor wishes.

The condition may also be reversed — as when teenagers go to a beach to see, be seen, and interact with others. In this case, the desire of the visitor is for high densities of human use (Bury, 1976: 24).

The link between social carrying capacity and the type of recreational experience is illustrated graphically in Figure 4.1. The satisfaction derived from a wilderness experience is reduced at very low levels of use — 'two's company and three's a crowd', indeed. The canoeists in Lucas's (1964) study of Boundary Waters Wilderness on the US-Canadian border, had no wish to see fellow humans. On the other hand, being the *sole* visitor to say, Disneyland, would hardly be an enjoyable experience. In fact, the satisfaction gained from such essentially gregarious occasions increases with the level of use, at least to the point where crowding and congestion begin to irritate. It could well be the waiting and the queueing which then become exasperating rather than the numbers of people in attendance.

Perhaps the most detailed study of recreational carrying capacity was carried out for the US Bureau of Outdoor Recreation (1977), in an attempt to set guidelines for determining 'optimum' carrying capacities for a range of recreational pursuits. In the discussion of social carrying capacity the study identified the major influential factors as: psychological, social and physical, or situational. Certainly, numbers of people alone do not cause visitor dissatisfaction. Reaction to crowding is variable and to some extent, self-regulating. This makes any measurement of social carrying capacity just that much more difficult because the non-gregarious individuals are absent or have redistributed themselves in space and time so as to avoid peaks in recreation usage.

How a person reacts to the presence of others is influenced by

Figure 4.1: The Effect of Crowding on Recreational Satisfaction

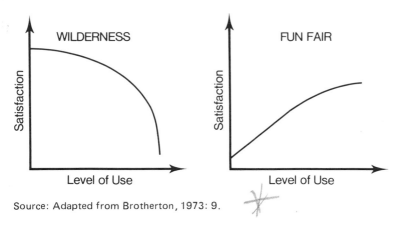

Source: Adapted from Brotherton, 1973: 9.

underlying psychological factors such as personal values, goals, attitudes, expectations and motivations. The level of satisfaction is also affected by other events or conditions incidental to the recreation experience, for example, vehicle troubles or traffic problems on the trip, illness, or even the weather.

Social circumstances, too, help shape perception of a particular situation and the way people receive and interpret information about a recreation environment. Human perception is, in part, a function of the psychological factors noted above, but also of demographic characteristics and socioeconomic background of participants. Once again, it is not so much the size of the crowd, but similarities or contrasts in social status, behaviour, or composition of the group which become a source of frustration and conflict (see below).

Perception of the quality of a recreation experience also reflects the characteristics of the physical environment or situation in which the activity takes place. Site features such as location, size, configuration, terrain, vegetation, proximity to compatible activities and the type of support facilities, can all influence satisfaction levels. In particular, they may affect the capacity of the landscape to 'absorb' users. It is the actual awareness of others which is important for social carrying capacity so that any objective measure of the density of usage may not be a true reflection of crowding. Out of sight *is* out of mind and if others present are not visible because of certain site characteristics, social carrying capacity may be considerably enlarged. Bury (1976) points out that carrying capacity generally increases with increasing density of vegetative cover. Visitors cannot see or hear one another and so the area *seems* less crowded. Wilderness above the timber-line, for example, has a smaller social carrying capacity than wilderness at lower altitudes where participants are screened by both topography and vegetation. This associated notion of 'landscape absorption' has obvious implications for management of existing recreation sites and design of proposed sites and facilities (see below).

In this discussion of recreational carrying capacity most emphasis has been placed on ecological and social aspects. Consideration of these two components separately and sequentially does not imply any order of importance, nor should it obscure the complex relationships between them. Wagar (1968) stressed that both resources *and* people must be taken into account when considering carrying capacity. It is important for decision makers to be aware of the dynamic, multi-dimensional nature of the capacity concept in order to adopt a balanced approach to managerial responsibilities.

This comprehensive viewpoint was emphasised in a recent comment by Lindsay (1980) who conceptualised outdoor recreation carrying capacity as:

. . . a function of quantity of the recreation resource, tolerance of the site to use, number of users, user type, design and management of the site and the attitude and behavior of the users and managers (Lindsay, 1980: 216).

Thus, a competent recreation management programme would incorporate both environmental considerations *and* human needs and desires. It remains a matter of judgement as to when degradation of the resource base or deterioration in the quality of the recreation experience reach the point where action is called for. The task of determining carrying capacities is matched by that of deciding when and where they are exceeded, and ultimately the choice of remedial management procedures.

The Environmental Impact of Outdoor Recreation

The intangible nature of social carrying capacity and the consequent difficulty in establishing when satisfaction has declined to an unacceptable level have already been stressed. Impacts on physical features of the environment may be easier to detect, but precise measurement of their magnitude can be just as elusive. Wall and Wright (1977) point out that it is almost impossible to reconstruct the environment minus the effects induced by recreation or to establish a base level against which to measure change. Moreover, the environment is not unchanging even without the intervention of man in speeding up natural processes. The problem then arises of disentangling the role of recreationists from the role of nature. Spatial and temporal discontinuities between cause and effect can further obscure the environmental impact of outdoor recreation. Erosion in one location may result in deposition elsewhere and considerable time may elapse before the full implications are apparent.

The problem of impact assessment is heightened by non-uniform patterns of recreation use (Glyptis, 1981). Visitor pressure within a site tends to be concentrated in space and time. Gittins (1973) documented the differential intensity of recreational activity in Snowdonia National Park in Wales where patterns of use varied with the time of year, seasonal conditions and popularity of certain park features. Gittins was able to produce a schematic grid map indicating where recreational use was high, medium, or low (Figure 4.2). The map showed clearly that the park was by no means crowded in the overall sense, but that the impact of recreation was concentrated in a series of corridors and nodal points.

A comparable study was carried out by Ovington *et al.* (1972) on the impact of tourism at Ayers Rock − Mt Olga (Uluru) National Park in central Australia. The study established that although contact areas for tourists within the park are restricted, each shows evidence of environmental change in terms of topography, soil, drainage patterns, flora, fauna, odour, noise and waste material accumulation. Ecological impacts included soil compaction, erosion and destruction of vegetation and wildlife habitat. Even the massive monolith of Ayers Rock itself has not escaped environmental damage from climbers, not to mention the well-intentioned installation of chain-railings and lines painted on the rock surface to assist visitors to reach the summit.

On a smaller scale the pattern and extent of wear-and-tear by recreationists on campground, picnic sites and sand dune vegetation have been demonstrated (Lapage, 1967; Boden, 1977, Slatter, 1978). Various methods were used to record changes in ground cover and in species composition and these were correlated with the level of visitor usage. Lapage used sequential photographs on a systematic grid system to reveal a progressive reduction in vegetative cover and number of species closely associated with concentrations of use around fixed site facilities such as picnic tables and barbecues. With continued use

Figure 4.2: The Intensity of Recreational Use in Snowdonia National Park

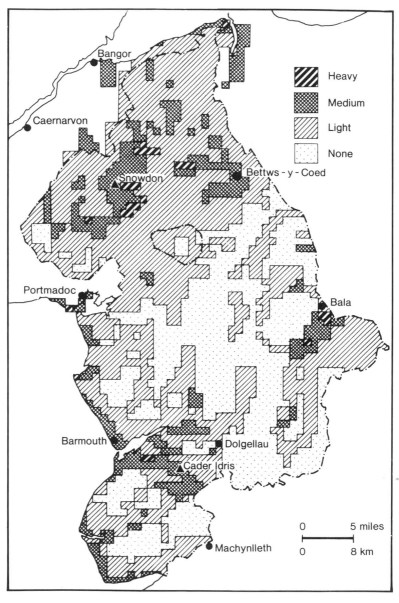

Source: Patmore, 1973: 238.

Lapage found a gradual rearrangement of plant species composition leading to a relatively recreation-tolerant soil cover. The ecological environment responds in different ways to visitor pressure and the possibility of beneficial changes should not be dismissed. It is considered by some observers that soil compaction around the roots of trees, for example, has a useful effect in terms of forest viability. Low intensities of trampling can stimulate plant growth and the opening up of forests with nature trails allows more light through the canopy and can contribute to an enhanced recreation landscape.

Studies of recreational impact highlight the need for close monitoring of visitor use, movement, concentration and dispersion. In their patterns of recreation, people *do* reveal preferences for certain sites within space and for particular paths and choice of routes to desirable territorial goals. In this regard the 'edge effect' is often prominent in the manner in which visitors distribute themselves over a site, favouring the edges in the landscapes, e.g. paths and areas adjacent to access points, trees, gardens and other features, and often ignoring the wide open spaces between. Once again a useful management tactic becomes obvious — create more 'edges' and thereby even out visitor pressure.

When comparisons are made between sites it becomes clear that some ecosystems are more tolerant of recreation activity than others. Some areas are virtually indestructible, while others are so fragile as to permit only minimal use. Goldsmith and Munton (1974) suggest that the ecosystems or habitats most vulnerable to recreation impact are:

*Coastal systems, such as sand dunes and salt marshes characterised by instability.

*Mountain habitats, where growth and self-recovery are inhibited by climate.

*Ecosystems with shallow, wet, or nutrient-deficient soils.

A comprehensive survey of the ecological impact of outdoor recreation was presented by Wall and Wright (1977) who itemised the consequence of recreational activities for specific attributes of the environment. Most emphasis was directed towards soil, vegetation, water and wildlife. However, the authors were able to show that even geology and the air are affected by certain forms of recreation and complex inter-relationships exist between types of recreational impact. One specific form of outdoor recreation which is capable of widespread repercussions for the environment is the use of off-road vehicles.

Off-road Recreation Vehicles

In recent years, off-road vehicles, such as trail bikes, dune buggies, four-wheel drive vehicles and specialised recreation vehicles such as over-snow vehicles and all-terrain vehicles, have become a significant feature of the recreation scene. Although still very much in a minority compared with other recreational pursuits, their use is increasing dramatically and with it their potential for destruction of the recreational environment and conflict with other users and uses.

A growing body of literature now exists to substantiate the extent of the impact of various types of off-road vehicles on specific components of the environment (Brander, 1974; Australian House of Representatives Standing Committee on Environment and Conservation, 1977; Bury *et al*., 1977; Neumann and Merriam, 1979; Nicholes, 1980; Godfrey *et al*., 1980). Much of the problem rests with the use of these vehicles in sensitive environments, e.g. coastal sand dunes, arid zones, steep slopes, alpine areas and wetlands.

Off-road recreation vehicles can also be responsible for the spread of noxious weeds and the invasion of despoiled areas by exotic vegetation normally unable to compete with indigenous vegetation. This is a particular problem in parts of Australia where seeds from weed-infested roadside reserves are easily spread by tyres and mud on vehicles. Damage has also been experienced at sites of archaeological and scientific significance in coastal areas of Australia where Aboriginal relics and middens have been destroyed or disarranged.

Quite apart from the physical effects of off-road recreation vehicles, the most persistent cricitism is the noise associated with their use. Trailbikes, in particular, can be heard over great distances and over-snow vehicles are also criticised for being excessively noisy. Other ancillary impacts attributed to off-road vehicles are the spread of litter and the risk of fire in otherwise inaccessible areas. Finally, there are considerable hazard risks with use of these vehicles and deaths and injuries are not uncommon.

Off-road recreation vehicles are only one of the more obvious sources of nuisance associated with outdoor recreational activities. However, if time and space patterns of potential effects can be identified, preventive and remedial measures can be undertaken. Perhaps the most constructive response is to set aside special areas for off-road vehicles, bicycle moto-cross enthusiasts and even skateboards, where their use can be controlled and environmental repercussions minimised.

Conflicts in Outdoor Recreation

Brief reference has been made to nuisance aspects of some types of outdoor recreation. However, it is not always a question of over-use of recreational resources, so much as incompatibility and resulting conflicts between opposing recreationists and between outdoor recreation and other forms of resource use.

The question of compatibility revolves around the degree to which two or more activities can co-exist in the use of a given recreational resource. Goodall and Whittow (1975) point out that the problem is linked with the resource requirements for particular recreational pursuits. Only where recreational activities have similar requirements is there a possibility of shared use of a site, or alternatively, of conflict. Noisy activities such as those involving off-road recreation vehicles or power boats conflict with fishing, bird-watching, use of wilderness and other activities requiring peaceful countryside locations. Nor is conflict necessarily confined in space or time; site disturbance can have a lasting effect and can spill over on to adjacent areas. Goodall and Whittow stress that the incidence of incompatibility is, in part, a function of the activity, the manner in which it is practised and the characteristics of the site or the resource involved. Trails, rivers and other constricted linear resources are particularly sensitive to use incompatibility. On the other hand, timbered land may increase compatibility by reducing visual intrusion and noise penetration.

Conflict and compatibility involve a good deal more than simple one-to-one comparison of selected recreational activities. According to Lindsay (1980), the conflict problem may be summarised as one of recreationists competing for the same physical, social and psychological space during the same time period. Thus, confrontation over use of recreation space should not be interpreted solely as inter-activity conflict. The complexities of human behaviour are such that conflict situations can develop between different types of recreationists engaged in the same activity.

Jacob and Schreyer (1980) believe that the key to conflict resolution lies in identifying the 'conflict potential' of various recreation resource *clientele* rather than in labelling certain *activities* as conflict prone. It is not merely a question of skiers not getting along with snowmobilers, or of 'motor versus muscle'. In this context four causal factors are identified as conducive to conflict in outdoor recreation:

Activity Style — The various personal meanings assigned to an activity, For some, participation may be intense; the activity becomes the focus of life interest, with acquisition of status and achievement of a high quality recreation experience prominent goals of participants. Such persons are prone to conflict because few recreation situations or fellow participants measure up to their high standards.

Resource Specificity — Some individuals attribute special values and importance to certain physical resources and develop possessive, protective attitudes to favoured recreation sites — a common trait of skilled fishermen and hunters. Tension can develop with lower status 'intruders' who do not share this appreciation and interpretation of site values, and who disrupt the exclusive, intimate relationship built up with a place. Once again conflict has little to do with activities themselves, but can occur between divergent classes of resource users.

Mode of Experience — The manner in which individuals approach a recreation experience can provide the ingredients for conflict. Jacob and Schreyer distinguish between 'focused' and 'unfocused' modes of experience, with the latter concerned with overall spatial relationships and environmental generalities rather than specific entities within that environment. Thus the 'focused' wilderness user, intent upon achieving an intimate relationship with specific aspects of the natural environment, has little in common with the 'unfocused' hiker for whom merely being in the countryside is sufficient. The greater the gap between recreationists along this continuum, the greater the potential for conflict.

Tolerance for Lifestyle Diversity — The suggestion is that individuals deliberately choose recreation settings and associations which reflect their societal outlook and behaviour and are unwilling to share resources with other lifestyle groups categorised as deviant, or merely different. Value-laden inferences are made about people indulging in alternative forms of recreation stereotyped as 'less worthwhile'. Thus, the trail-bike, the power boat and the snowmobile are seen 'as symbolic of a society that arrogantly exploits and consumes resources'. Ethnic, racial and social class distinctions can also be the basis for lifestyle-based conflicts. Such people are often labelled out-of-hand, as 'inferior', so that even when pursuing the same activity and following the same rules, conflict still ensues, especially as the number and variety of people desiring access to recreation resources increase.

Jacob and Schreyer suggest that the degree to which these four factors are present, singly or in combination, represents the extent to which the *potential* for conflict exists. Conditions for conflict may just as readily occur in the mind and be part of the mental state and attitude of the participant, as in the nature of the recreational activities. The authors conclude with a warning for management:

Unfortunately, the tendency to define conflict as confrontations between activities has left the sources of recreation conflicts unrecognized. In failing to recognize the basic causes of conflict, inappropriate resolution techniques and management strategies are likely to be adopted (Jacob and Schreyer, 1980: 378).

Outdoor Recreation Management

The foregoing comments emphasise the dual importance to outdoor recreation management of the physical *and* the social environment. The primary aim of outdoor recreation management, presumably, is to bring together supply and demand — to attempt to equate resource adequacy and human recreational needs and desires. In so doing the manager obviously must have regard for the character and quality of the resource base ensuring that capacity is not exceeded and that environmental degradation is minimised. At the same time, the managerial role extends to visitor enjoyment and satisfaction. Action must be taken to reduce conflict and to maximise the quality of the recreation experience. These dual responsibilities hold whether for the economic success of commercial enterprises, or for the protection of public investment in parks and recreation areas.

A first step then in the management process is the establishment of broad management objectives. From these will flow the determination of carrying capacities and the selection of specific management procedures. Modification of the system may well follow implementation of the management approaches decided upon. An important element in this phase is evaluation of the system based on monitoring of its operation by managers and feedback from users.

The management process is set out in Figure 4.3 (adapted from Brown, 1977). A set of objectives is delineated first with reference to the capabilities of the resource base. Information on resources should indicate which activities are physically possible as well as some of the resource constraints on recreation opportunities.

Figure 4.3: The Recreation Management Process

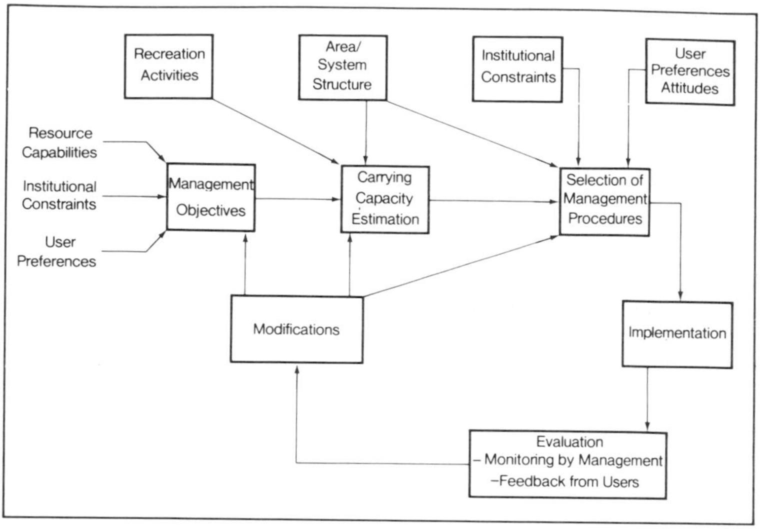

Source: Adapted from Brown, 1977: 194.

Institutional constraints also have obvious implications for management and set limits on the range of recreation opportunities possible. Legal restrictions and standards, administrative policies and guidelines and budgetary and personnel considerations, can all influence the selection of realistic management objectives. In some situations additional problems are created for management by overlapping Federal, State and local jurisdictions, each of which may have different interpretations of what is appropriate recreational use.

Ideally, management objectives should reflect user preferences if they are to receive support at the implementation stage. A good example is the 'battle' fought in Yosemite National Park in 1970 between hundreds of young campers and a combined force of park rangers and state police. The dispute centred on what were seen as restrictive park zoning regulations and excessive fees and the demonstrators felt they were discriminated against by the park administration. A significicant outcome of the confrontation was the admission that park planning authorities were out of touch with public opinion on many matters relating to national parks. As a result, provision was made for a much greater degree of public involvement in the park planning process for Yosemite and other sites (Mercer, 1980a).

More and more people are now demanding the right to participate in decision making and public involvement is increasingly seen as a necessary and desirable input to management. This does not mean that the process must be totally democratic in the sense that the user population 'calls the tune'. Identifying the population to be consulted is always a problem and, in any case, it would be foolish to disregard the expertise of management entirely in reaching a decision. As is often the case, compromise in the form of 'guided democracy' is probably the best approach. User preferences regarding resource attributes, social characteristics of the recreation environment and preferred management approaches, should certainly be canvassed, but interpreted in the light of managerial experience of what is desirable and possible. It is important, however, that the exercise of involving the public be perceived as more than good public relations. Whereas user preferences are only one of many inputs to the formulation of management objectives, there should be clear evidence that they have been considered and integrated into the final decision.

That said, it must be conceded that many factors inhibit and distort the clear expression and articulation of user preferences and a range of approaches may need to be used to encourage participation and combat apathy and indifference (Jubenville, 1978). Even when success has apparently been achieved in provoking a constructive response from communities affected by recreation management proposals, there are risks involved in the process of public participation. Care must be taken to ensure that not only vocal pressure groups and politically active professional lobbyists receive attention. The 'squeaky wheel syndrome' may not truly reflect majority preference. Conversely, the imposition of 'elitist' managerial attitudes on users could lead to management objectives which are unrealistic and unacceptable. A good measure of genuine public participation is essential, but a balance should be struck between uninformed reactions, perhaps merely reflecting current trends and fashions and a more objective appraisal by supposedly detached experts in management.

The second stage in the outdoor recreation management process (Figure 4.3), that of setting appropriate carrying capacities consistent with the management objectives adopted, should be related to the structure of the management area or system. As was noted earlier in this chapter, limits on ecological and social carrying capacity are, in part, a function of the natural features of the site (configuration, terrain, ground cover and the like), man-made facilities and amenities which influence visitor distribution and behaviour and the recreation activities to be accommodated. It is also worth reiterating that carrying capacities, once set, are not inflexible but are open to manipulation by management; hence the feed-back loop in the flow chart (Figure 4.3) from management procedures.

The range of approaches possible for actual management of recreation sites or visitors is discussed in more detail below. In this view of the management process it should be noted that several of the factors which contribute to the formulation of management objectives also influence the choice of specific tactics or tools to achieve those objectives. It is not always a case of what managers may see as necessary, or *wish* to do, so much as what they are *able* to do.

Once again institutional directives can act as constraints in the selection of management procedures. Obviously too, the characteristics of the recreation area or site set limits on which combination of approaches is likely to be most successful. Linear sites call for a different approach from those with more regular dimensions, and remote forested areas with rugged terrain may not need as strict regulation as would more open accessible sites with fewer natural deterrents on recreational usage. Brown (1977) also stresses the value of knowledge of user preferences and attitudes in the choice and effectiveness of specific management tools. Some may respond kindly to appeal and inducements, others may react more favourably to direct regulation.

A desirable characteristic of efficient management is flexibility, so that, if in the implementation of the management procedures selected deficiencies are detected, the management process should allow for modifications (Figure 4.3). The need for adjustments may be discerned by management or become apparent in feedback from users. Subsequently, modifications can be made at various points in the system and the management process becomes self-regulating.

Once objectives have been formulated and estimates made of carrying capacities, the primary task of outdoor recreation management emerges — that of selection, implementation and modification of on-site management procedures. However, effective management begins at an even earlier stage with proper site selection, planning and design. If these preliminary considerations receive adequate attention, the most appropriate sites and the more resilient components of the environment (in terms of low vulnerability and high tolerance to visitor usage) will already have been set aside for recreation and laid out and equipped, so as to minimise management problems.

Recreation Site Selection

This is a most important first step to which much of the ease or difficulty in subsequent operations can be attributed. Fundamental considerations are access to users and the suitability of the resource base for
the recreational activities envisaged. This should already have been
established by application of the site evaluation techniques described in
Chapter 3. However, the fact that a site apparently meets the basic suitability criteria laid down may conceal certain shortcomings in specific
resource attributes which will prove costly to management in later use.
Where more than one site meets basic requirements, a detailed examination of site characteristics is needed to determine priorities for development. This examination should focus on the features of competing sites
which affect the task of management in producing and sustaining worthwhile recreation values (McCosh, 1973; Jubenville, 1976).

Assuming that questions of location and convenience of access to
potential users have been satisfied, many physical features of the site
itself can impinge upon the quality of the recreational experience and
hence the role of management. Not only the size of an area, but its configuration are important. It is almost always helpful to have an area
somewhat larger than required to allow rotation of usage and provision
of a buffer zone to segregate the site from adjoining developments. In
most cases too, a long narrow site is less efficient in terms of internal
arrangement of attractions, facilities and services, than one of more
regular configuration.

The nature of the terrain, degree and direction of slopes, rock types
and presence of rock outcrops, soil stability and compactibility,
drainage and susceptibility to flooding and availability of construction
materials, can all have engineering implications for site development
and maintenance. So too, can the size, variety and density of the
vegetation and the extent and location of open space.

The importance to the recreation landscape of water of the right
quantity, quality and characteristics is noted in other chapters, but
several ancillary aspects of water also have to be considered in site selection. Water is needed for drinking, sanitation and possibly irrigation, so
that sources and suitability of water supply need to be determined
along with the costs of pumping, treatment, storage and disposal.
Adequate estimates of water availability require knowledge of ground-
water and of climate and weather patterns over an extended period,
e.g. precipitation, evaporation and snow cover. Other climatic factors
which may have a bearing on decisions concerning a recreation site

include aspect, exposure to winds and even related seasonal conditions such as the length of shadows in winter and the incidence of high spring pollen counts. Finally, a site could have certain negative or undesirable features which could influence selection. Jubenville (1976) suggests that a hazard survey be carried out for each potential site to identify possible hazardous conditions such as avalanches, falling trees, precipices, dangerous waters, poisonous plants and insects and dangerous animals. Other annoyances, such as noise, dust, fumes and aquatic weeds and algae can represent problems in the making for management; problems which, if foreseen, might be avoided.

McCosh (1973) stresses the value of prior study and sound judgement in recreation site selection. Poorly-chosen sites will become inefficient areas with problems that cannot easily be solved. Of course, some of the negative site characteristics noted may be offset by good planning and design. Use of design in this way as a compensatory device is fine, providing the cost is not excessive. However, it is preferable to implement design measures which are complementary to and reinforce the natural features of the site. The idea is:

. . . to utilize the features of the landscape to enhance recreational experience, minimize site maintenance and maintain natural aesthetics. Although fitting the development to the natural lay of the land may be more expensive and require more attention to detail, the resulting site should be more attractive, more able to handle larger visitor-use loads and less expensive to maintain (Jubenville, 1976: 155).

Recreation Site Planning and Design

Albert Rutledge (1971), in his seminal work *Anatomy of a Park*, put forward what he calls a set of 'umbrella considerations' or principles of design. These include:

Design with purpose — so that the appropriate relationships are established between the various parts of the recreation complex — natural elements, use areas, structures, people, animals and forces of nature.

Design for people — rather than to meet some rigid standards, or the impersonal demands of machines, equipment and administrative convenience. More attention to the 'why' of design would go a long way towards structuring outdoor areas to satisfy human behavioural needs.

Design for both function and aesthetics — striking a balance of dollar values and human values with the achievement of efficiency interwoven with the generation of a satisfying sensory experience.

Rutledge was writing of park design, but the principles and detailed procedures he describes have application in many other situations. For example, Lime (1974) has demonstrated the relevance of good location and design to the affective functioning of campgrounds. While it is probably true to say that aesthetics are often only considered after functional aspects have been satisfied, the two should go together in the design process so that attention to aesthetics actually strengthens functional efficiency. In practice, functional elements of design tend to receive emphasis because of their more tangible nature — 'it works or it doesn't'. Aesthetics, on the other hand, are like beauty, very much in the eye of the beholder!

A further source of confusion can arise from overlap between the planning and design phases. In general terms, recreation site planning could be said to be concerned with the broad arrangement of site features, support facilities and circulation patterns necessary for the type of recreation envisaged. Design is related to micro-location and the moulding and fitting of the plans to specific topographic and landscape features of the site, while maintaining the desired positions of the facilities and circulation patterns (Jubenville, 1976). For convenience, the criteria to be observed during both phases are considered together in the following discussion.

In the first place, planning and design of the recreation site should conform to known user preferences for given environmental conditions or situations (Christiansen, 1977). Merely providing a picnic site is not enough. Service requirements, supporting facilities, equipment and site refinements should reflect the style and characteristics of participants. They should also be located to fit in with normal behavioural patterns, minimise conflict and confusion and facilitate movement within the site.

A basic functional criterion of planning and design is that the recreation site and associated developments satisfy technical requirements, i.e. that they be usable in the sense of meeting standards of size, spacing and quantities. Operating needs and conditions are also important and apart from meeting health and safety regulations, site developments should provide for the comfort and convenience of users. Rutledge (1971) illustrates the relevance of orientation to natural forces in the layout of recreation sites, e.g. the elevation and path of the sun's rays and the direction of prevailing winds. Rutledge also stresses a common sense approach to avoid unnecessary costs and provide for ease of supervision.

Recreational use of a site inevitably involves movement and the circulation system adopted can have a pronounced effect on efficiency of use, safety, satisfaction levels and supervision of visitor behaviour. Rutledge points out that the aim should be to get people where they want to go readily and in doing so, not interfere with other activities. The task, therefore, is to anticipate flows, eliminate obstacles and confusion and provide unobstructed, well-defined, logical routes. Proper circulation planning and design can become an arm of recreation site management, not only in protecting the natural environment and visitors, but in promoting and facilitating desirable patterns of recreational use.

Sound site planning and design can minimise the task of supervision and the need for restrictive control measures over visitor behaviour. Public welfare should always be a concern and if provision for visitor health and safety is built into a recreation site, many hazardous situations can be prevented. By definition, accidents are unplanned, but planning and design can go a long way towards eliminating the factors likely to generate emergencies.

Maintaining law and order at public recreation sites is also a serious problem for management. Depreciative behaviour can reduce or destroy the resource base and facilities and interfere with the experience and satisfaction of other participants. Vandalism, acts of nuisance, violation of rules and crime, unfortunately, must all be anticipated. The monetary impact is staggering. In the United States the total yearly loss from vandalism alone has been estimated at US $4 billion (Clark, 1976).

The problem can at least be contained by prior attention to planning and design. Weinmayer (1973) believes that proper design can reduce vandalism by 90 per cent and some observers suggest that much antisocial behaviour actually represents a protest against poor design and management of parks and other recreation sites (Gold, 1974). So-called 'vandalism by design' is blamed for providing the opportunity for misuse by equipping recreation sites with objects, facilities and materials which invite disrespect and ultimately, destruction. The inference is that opportunities for vandalism and other forms of undesirable behaviour can be removed or reduced at the planning and design stage. It is possible, of course, to attempt to devise structures which are vandal-proof and virtually indestructible. It is preferable and more positive to provide sturdy, but attractive recreation environments which will be valued and protected by the users themselves. Site developments should be designed for easy maintenance and quick restoration if damaged. Rutledge (1971) suggests that thought be given to the clustering of potentially vandal-prone features, the opening up of sites to external inspection, more adequate lighting and the encouragement of higher levels of use as a deterrent to anti-social acts. On-site control of vandalism and other forms of depreciative behaviour is a particular facet of visitor management and this is discussed later in this chapter.

Recreation sites which are properly selected and located and which have had the benefit of thoughtful planning and design should almost manage themselves; certainly, the task of management should be made much easier. Unfortunately, it is probably more often the case that managers inherit a poorly selected site where little attention has been given to adequate development planning or design. Subsequent problems emerge, either because of overuse, deliberate misuse (above), or unintentional damage through ignorance and inappropriate use. Careful management of resources and visitors then becomes an on-going concern.

Recreation Resource Management

Jubenville (1978) sees the managerial role in outdoor recreation as incorporating *resource management*, concerned with the reciprocal relationships between the recreation landscape and the visitor; *visitor management*, enhancing the social environment in order to maximise the recreation experience; and *service management*, involving the provision of necessary and desirable services so that the user can enjoy both the social and resource environment. Whereas the three are important components of the overall recreation system, Jubenville considers visitor management to be fundamental since it is the visitor who 'creates' (expresses?) demand for recreational experiences which require the other two elements. In the ensuing comments provision of services will be regarded as a complementary, but ancillary aspect of outdoor recreation management and discussion will concentrate on resources and people. That said, it will soon become apparent that there is much scope for overlap between the two.

Recreation resource management implies close monitoring of the recreation site to chart the rate, direction and character of change. It is vital that negative changes be detected early so that appropriate and positive management procedures be taken before site degradation proceeds to the point where the recreational environment becomes a source of dissatisfaction to visitors. Without a systematic monitoring programme, management has no basis for comparison to determine change. Once deterioration becomes evident resource management procedures must be introduced.

Resource management involves the manipulation of elements of the resource base to maintain, enhance, or even re-create satisfying opportunity settings for various recreational pursuits. Jubenville (1978) sees the programming or implementation phase of recreation resource management as including:

Site management — manipulation of the developed site to maintain the quality of the resource setting and rehabilitate it where necessary.

Vegetation management — silvicultural practices related to the management of intensive use areas, such as roads, trails, site developments and around waterbodies.

Landscape management — designed to assess the visual impact of developments on the aesthetic appeal of the landscape.

Ecosystems management — defining ecosystems and their boundaries and determining possible effects of human use including fire management.

Hazard management — inventory and reduction of potential natural and man-made hazards associated with recreation use.

Jubenville goes on to suggest five basic procedures for the management of developed recreation sites. In selecting the most appropriate course of action, the recreation site manager needs to balance concern for the resource base against commercial considerations and the costs involved in loss of patronage. Leaving aside Jubenville's first suggestion — 'cut out and get out' — which is hardly a positive approach to management in permitting uncontrolled use and site degradation, the choice is between either:

*Site closure and rejuvenation through natural processes or cultural treatments. Site closure will certainly minimise recovery time and inconvenience and may be justified for heavily deteriorated sites, especially where alternative opportunities are available.

*Rest and rotation of sites, or perhaps areas within a site, so that some recreation opportunities are always available.

*Leave open and culturally treat the site, i.e. keeping the site operating while implementing rehabilitation measures. If possible, this is clearly the ideal situation, but can only succeed if treatment begins before site deterioration is well advanced.

Resource management procedures primarily involve technical and engineering type actions, or landscaping techniques. Examples include various soil treatments and ground cover improvements such as irrigation, use of fertilisers, re-seeding, replanting or conversion to hardier and more resilient species, judicious thinning of vegetation and removal of noxious species. These measures are aimed at increasing the durability of the biotic community as well as inducing its recovery.

On-site patterns of recreational use can be influenced in various ways. These could involve channelling the movements of visitors along selected paths — thorny bushes are quite effective in achieving this purpose (James, 1974), or discouraging recreationists from entering a particular area by fencing or the erection of some barrier designed as a 'people-sifter' (Miles and Seabrooke, 1977). The effect may be discriminatory, but obstacles such as ditches and stiles, which prove a deterrent to some classes of visitor, are not insurmountable to all.

Vehicular traffic can be regulated as to mode and route and many heavily-used sites no longer permit use of private vehicles. Shuttle buses and other forms of communal transport are becoming more common in national parks (Chapter 7). One-way traffic can be made mandatory especially where parallel routeways exist and separate trails can be designated for different classes of movement, e.g. skiers and snow-mobilers.

Such action may be complemented by landscaping to enhance carrying capacities. This could involve the hardening or surfacing of intensively used areas such as viewing points; rotation of site furniture (barbecues, picnic tables) and movable facilities such as kiosks and shelters; rotation of entrances, trails and campsites; and provision of more effective waste disposal systems. As noted earlier in this chapter, social carrying capacity can also be stretched by imaginative plantings to create more 'edges' or borders and by breaking up the site with artificial mounds and buffers to boost the capacity of the landscape to 'absorb' visitors. Van Lier (1973) noted the importance of the 'border effect' in the size and layout of inland beaches in the Netherlands. By creating more levels or zones, a greater number of users could be accommodated on a beach. In the same way, Lime and Stankey (1971) indicate how recreational use can be redistributed and carrying capacity increased by improving access to previously under-used areas. Additional roads and trails and the installation of lighting, elevated pathways, bridges and the elimination of hazards are effective in redirecting visitor pressure.

With recreational waterbodies, capacity can be enhanced by providing more access points and ancillary facilities and by manipulating the type and form of landscape features, e.g. addition of sandy beaches. Wildlife capacities which indirectly impinge upon certain recreational pursuits can also be built up by provision or improvement of habitats to encourage greater abundance and variety of animals, birds and fish. Widlife populations will also respond positively to more reliable food and water supply, control of diseases and pests including predators such as feral cats, controlled use of biocides and minimisation of pollution and reduction of fire and other hazards.

Recreation resource management is directed towards maintaining and enhancing the site as a viable setting for outdoor recreation. Ultimately, however, it is the reaction of the visitor to the site which determines the success of the management programme. Ensuring a satisfying, high quality recreation experience is the prime reason for developing an outdoor recreation management system and specific procedures for visitor management contribute to this aim.

Recreation Visitor Management

Once again, monitoring of visitor behaviour and user preferences plays an important part in visitor management, for only through knowledge of what visitors do and want to do can appropriate management tactics be devised (Miles and Seabrooke, 1977). Monitoring may be formal or informal, overt or covert and it should be a two-way exercise concerned as much with the impact of the site on the visitor as how the visitor affects the site. The managerial process is complicated because it is not merely a question of ecological carrying capacity and over-use, but social carrying capacity can be involved along with the various sources of conflict identified earlier in this chapter.

Paradoxically, one way to approach the problem of excessive visitor pressure is to concentrate recreational use even more. Concentration of use can help control general site deterioration by attracting visitors to selected locations able to sustain high levels of use. It is the antithesis of load spreading and is the principle that has guided construction of sites such as Canyon Village in Yellowstone National Park (Garrison, 1977). In that case land with no primary park values was chosen for a townsite type of centre where great numbers of people and accompanying congestion could be accommodated while reducing pressure elsewhere.

More typically, efforts are made to overcome 'people problems' by spreading the load in space and time. Dispersal of use seeks to redistribute recreationists in order to bring about more uniform patterns of visitor pressure. Time-wise, attempts can be made to reduce seasonal or daily peaks of usage by extending operations into slack periods, with or without incentives, and even utilising the night hours in some circumstances. Staggering of vacations is another approach to spreading use more evenly throughout the year. Alternatively, additional opportunities can be created space-wise to divert some visitors from overused sites.

When these essentially voluntary means of bringing about dispersal of use fail to achieve that objective, it becomes necessary to adopt a more direct approach to regulating visitor behaviour. Regulation of use implies some restriction over what recreationists are permitted to do. Attempts at people control come down to a choice between 'do' and 'don't' — the carrot or the stick. Most recreation managers would be aware of the value of allowing the user to retain some sense of freedom of choice and the role of persuasion in modification of visitor behaviour is discussed presently. However, with certain management problems such as vandalism, enforcement of rules backed up by strenuous efforts at detection and punishment of offenders may be the most effective means of control (Priddle and Wall, 1979).

In regard to managerial directives, several of the tactics already noted in connection with resource management also require visitor regulation as a concomitant of site protection. The admonition to 'Keep off the Grass', for example, is clearly designed to bring about a particular response in recreational use patterns and thereby help maintain the condition of the site. Regimentation for its own sake is indefensible and there are some situations where recreational use should *not* be regulated. In most instances, a positive approach is possible and preferable to an endless array of signs informing users of what they *cannot* do.

On-site control involves directions as to location, time and duration of recreational visits and activities in order to attain the desired intensity of use for the area. Among the most common procedures for visitor control are zoning or scheduling. These have the advantage, not only of limiting use, but of promoting dispersal of use and reducing conflicts by separation of incompatible forms of recreation, such as fishing and water-skiing.

Zoning involves the clustering of compatible uses in selected parts of a recreation site. National parks are a form of zoning to begin with and the designation of certain areas within parks for special purposes, e.g. wilderness, is often practised (Chapter 7). Different stretches of a river or lake can also be zoned for different uses, sometimes on the grounds of safety, or because the resource attributes do not lend themselves to all types of recreation, or simply to avoid mutual interference and maximise satisfaction between users. Craig (1977) gives the example of the Chattooga River in South Carolina, USA, where the headwaters are narrow and shallow providing difficult conditions for boating, but ideal for cold water trout fishing. By contrast, the lower river is too warm for optimum trout production, but offers some of the best boating in southeastern United States. Accordingly, the Forest Service has zoned the upper reaches for fishing only and permits both uses in the lower portion of the river. Spatial zoning is likely to be more successful where there is a logical and accepted basis for partitioning of the site. It is useful, too, if zone boundaries can be aligned to some natural or recognisable feature, e.g. different activities allocated to the opposite banks of a river.

Scheduling, or zoning by way of time limitations, is another useful procedure for visitor control. Recreation activities using the same site are allocated to specific time periods on an hourly, daily, weekly, or seasonal basis in order to reduce conflicts and to ensure adequate rotation of use. The time frame chosen depends upon the degree of conflict and the level of competing uses. A variation of time zoning, especially with linear recreation resources, is the staggered scheduling of departure times, e.g. river trips. Ideally, schedules should be drawn up after consultation with user groups, and if possible, tailored to fit normal recreational patterns.

The term 'density zoning' is sometimes applied to a procedure for space limitation whereby recreation density levels are linked to predetermined upper limits of use for particular management zones, relative to ecological and social carrying capacities. Jubenville (1978) notes that some national parks and lakes in the United States have recently been zoned in this way and their use limited to certain density patterns, based on the resource, the activity and the perceptions of users. To be effective the procedure usually requires a well-supervised permit system or some other equitable means of rationing available recreation space. Rationing refers to the mechanisms through which opportunities to use designated recreation resources are distributed to users (Stankey, 1977). Implementation of rationing assumes that reasonable estimates of carrying capacities can be established; that in the absence of rationing usage would exceed capacity at some sites; and that a reduction in usage through rationing is the preferred management option (Grandage and Rodd, 1981). Recreational use can be rationed by various means. Chubb and Chubb (1981) suggest three broad approaches:

*Sharing the limited supply of recreational opportunities among potential participants by measures such as the issue of permits and licences; use of a reservation system; queuing and participation on a 'first-come, first-served' basis; or allocation of opportunities by lot.

*Providing a limited experience to as many participants as possible even though this may affect the quality of the experience, e.g. placing limits on the size of parties; and rotation or regulation of use to encourage high turnover.

*Making it more difficult for people to participate. Use can be discouraged by restricting access; making reservations harder to obtain; insistence on merit standards (certain skills or knowledge) as the basis for entry; and the imposition of fees. Differential fee structures can also be used to redistribute recreational use patterns.

Any form of rationing discriminates to a certain extent against some participants and some forms of recreation. The use of fees or eligibility standards to apportion recreational opportunities has been soundly criticised on the grounds of equity and effectiveness. Moreover, all rationing systems have shortcomings and in Stankey's (1977) words, can be 'beat'. To complement procedures for visitor regulation, management can seek to modify recreation behaviour by persuasion and the provision of information through interpretative services.

Information and Interpretation

In the dissemination of information about recreation opportunities Jubenville (1978) makes the distinction between advice reaching the potential visitor before arrival at the site (Regional Information System) and information provided at the site (Area Information System). Prior information should reach the individual when choices are being considered concerning recreational participation. It is more often the task of government or regional organisations than the specific site manager and can even involve zero, minimal, or negative information aimed at diverting attention or making heavily patronised sites less attractive. Thus, certain sites or facilities may be omitted from a map, or reference may be made to popularity and associated crowding; conditions which some will try to avoid.

Much more effort is directed positively into inducing desired patterns of behaviour on-site by increasing public awareness through publicity, education, interpretation and other less obtrusive methods or persuasion. Freedom of choice is seemingly not directly involved, yet the behavioural response sought is produced. Various means are available for transmitting information and communicating information between management and visitors. Typical approaches involve the use of maps and signposting, publications and brochures, electronic media and on-site contact by way of visitor information centres and guide services. These last methods for getting the message across are more often in the nature of interpretation than mere passive provision of information.

Interpretation has been described by Tilden (1967) as more than just instruction or communication of information. Tilden sees the chief function of interpretation as provoking and stimulating interest and awareness among visitors to a recreation site. This is to be achieved by revealing meanings and relationships in nature by reference to original objects and from first-hand experience with common easily understood examples and materials.

A second function of interpretation is to assist in accomplishing management objectives. It can do this by encouraging appreciation of the recreation environment and promoting public co-operation and responsibility in conserving recreational values. Lime and Stankey (1971) suggest that much destructive behaviour results from ignorance rather than malicious intent so that increasing the flow of information to the public is a preferable and probably cheaper means of reducing depreciative acts than prohibitions and censure. As Clark (1976) and Harrison (1977) explain, the key is often in pointing out 'why', when certain norms of behaviour are required.

Why can't cars be driven off parking pads?
Why can't tables be moved . . . ?
Why can't a tree be chopped down for firewood?
Why can't initials be carved on benches or tables or trees?
(Clark, 1976: 66).

On the premiss that 'an informed public is a caring public', the Countryside Commission (1978) in Britain has designed a number of self-guided trails around forests, farms, urban centres, ancient monuments and natural areas to increase understanding and appreciation of these features and thereby engender improved standards of behaviour and greater respect for the environment.

A basic objective of recreation management is to provide a sustained flow of benefits for users (Wagar, 1964). Concern for the quality of the visitor experience then, is another justification for effective interpretation programmes.

Increasing our contact with visitors can help them find out what the range of recreation opportunities and attraction is . . . recreational experiences may also be enhanced if visitors can be taught an understanding of basic concepts of ecology and other outdoor values . . . By deepening their sense of appreciation and awareness for the natural environment, more recreationists could take better advantage of an area's recreation potential (Lime and Stankey, 1971: 181).

Care is needed in the selection and implementation of interpretative methods and mention has already been made of some of the means of communication available. Basically the choice is between personal services of some kind (talks, demonstrations, guided tours, information services at a visitor centre) and self-directed services involving printed materials or audio-visual media. The advantages and disadvantages of each method are canvassed by Hanna (1975) and the choice of medium will be influenced by philosophical and practical considerations pertinent to a particular site. The method selected should be capable of interpreting the recreation environment to the anticipated audience in an exciting, aesthetically pleasing fashion, as well as being reliable, flexible, compatible with other media and reasonably vandal-proof (New Zealand National Parks Authority, 1978).

Interpretation is more than mere mechanics and a certain amount of caution is called for in the implementation of an interpretation programme. Too much interpretation can be counter-productive and destroy the sense of spontaneity and discovery in recreational activities. Participation can become 'over-programmed' and people may resent what they perceive as attempts at 'brain-washing' and efforts to force them into designated modes of use and enjoyment. Managerial attitudes can also intrude; elitist overtones and pre-conceived obsolete notions of what constitutes acceptable patterns of recreation behaviour, or of deviance, can distort the orientation of interpretation initiatives.

All procedures aimed at recreation visitor management, whether direct regulation or indirect modification of user behaviour, involve some loss of freedom. Some trade-off is required between freedom of choice and the adequacy of the resource base to meet the requirements of users and the objectives of management. However, positive manipulation of the physical and social environment to create and enhance recreation opportunities is surely preferable to reliance on negative forces or congestion, frustration, dissatisfaction and ultimately self-regulation, to produce their own solution.

5 OUTDOOR RECREATION AND THE CITY

The trend towards urbanisation in western industrial countries is well established. Some three-quarters of the population of the United States lives in urban areas and that figure is exceeded in Britain and parts of Western Europe. In Australia too, another highly urbanised nation, life is centred on the cities and most of the people are born and spend their lives within the confines of the built environment.

Despite this concentration of humanity the major policy and research emphasis in outdoor recreation, until recently, has been beyond the major cities (Mercer, 1980b). Only in the past decade has growing concern for quality of life issues focused attention on the relative deprivation of city dwellers and the need for more enlightened planning of the urban environment.

> Many of our great cities are sick — losing population, losing jobs, losing fiscal solvency, losing the experience of neighbourhood and community, losing the convenience, safety and attractiveness which are the reasons for their existence . . . they are short on justice, short on tranquility, short on general welfare (Reuss, 1977: 2).

Whereas parks and recreation are obviously not the highest priorities on any programme to meet such urban problems, efforts to enhance recreational opportunity and reduce recreational deficiency can contribute substantially to the quality of city life.

Perhaps the most comprehensive attempt to document concern for urban recreation was made by the United States Heritage Conservation and Recreation Service in its National Urban Recreation Study carried out in 1978. Primary objectives of the study were:

*To examine perceptions of needs and opportunities held by recreation users and administrators in urban areas across the country from the neighbourhood to the metropolitan level.
*To identify major problems of recreation and open space providers in meeting needs.
*To explore possible solutions to problems with a wide variety of citizen and governmental interests.
*To identify a variety of open space areas with potentials for protec-

tion.

*To define a range of options for all levels of government with emphasis on Federal alternatives which could assist or facilitate local, State and private efforts (US Department of the Interior, 1978: 20).

The study concentrated on seventeen of the nation's largest cities along with smaller towns and counties within their immediate vicinity. The sample field study cities were considered to reflect the dominant recreation issues and problems facing highly populated urban areas in USA. With allowances for scale and local circumstances, the findings have relevance for other parts of the developed world.

The report established that no coherent national policy exists for a balanced system of close-to-home recreation opportunities for all segments of the urban population. The study also found that recreational deprivation was not always a function of lack of facilities. In many cases existing or potential recreation resources were not being fully utilised because of inappropriate locations or physical characteristics, deteriorating conditions and poor quality management and programming.

Despite the broad spectrum of urban recreation issues addressed the report was able to set out some common guidelines to indicate nine major directions for public action:

*Conserve open space for its natural, cultural and recreational values.
*Provide financial support for parks and recreation.
*Provide close-to-home recreation opportunities.
*Encourage joint use of existing physical resources.
*Ensure that recreation facilities are well-managed and well-maintained with quality recreation programmes available.
*Reduce deterrents to full utilisation of existing urban recreation facilities and programmes.
*Provide appropriate and responsive recreation services through sound planning.
*Make environmental education and management an integral part of urban park and recreation policies and programmes.
*Strengthen the role of the cultural arts in urban recreation.

At the same time, the report recognised the great disparity in the wealth of urban communities and the unevenness in the resource endowment which makes any common strategy for meeting these guidelines difficult. Not only are there obvious physical and social differences between individual cities, but intra-urban contrasts develop over time in morphology, functional land use and population characteristics and hence, in recreation needs and opportunities. At least some of the shortcomings in the urban recreation environment can be related to this dynamic element in the character of towns and cities. An evolving pattern of urban growth and development can be recognised, marked typically by inner decay, peripheral sprawl and increasingly mobile and sophisticated groups of inhabitants. The implications are that any corrective measures proposed must be adjusted for a particular geographical setting, area and population. A distinction should, at least, be made between the inner city, the suburbs and the urban fringe.

The Inner City

A specific finding of the US National Study was that the greatest urban recreation deficiencies for land and facilities exist in the inner cores of the largest cities.

> The larger older cities face particularly serious physical problems relating to the age and design of their recreation facilities. These facility-based problems, intensified by a lack of investment over the last 20 years, are worsened when coupled with new recreation demands from rapidly-changing neighbourhoods (US Department of the Interior, 1978: 43).

Population dispersion has tended to take place from the centre leaving behind diverse ethnic and cultural heritages, but typically less affluent, elderly and similarly disadvantaged groups. Any reverse movement of population is often representative of dissimilar and incompatible lifestyles and merely adds a further dimension to the task of recreation provision. Basic deficiencies are aggravated by a new set of recreation demands from a diverse and rapidly changing clientele.

Some of the older core city areas are fortunate to retain a sound financial tax base with an established network of parks and open space. Other declining fiscally-troubled core cities are forced to allocate a larger share of their recreation budgets to operation and maintenance at the expense of acquiring and developing new facilities and programmes (Table 5.1). US census data show that in 1975, Cleveland, Boston and

Camden — all declining cities — spent more than 95 per cent of their recreation funds on operations; whereas Houston — a city which is growing by 50,000 annually — spent less than 50 per cent on operations. Those capital funds which are available for recreation purposes in older cities are spent on rehabilitation of ageing facilities. In 1976, Boston spent approximately 95 per cent of its capital budget on rehabilitation; New York City spent an estimated 85 per cent. Many older cities such as New York, Cleveland, Akron, Wilmington and Boston spent nothing at all on land acquisition in 1976.

Table 5.1: Capital and Operating Park and Recreation Expenditures, USA 1975-76 (by type of city)

Core Cities	Average *Operating* Expenditures as % of Total Recreation Budget (weighted mean)	Average *Capital* Expenditures as % of Total Recreation Budget (weighted mean)
Growing	43%	57%
Declining/Fiscally Healthy	74%	26%
Declining/Fiscally Troubled	71%	29%

Source: US Department of the Interior, 1978: 89.

In some of the world's larger cities, both inside and outside USA, further difficulties are encountered in attempting to cater for the recreation needs not only of residents, but also of commuters and visitors, all within the same inner city environment. A good example is the City of Westminster in central London where apart from permanent residents who number about 240,000, some 500,000 workers commute to the city daily, and many millions of visitors are constantly present from all parts of Britain and the rest of the world (City of Westminster, 1975). In this case, the Westminster City Council recognised its particular responsibility was towards its resident population, especially in providing recreation opportunities close to home for this group.

However London, in common with most of the world's great cities, developed without the benefit of a comprehensive recreation plan. By the time the need for planning was evident many options were closed off by the massive social and dollar costs of acquiring recreation space. Skyrocketing land prices and finite funding sources placed any available recreation space beyond the reach of urban authorities. In downtown Atlanta, for example, a 1.7 acre (approx. 0.6 ha) site acquired by the city was valued in excess of $ US 9 million. Its acquisition was only made possible by donation. As a result, traditional recreation activities requiring large expanses of land are now simply not possible in the densely populated neighbourhoods of most core cities.

In such circumstances recreation needs can be met partially by providing indoor facilities or by innovative programmes to create additional urban recreation opportunities. Seattle, Washington for example, has transformed the air space over a ten-lane interstate highway into a 3.5 acre (approx. 1.4 ha) Central Freeway Park. Spanning the 'concrete canyon' on a bridge structure, the park offers an unusual retreat in downtown Seattle. Sydney, Australia is another example of a large modern city where a proposal has been made to transform hectares of wasted space on the rooftops of city buildings into sporting and recreational facilities for office workers and residents. New buildings are to be the prime target of this policy with incentives for developers to incorporate use of rooftop space into their plans.

The Suburbs

If it is difficult to make useful comparisons of recreation provision between inner cities, it is impossible to generalise regarding the recreation environment in the suburbs. Clearly, the dispersion of population from the core area referred to earlier is stimulated by a perceived improvement in the quality of life, part of which is reflected in a better range and standard of recreation opportunities. However, the extent to which this is experienced depends upon the particular local mix of such factors as location, resource base, socioeconomic status, community spirit and the affluence and initiative of the local government authority (Mercer, 1980b).

Suburbia has, or should have, one advantage; relatively newer facilities are likely to mean lower operating and maintenance costs leaving more funds for investment in capital projects and acquisition of land. However, recently settled suburban communities with small, but rapidly growing populations and limited financial resources are more concerned with the availability of basic services than with the 'luxuries' of amenity provision (Mercer, 1980b).

Again, the very nature of the suburban environment, typified by areal sprawl of dispersed housing units and dormitory style subdivisions with heavy reliance on the motor car, makes it difficult and expensive to provide a full range of recreation facilities. Site design of most early suburbs precluded the establishment of large open spaces for community recreation and both private developers and public housing authorities appear to have given only minor consideration to this aspect, apart from labelling the mandatory minimum area as 'recreation reserve' (Mercer, 1974). There seems little evidence of any comprehensive planning of recreation facilities as an integral part of emerging neighbourhood and community development patterns. Where tracts of recreation land are set aside, they are developed on an *ad hoc* basis with scant regard for other than the immediate needs of the existing population.

Large modern cities typically spill over unimpeded into the surrounding countryside in a process aptly termed 'metropolitan scatteration' (Wingo, 1964). The rapidly diffusing residential frontier is allowed to outpace provision even for basic service needs, the urgency of which merely reinforces the traditional low priority given to recreation planning. Unimaginative land subdivision perpetuates the conventional grid street system with associated large scale alienation of potential recreation space. Little thought is given to the most appropriate size or form of the overall neighbourhood or its relationship to the rest of the city.

Australian cities, in particular, are much less compact than their older European counterparts with corresponding lower residential densities. This has nothing to do with a relative scarcity of land, but rather reflects a preference for maximising private space at the expense of public amenity (Kemeny, 1978).

> Urban areas are necessarily a compromise between private space (size and quality of dwellings) and public amenity (parks, public transport, libraries, community centres.) In some societies, and Australia is one, the emphasis is heavily on private space — private gardens rather than public parks and extra household space rather than public facilities. In others, such as West Germany and Scandinavia, private space is sacrificed for public amenity (Kemeny, 1978: 5-6).

The resulting featureless sprawl promotes a degree of introspection in urban Australia or a tendency towards 'privatisation' as Mercer (1980b) calls it. In the absence of local clubs or pubs, community meeting centres or sports complexes, cinemas, or even shopping centres in some cases, the inhabitants place greater emphasis on the home environment for their leisure pursuits. The very poverty of public facilities forces households to maximise private space by way of compensation.

Moreover, the only practical means of transportation in a highly dispersed, rapidly expanding, low density urban area is the private automobile. This means that those without a car are severely disadvantaged with respect to leisure options and its also means that the scale of metropolitan planning is geared to the car and not the human being (Mercer, 1980b). As the metropolis spreads, pressure to construct intra-metropolitan freeways to accommodate the car and overcome traffic congestion also increases. Mercer points out that in addition, freeways accelerate residential development towards the periphery so that ex-urban recreational opportunities are pushed further and further away from the centre of gravity of the population to the detriment of people living in the inner suburbs and those without access to private transport. Thus freeways, proposed as a solution to one urban problem, merely give rise to others and recreation opportunities decline still further.

It appears then, that the modern city has let its inhabitants down as far as outlets for leisure in any communal sense are concerned. What seems to be lacking are the essential ingredients to create the 'village' atmosphere of earlier times — a setting which will generate a sense of togetherness and belonging and place. Features which once had an important recreational function as part of that setting have no place in present day suburbs. The town square, the village green, the dance hall-cum-cinema, even the local 'pub' or bar in some cases, have given way to home-based recreation centred on the television set, perhaps the backyard pool and all manner of electronic gadgetry. The sterile facilities which serve for community recreation purposes do little to offset urban alienation. It is difficult to identify with a slab of concrete or fibre glass and it is no wonder that the potential users attempt to humanise these structures with graffiti. They see nothing wrong with vandalism of incongruous features to which they cannot relate and which apparently cannot satisfy their recreation needs.

As Gold (1973) sees it·

There is evidence to suggest that the residents of most cities have not been able to communicate their outdoor recreation preferences to the planner and decision-maker and when preferences have been expressed, there is no sensitive technique for translating them into opportunities (Gold, 1973: v).

In a more recent paper, Gold (1980b) argues that local authorities which have the prime responsibility for recreation face a deepening cost-revenue crisis in the last decades of the twentieth century. This likelihood, coupled with steady state economic conditions, continuing high inflation and unemployment and a general indifference on the part of the higher tiers of government to the problems of cities, serves to underline the need for fresh initiatives in urban recreation planning. Part of this strategy should be a broader approach to the provision of leisure opportunities in the suburbs with greater emphasis on self-help and community involvement. Out of necessity planning bodies may come to realise that some of the deficiencies inherent in suburban life and living may be remedied by encouraging fuller utilisation and management of communal recreation resources.

The Urban Fringe

According to the US National Urban Recreation Study no land areas in the United States are being developed faster than those at the urban fringe (US Dept. of Interior, 1978). It has been estimated that every year some three million acres (approx. 1.2 million ha) of rural land are converted to urban and built-up uses across America (US Department of Agriculture, 1981). In these urbanising areas, local initiatives to direct development away from critical agricultural, environmental and recreational uses are often weak or non-existent. The city periphery thus becomes the focus for some of the most urgent programmes for open space retention purposes.

One of the problems in discussing peri-urban recreation is to decide where suburbia ends and exurbia or the urban fringe beings. Yet it is important to consider recreation opportunities in this transition-zone because mobile city populations readily incorporate nearby fringe areas into their effective recreation space. Despite the growing importance of home-based recreation noted earlier, the neighbouring countryside is increasingly perceived as an extension of life in the city. As Cracknell (1967) has observed, referring to Britain:

> . . . it is the garden for children to play in, a vista people can enjoy from their mobile room − their car . . . For every city dweller it has become . . . an integral part of his environment . . . In a very real sense the belt of countryside around a city has become its 'living space' (Cracknell, 1967: 153).

It has been suggested that preoccupation with specifically *outdoor* recreation on the part of city people is motivated in part by the urbanisation process itself (Woolmington and Hart, 1977). Much the same sentiments have been expressed by Janiskee (1976) who explained the recreation appeal of extra-urban environments in the context of a push-pull model of motivation. Periodically, environmentally undernourished urbanites are 'pushed' from the city because of stresses imposed by their lifestyles. At the same time they are 'pulled' into the more natural hinterland by the opportunity to experience compensatory alternative surroundings and activities. Apparently, urban dwellers, who have voted with their feet for city living, are not fully adapted to the urban environment. They have a physical and social need to seek novel, irregular and opposite situations and this need is reinforced by growing awareness of what the surrounding countryside has to offer, together with enhanced means of making use of its recreation potential. This striving for self-renewal in a different, specifically outdoor setting inevitably leads the city dweller to the urban fringe and beyond for recreation.

In many respects then, the hinterland of the modern city can be regarded as part of its playground. Yet, despite its obvious advantages, Davidson (1976) suggests that in Britain, at least, its potential may have been overlooked in urban recreation planning.

> The amount of land devoted to public and private recreational use on the edge of towns is less than might be expected and surprisingly few country parks have been created in an environment potentially so suitable for them (Davidson, 1976: 4).

Instead of treating the fringe as a sort of undesirable no-man's-land or a speculator's paradise, Davidson advocates the creation of recreation landscapes blending both urban and rural environments:

> . . . providing the missing link — geographically and environmentally — in a recreation system which extends from the city centre to the national parks . . . (Davidson, 1974: 890).

Implementation of any plan to exploit the recreation potential of the peri-urban countryside cannot succeed without the co-operation of the more traditional landusers involved. These aspects are explored in more detail in the following chapter, but it is clear that a more flexible approach to management of the resources of the urban fringe will be necessary if it is to fulfil its role as an integral part of the urban recreation environment. In particular, the ex-urban zone should be related to other components of the city structure — the suburbs and the inner core — and the contribution each can make to meeting the recreation needs of the population considered in the context of the overall functioning urban system.

The Urban System

The US National Urban and Recreation Study, referred to earlier, recognised that the existence and quality of urban recreation depend upon and affect many other components of the urban system — housing, transportation, education, employment, health and social services, crime prevention, environmental protection and many others. This approach echoes that of Perloff (1969) who argued that the urban community may be viewed as a set of interacting subsystems. One of these environmental subsystems is the recreation environment which includes all the places and facilities with which city-dwellers involve themselves for leisure and recreation (Atkisson and Robinson, 1969). The recreation environment or 'cell' ranks alongside other subsystems — residential, occupational, service, commuter — making up the 'setting' for people's lives.

Much of the dissatisfaction with urban living and many of the concomitant social problems can be traced to gross deficiencies in and between these subenvironments of the urban system, i.e. to the apparent inability of the modern city to meet the basic needs of the inhabitants. The objective of urban environmental planning then becomes enhancement of these settings by manipulation of selected environmental variables to increase the 'livability' of the whole city for those inhabitants.

In the context of the recreation subenvironment the aim is to produce a more satisfying array of amenity stimuli and responses. The range and intensity of amenity responses generated are, in turn, a function of the nature, characteristics and location of what Atkisson and Robinson (1969) call 'amenity precipitants'. These can include all manner of natural and cultural features and any programme to promote leisure opportunities should begin with an assessment of the attributes of the recreation subsystem which can generate an amenity response. In an urban situation a fundamental component of a favourable amenity response system is the availability of open space for recreation.

Urban Open Space

Open space is one of the major influences on the profile of an urban community and most observers agree that it is basic to the structure of the built environment in meeting human needs. Yet, the concept of open space requires some elaboration and various factors can impinge upon its function as part of the urban outdoor recreation resource base.

Too many planning bodies appear to equate *open* space with *recreation* space. Obviously one is a pre-requisite for the other, but the two need not be synonymous. Nor is this distinction mere semantics. Many of the world's cities, especially those recently developed have ample open space. However, *open* space is exactly what it is: there is nothing present to facilitate or even permit recreation. Modern planned national capitals such as Brasilia and Canberra are blessed with vast areas of open space, geometrically arranged, trimmed and manicured, yet often devoid of any feature which would encourage outdoor recreation. Indeed, any recreation function, apart from perhaps passive viewing, is specifically excluded in many cases, either by physical barriers, equally forbidding signs, or other effective means of discouraging participation. Open space it may be — recreation space it is not.

This is borne out by the US National Urban Recreation Study which found that in the United States:

> The primary benefits of most open lands in and near urban areas are non-recreational, but they serve critical environmental, aesthetic, cultural, agricultural and other productive purposes . . . Most of the large open space areas now being proposed for public acquisition and protection are located at the edge of urban areas and cannot provide intensive close-to-home recreation . . . meeting recreation needs is not the primary reason for their protection (US Department of the Interior, 1978: 34).

Thus, it is not always a useful exercise to calculate the amount of open space set aside in an urban area and presume it to be available for recreation. In the rural city of Armidale, Australia, where this was written, some 37 per cent of the urbanised area is designated open space; an impressive figure until it is revealed that a substantial portion is made up of streets and other routeways, or forms part of the enclosed grounds of schools, institutions and private sporting bodies. In terms of functional public recreation space the true measure would be closer to 15 per cent. This is not to deny that urban open space *per se* has value apart from a potential recreation role. Demands from the affluent for lower residential densities and from planners for larger landscaped sites for public buildings and industrial estates, add to a growing social awareness of space as a community asset. Links are frequently suggested between environmental quality and urban scale and population density, although whether these are casually related is open to debate. However, there seems to be general agreement that open space in urban areas is a 'good thing', as the essential context to which complementary city structures relate and to provide the opportunity for outdoor recreation.

Yet, it is surprising that not all undeveloped areas of urban land and water are perceived as recreation resources or used as such. Many city authorities apparently lack the imagination or the means to capitalise on the potential of neglected areas such as floodplains, water supply reservoirs and catchments, waste treatment facilities, waterfronts, parking lots, service corridors and abandoned rights-of-way. Especially valuable are strips of linear open space where the edge effect promotes greater recreation use (Whyte, 1969).

The US Bureau of Outdoor Recreation has identified several successful space-conversion projects which have resulted in useful additions to the urban recreation resource base:

*In Baton Rouge, Louisiana, 35 acres (approx. 14 ha) of unproductive land beneath an elevated highway interchange have been transformed into Interstate Park as a neighbourhood recreation area.

*San Francisco has at least three park areas atop underground parking facilities, including Union Square and in downtown Los Angeles two large corporations have created a 2.5 acre (approx. 1 ha) rooftop park above a garage as part of an urban renewal project.

*In Albuquerque, airport buffer lands have been transformed into a community golf course.

*Along the lower Rio Grande, the city of El Paso has recognised the potential of the river's floodway in developing a linear park incorporating recreation activities and facilities capable of withstanding periodic flooding.

*The surface of covered water storage facilities in Denver is used for

public tennis courts and sports fields.
*In Washington DC, a sanitary landfill site has been transformed into a useful and valuable recreation resource.
*In New York City, construction of a 30 acre (approx. 12 ha) park is under way on the roof of a new sewage treatment facility. Scheduled for completion in 1983, the park will include a picnic area, baseball diamonds, tennis courts, trails, swimming pools and an ice rink.
*Northwestern State University, Louisiana is developing a public recreation complex on university land to provide for the recreation needs of local citizens as well as its own scheduled requirements.

Implicit in several of these projects is the waste involved in the setting aside of resources for some exclusive use. Public institutions in or near urban communities frequently provide opportunities for innovative recreation programmes. Establishments such as schools, hospitals, childcare centres, health clinics, religious and cultural facilities, fair grounds, sporting arenas and even military bases can all have significant potential in multiple use as cost-effective communal recreation space.

Schools, in particular, represent a sizable porportion of readily accessible publicly-owned resources. They are usually well distributed within cities and occupy strategic locations in residential neighbourhoods. Most have playgrounds or playing fields attached and many have indoor gymnasiums and pools. Yet aside from their primary role, they are often one of the least utilised public facilities, remaining empty when recreation pressures are greatest — after working hours, at weekends and during vacations. Only 65 per cent of the urban jurisdictions sampled in the US National Urban Recreation Study had formal cooperative arrangements for joint use of schools for recreational purposes. In many areas opportunities were also found to exist for reclamation or conversion of abandoned public buildings to provide indoor recreation centres.

Use and Non-use of Urban Recreation Space

Failure to recognise urban recreation opportunities is not always confined to city administrators. Potential users, too, seem reluctant at times to avail themselves of the facilities which are provided. Field observations suggest a surprisingly low level of utilisation of recreation space especially in the inner core of some cities. An Australian study in the inner suburbs of Melbourne found that a neighbourhood park was not 'a particularly vital part of most residents' perceived environment' (Cole, 1977: 93). Although considerable diversity was discovered in user groups and activities, the dislike for the park displayed by children in particular, was traced to constraints on natural patterns of active child behaviour; possibilities for creative play in the park were virtually non-existent.

Gold (1973) explores the reasons for such under-utilisation of urban recreation space and concludes that the major causes can be grouped into three categories — behavioural, environmental and institutional (Table 5.2). Not all of these inhibiting factors are easily countered, but obviously convenience of access, site characteristics, location, level of

Table 5.2: Major Causes of Non-use in Neighbourhood Parks

Behavioural	Environmental	Institutional
User Orientation*	Convenient Access*	Goal Differences*
Social Restraints*	Site Characteristics*	Personal Safety*
Previous Conditioning	Weather and Climate	Relevant Program
Competing Activities	Physical Location	Management Practices
User Satisfaction	Facilities and Development	Maintenance Levels

*Most significant in each category relative to all factors.
Source: Gold, 1973: 103.

facilities, safety considerations and management and maintenance are subject to manipulation. Certainly, Gold's comments support the view that non-planned designation of open space in urban areas with little thought to effective location, size and quality, will probably ensure that it remains *open* space — empty and ignored.

Yet remedial measures need not be elaborate. Recreation space can and should reflect the characteristics and aspirations of users and potential users. As Bannon (1976) sees it, the planning and design of recreation areas:

> should be premised on the concept of 'openness': open to choice, open to active use and manipulation, open to view and understanding, open to access, open to new perceptions of experiences. (Bannon, 1976: 187).

Key elements are *diversity* and *flexibility*, so as to offer a range of recreation opportunities likely to attract wide use from a broad cross-section of the community, yet remaining amenable to change of function and orientation.

The contribution which the urban dwelling and its surrounds can make to the total stock of available recreation space also cannot be ignored. An Australian study, for example, found that 51 per cent of suburban children spend half or more of their outdoor leisure time in their own yards (Halkett, 1976). These areas are often the most intensively used for recreation and where this private space factor is inadequate or reduced in quality, the extent and variety of play are curtailed.

The streetscape, too, tends to be popular for recreation purposes despite obvious hazards; in fact it appears the busier the street, the more appealing it is (Young, 1980). The unstructured nature of city streets and footpaths with their clutter and ever-present element of danager, apparently offer an exciting and challenging contrast to conventional playgrounds. Rather than attempt to counteract this appeal directly, it would seem more productive to take advantage of the opportunities at the street scale for design of imaginative *and* safe play areas (Rudofsky, 1969). Bannon (1976) uses the example of Central Harlem, New York, to illustrate the potential for transformation of small blocks of vacant land in built-up areas into 'vest-pocket parks' and 'tot-lots' as a viable alternative to the streets for play, or for quiet relaxation by older residents. Bannon also sees 'adventure playgrounds', where children are allowed and encouraged to create their own play environment under non-restrictive supervision, as providing an unorthodox setting for spontaneous enjoyment:

> In urban areas where space of any kind is at a premium . . . adventure playgrounds are the closest we have come to emulating some of the mysterious and exciting pleasures of childhood . . . The land is left in its original state, with building materials (such as wood, cardboard boxes, logs, planks, bricks and so forth) provided for the children to build almost anything they desire . . . Building a house, planting a garden, digging a tunnel, cooking a meal, swinging on ropes from trees, creating a mysterious artifact, anything children enjoy which does not endanger them or others is permitted (Bannon 1976: 205-6).

Street closures for an hour, or a day, or for longer periods, perhaps with the introduction of mobile recreation programmes, are another means of harnessing and redirecting the attraction of the streetscape as a neighbourhood recreation resource and counteracting the tendency towards non-use.

Urban Recreation Space Standards

According to Balmer (1974), three questions are fundamental concerning urban recreation space: how much is needed, what form it should take and where should it be located? The first of these questions concerns measures of quantity and this inevitably involves reference to space standards — specific numerical indicators of the adequacy of recreation provision.

From time to time attempts have been made to arrive at desirable and practical standards for parks and open space relative to user populations. Some of these are examined by Seeley (1973), Gold (1973) and Bannon (1976). In urban situations the most frequently cited standards range from seven to ten acres (approx. 2.8 to 4.0 ha) per 1000 people, the total encompassing parks and playgrounds under various categories (Figure 5.1).

Figure 5.1: Area Standards for Park Planning in Canberra, Australia

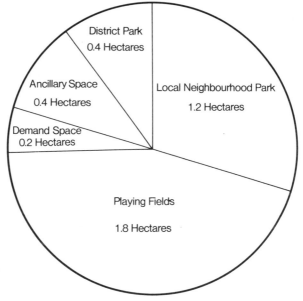

Note 1: *Ancillary space* refers to space for screen and shelter planting, sound-reducing planting, landscape development, and easements for overhead power-lines and floodways.
2. *Demand space* refers to space for tennis courts, swimming pools, bowling greens, squash courts and 'concessional entertainment' for organised and social sport.
Source: National Capital Development Commission, 1978: 10.

The space standards indicated for Canberra in Figure 5.1 are considered by the planners to be appropriate for the particular type and size of population of that city. However, it is obviously unrealistic to attempt to apply *common* standards across contrasting communities — standards which are inflexible and unrelated to changing socioeconomic profiles of potential users or to varying space needs for different recreation activities. The fact that supposedly universal norms have not always been attained reflects the many factors which should influence a more realistic definition of definition of space standards.

Clearly, any set of recreation space standards should only be used as a guideline to be modified as required and applied sensibly in the context of the sociocultural characteristics of the community involved and the resource attributes of the subject urban environment. In particular, rigid adherence to uniformity should not be allowed to obscure the many possibilities for innovative planning, management and design of leisure opportunities less demanding of space (Burton, 1974). In other words, a strict standards approach confuses recreation opportunity with area and recreation space *per se*. Standards, originally prescribed as minimums, become maximums and even optimums in some cases.

Again, the pace of modern city development quickly makes redundant the setting of inflexible standards. It is not always a lack of conviction on the part of recreation planners regarding the desirability of departing from space standards advocated, so much as the unavailability and cost of available land. Although application of standards might be marginally better than a completely *ad hoc* process, it cannot cope with the emergence of 'new' recreation resources and makes no provision for community input, or the involvement of private or commercial enterprises (Marriott, 1980).

Moreover, mere figures have little to say about the form, quality and essential characteristics of the recreation space designated under the idealised standards adopted. Too often the urban recreation system has to make do with 'left-over' or derelict areas for which no other use can immediately be found (Mercer, 1974). Minute, isolated parcels of low grade land, devoid of vegetation or other natural features, with unimaginative site design and inadequately equipped, may meet the arbitrary space standard set, but do little to meet the recreation requirements of a neighbourhood.

Such land is often given over to recreational use for a greater or lesser period of time for no other reason than that nobody can think of anything better to do with it for the time being ... land such as this remains classified as 'recreational' for several decades . . . until more 'profitable' uses can be found (Mercer, 1974: 25).

This is not to deny the potential of derelict lands as recreation space, but it does underline also the importance of allocating better quality resources, with appropriate characteristics and suitably located, to outdoor recreation. It follows, therefore, that satisfaction of recreation needs requires more than attainment of abstract space standards. In the provision of open space in cities, it is not a matter of how much, but how good the space is. In particular, consideration must be given to the important questions of location and accessibility for effective use of urban park and recreation resources.

Outdoor Recreation Opportunities and Urban Planning

Access to a diversity of recreation opportunities within urban areas is generally assured for those with automobiles who are willing to travel reasonable distances. Such opportunities are often severely limited for people without access to a car — the elderly, the young, the poor and the handicapped. The 1978 US National Urban Recreation Study estimated that approximately 45 million Americans live in households without cars. In the areas surveyed in that study, the proportion of households *without* cars ranged as high as 57 per cent in New York City. These people, together with those who cannot drive or prefer not to use their cars, rely on public transportation, which is usually commuter-orientated to work places and shopping centres rather than recreation outlets. Services are often reduced or eliminated during evenings and weekends when recreation demands are heaviest. This means that millions of city-dwellers are denied access to park and recreation facilities beyond walking distance. In these circumstances the provision of close-to-home recreation opportunities is even more essential if equity in delivery and performance of recreation services is to be achieved (Hillman and Whalley, 1977).

According to Cushman and Hamilton-Smith (1980), a spatially equitable distribution of urban recreation facilities would ensure that no person was deprived of access by reason of distance, time, travel cost, or convenience. However, confusion can arise between efficiency and equity in location decisions. A recreation policy based on efficiency-related criteria of minimising costs and aggregate travel and maximising attendance, would result in the location of a small number of large-scale facilities in high density residential areas. At the same time, consumers living in lower density areas would be worse off. Cushman and Hamilton-Smith advocate a compromise where efficiency is balanced against maximum equality of recreation opportunity. They believe that the degree of equity or inequity can be determined by reference to measurable elements of relative opportunity or relative deprivation, such as travel costs, constraints on recreation options arising from facility characteristics and demographic variations in the population's ability to use services offered.

Equity in location and access within an urban recreation space system must take account of these time/distance constraints and the circulation patterns of user groups. Studies of children's playgrounds, for example, indicate a highly localised service area of up to a quarter of a mile (approx. 0.4 km), and 75 per cent of all visitors to urban parks are said to come from less than a half-mile (approx. 0.8 km) radius (Balmer, 1974). Distance, of course, is only one barrier in the way of individuals wishing to make use of a particular facility. Access to neighbourhood parks is often restricted by physical barriers such as highways, railroad tracks, or industrial development. Chicago's lakefront parks, for example, have limited pedestrian access from surrounding neighbourhoods due to the presence of Lake Shore Drive. Yet, these same parks can be easily reached by car. Similarly, a 'tot-lot' separated from its pre-school users by distance or busy streets can have little role to play in meeting their need for recreation space.

Cushman and Hamilton-Smith (1980) suggest that the first step in reducing inequity is to identify, classify and map the spatial distribution of all recreation facilities in the city and the nature and level of services provided. Deprived residential sectors can then be determined and deficiencies rectified.

> For urban parks, for example, the spatial patterns of playgrounds, neighbourhood parks, district parks and large urban parks can be visually correlated and statistically analysed according to the degree of dispersion and clustering of parks in each of the park types. In this way, the areas of the city being served and the areas of the city not being served by parks in each of the park types may be determined (Cushman and Hamilton-Smith, 1980: 171).

A somewhat similar approach was used by Mitchell (1968, 1969) to evaluate spatial aspects of Christaller's central place theory in an urban recreation context. Part of Mitchell's purpose was to seek understanding of the variables and processes which interact to affect the distributed pattern of public recreation sites within the city of Columbia, South Carolina.

Such variables as relative location, distance, time and facilities appear to be significant to consumers of recreational activities. On the other hand, public demand or pressure, available personnel, budgetary limitations and philosophical orientation are also factors that seem to be important to producers of recreational services (Mitchell, 1969: 104).

Mitchell discussed spacing of recreation facilities within a four-tier hierarchy of recreation units based upon the criteria of function, size and service — playgrounds, play fields, parks and large parks. He proposed a theoretical spatial distribution for each class within the hierarchy, based on uniform hexagonal patterns, equal spacing, regular size and shape service areas and standard threshold populations. When simplifying assumptions concerning the strict residential character of the city and its uniform population distribution were relaxed, a more complex distribution pattern emerged which reflected the overriding significance of population density as the key explanatory variable in understanding the location of public urban recreation sites.

As with Christaller's original work the value and practical application of hierarchy techniques in the study of urban amenity provision rest in discovering, explaining and correcting departures in an existing system from the idealised theoretical framework. Such remedial action should not be necessary if sufficient regard was given to urban recreation requirements at the planning stage.

In many cases, the urban recreation planning process does not address the deeper behavioural needs of a leisure-orientated society. More often it recognises and develops only conventional resources to accommodate present users and uses in stereotypical activities. Some of the best opportunities for departure from traditional approaches to planning would seem to exist in provision of recreation facilities in the urban environment of 'new towns' and communities.

Outdoor Recreation Planning in New Towns

The emergence of the new town movement as a response to urban growth pressures in established centres is well-documented (Perloff, 1966; Burby et al., 1976). New towns have been established in Britain, the Americas, Scandinavia and Australia. One of their advantages is that they can be planned holistically and can serve as a means of testing new systems of urban land-use planning. In this way new towns provide opportunities for recreation planning from the ground up with fewer constraints than in existing communities.

Typical of the attention given in new towns to planning and design of a stimulating leisure environment is the settlement of Tapiola in Finland (Von Hertzen and Spreiregan, 1971). Labelled the 'Garden City', Tapiola represents an attempt to create a city as a living park with all facilities and activities placed within the park structure itself and complementary to it. Each village within the city has several neighbourhoods clustered around a shopping and cultural centre and 54 per cent of the total area is designated open space.

The question of recreation provision has also received attention from the planners of new towns in Britain (Veal, 1975). In the planning and design of the new city of Milton Keynes north-west of London, for example, goals and objectives for recreation were identified at an early stage (Barron, 1974). These included:

*Provision of a wide variety of social, community and recreation facilities to give all residents a real choice of leisure time activities.
*Encouragement of both private enterprise and local initiative to provide as many of these facilities as possible.
*Making the new city's recreational opportunities as attractive to residents and potential newcomers as the availability of jobs and homes.
*Phasing provision in line with the build-up in population.

These primary goals were supported by a number of ancillary objectives which stressed:

*Unrestricted access for all, including disadvantaged groups, at acceptable charges.
*Satisfactory transport services and adequate car parking.
*High quality attractive facilities including landscaping.
*Increased awareness of recreation opportunities.
*Development of multi-purpose facilities and joint provision/dual use of institutional buildings.
*Public participation in the planning process.

In addition, provision was made for the arts, culture and entertainment, indoor and outdoor sporting areas, parks and open space embracing waterbodies and linear greenways and community recreation facilities including a City Club as a comprehensive leisure complex.

If these goals and objectives are realised, the new town experiment should succeed in creating for Milton Keynes a range of recreation facilities and opportunities appropriate to the needs of all its citizens.

Despite the advantages noted earlier which new towns enjoy over established communities as far as recreation planning is concerned, one problem is common to both — coping with the inevitability of *change*. Unless a dynamic element can be injected into the planning process in either situation, any recreation development programme will lose impetus and be unable to respond to changing emphases in leisure behaviour and associated pressures on resources and management policies. A flexible approach is the key to successful urban recreation planning, in which priorities are set down rather than rigid programmes and in which machinery exists for rapid review in the light of changing circumstances (Veal, 1975). Given this commitment, the recreation planner can make a useful contribution to generating a satisfying leisure environment for city dwellers in both new and old urban communities.

6 OUTDOOR RECREATION BEYOND THE CITY

In highly urbanised nations of the western world the city functions primarily as a place of residence and a base for work commitments. That growing segment of daily life given over to leisure appears to find only restricted expression in the urban environment, so that more and more people look beyond the city limits and find their action space for outdoor recreation identified increasingly with the rural scene.

As noted in the previous chapter explanation of the recreational appeal of extra-urban environments may be found partly in reaction to the crowding and other environmental stress associated with everyday urban living. Outdoor activities in a rural setting apparently allow city residents to escape; to exchange the routine, the boredom and the familiar, for the recreation opportunities perceived to exist in the surrounding countryside.[1] Even knowledge or 'cognitive awareness' of such outdoor opportunities is considered to act as a psychological safety valve for some in coping with environmentally induced stress (Iso-Ahola, 1980).

Rural Landscapes and Recreation

The role of rural landscapes in satisfying the aesthetic and recreational needs of a leisure-conscious society has long been recognised in Britain. Since 1949 the Countryside Commission has been active in promoting the conservation of the natural beauty and amenity of the English countryside within the framework of efficient agricultural land use (see Chapter 3). A survey sponsored by the Commission in 1977 found that visiting the countryside was the most popular form of outdoor recreation for the people of England and Wales (Countryside Commission, 1979). This finding was confirmed in the United States, by Cordell *et al.* (1980), who reported that much of the rural land in that country seems to have visual appeal to drivers and walkers. Both Americans and visitors to USA are likely to seek the more naturally aesthetic environment away from urbanised areas and it is these lands which it is suggested should be managed primarily as a scenic visual resource.

In Britain the Countryside Commission (1973b) has studied the effects of modern farming techniques on the scenic beauty and recreational appeal of rural landscapes. The Commission is endeavouring to convince landholders that, in the creation of new functional agricultural landscapes, many opportunities exist to maintain and enhance the aesthetic qualitites of the countryside and hence its role in outdoor recreation.

Recognition of the strong correlation between participant satisfaction and scenic quality of the recreation environment is an important step towards realisation of the contribution which rural landscapes, in both public and private hands, can make to the leisure opportunities of the city dweller. However, available *public* resource-based recreation areas such as national parks and forests are limited in supply and not always close to centres of population. On those public lands which are accessible, visitation rates at peak periods are often pushed beyond carrying capacity so that fees, permits and other strategies for rationing use become necessary. At the same time, attempts to expand the resource base are frustrated by lack of land of suitable location and quality, and by budgetary constraints on park management services wishing to undertake further land acquisition programmes. Attention, therefore, has switched to the potential of *private* land for the provision of recreation opportunities within reasonable proximity of cities.

Acquisition of Recreation Space

From the government and users' point of view, public use of private land represents a cheap and sometimes free addition to the supply of recreation resources which can help reduce the pressure of numbers in public areas (Cullington, 1981). Private land also provides variety in the recreation system for those who prefer man-made landscapes or whose activities are more suited to farmland and occupied countryside than to national parks or wilderness. Cullington points out that private land forms a useful complement to publicly-owned land for recreation in that it can cater for the many forms of linear outdoor activities, such as hiking and skiing, with minimal disruption to more traditional land uses.

These circumstances have prompted consideration of alternative approaches to retaining the essential character of countryside and extending community access to tracts of private rural land. In particular, park and recreation agencies have shown increased interest in less-than-fee simple methods of acquiring recreation space in the hinterland of cities (Howard and Crompton, 1980). Among these are:

Differential Property Tax Assessments whereby property taxes are levied on use value rather than market value as an incentive to open space preservation and farmland retention especially on the periphery of cities. Differential assessment laws are now in force in nearly every state of America. However, their effectiveness in influencing landholders to withhold their land from development varies with pressures (and prices offered) for subdivision and sanctions imposed for withdrawing from the programme (Coughlin *et al.*, 1978). The approach constitutes something of a holding operation rather than a permanent solution, unless combined with direct land use control (agricultural zoning or districting) or easements of some type.

Easements which place limits on certain ownership rights are the most popular less-than-fee procedures and offer some tax advantages to the landholder (Howard and Crompton, 1980). A *negative* easement may prohibit subdivision, surface mining, or the removal of vegetation and historic features. An *affirmative* easement may permit limited public access along trails or streams for specified recreational purposes. Negative easements are most useful in preserving scenic areas around public lands and along linear corridors, especially when combined with an affirmative easement which allows right of access.

Transfer of Development Rights which is based on the concept that the development potential of a parcel of land can be separated from that site and used somewhere else (Glotfelty, 1978). The receiving owner gains the right to develop his land to a greater degree, while the seller is compensated for not developing his land. The shifting of rights from one parcel to another not only concentrates development into planned areas, but also permits preservation of farmland, open space, wetlands, wildlife habitat and historic sites.

National Reserves which contain a mix of public and private land comprehensively planned and managed to maintain recreational, aesthetic, ecological, historical and cultural values (Howard and Crompton, 1980). By this means, coherent recreational landscapes can be created convenient to urban areas in which both negative and affirmative easements, coupled with fee simple acquisition or donation of intensively used sites, help ensure public access to high quality rural environments (see Chapter 7).

Procedures such as those outlined above, used singly or in combination, represent efficient, cost-effective means of making available extra-urban leisure opportunities without the expense and disruption entailed in public acquisition of additional resource-based recreation areas.

Land Use Conflicts

Recreational use of private land represents multiple resource use and as such can generate conflict between recreationists and landholders. The basis for conflict lies in the several functions seen for rural land and the contrasting attitudes associated with these roles. Davidson and Wibberley (1977) suggest a strong polarisation between those whose dominant concern is the efficient production of food and fibre or other economic uses and those who value more highly the intrinsic character of rural landscapes and wish to preserve this heritage unchanged. Between these two are other groups for whom different attributes of the countryside are significant. City planners, for example, often view land especially in the rural fringe merely as a space and development reserve for urban expansion. For others, the primary role envisaged may be for communications facilities or specific resource uses such as extractive industries or water conservation. Transcending all of these in numbers are those who link the resource function of countryside with leisure and outdoor recreation.

To some observers this multiplicity of roles makes conflict almost inevitable if recreationists press their claims to private rural land (Green, 1977). Whether conflict and confrontation are avoided depends essentially upon the goodwill and co-operation of the landholders. Their attitudes are of fundamental importance in determining the amount of land available to the public for outdoor recreation. These attitudes, in turn, are a function of the landholder's personal beliefs and experiences, together with legal, economic, social and ecological considerations, national traditions and government policies and the type and volume of the recreation activity involved (Cullington, 1981).

The relationships between these factors are depicted in Figure 6.1. Essentially, the issue is one of the balance between incentives and disincentives. Put simply: 'To increase the supply of private land for recreation, it is necessary either to increase the incentives, or to reduce the disincentives, or preferably both' (Cullington, 1981: 8).

Incentives may be provided by governments in an effort to encourage wider recreational use of private land and can include such measures as direct financial support, compensation payments, or the

Figure 6.1: Factors Influencing Availability of Private Land for Recreation

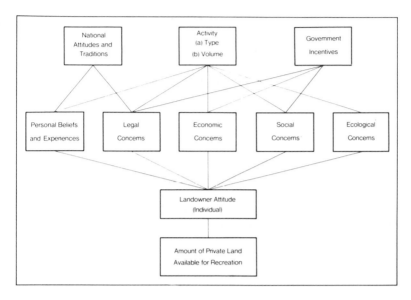

Source: Cullington, 1981: 9.

sponsoring of access agreements. Disincentives arise from the landholders' concern over such matters as:

*Legal liability for injury or damage to recreationists. The degree of the liability and the landholder's responsibility vary between jurisdictions and whether the visitor is an invitee, a licensee, or a trespasser. Several countries have enacted laws which attempt to allay landholders' fears of the liability problems should accidents occur (Harrington, 1975).

*Economic or financial implications associated with the costs of providing access and possible damage or changes in farming practices, set against any compensation payments or the opportunities to derive income from recreational ventures.

*Social considerations such as loss of privacy and problems with trespassing, which may be mitigated to some extent by the landowner's personal satisfaction from providing a community service.

*Ecological impacts on the farm environment as a result of recreational activities (see Chapter 4). These will depend to some extent upon how the farmer's perception of the problem is affected by the particular nature of the recreation activity and its incidence in space and time.

All of these concerns are interrelated and the degree to which they influence the landholder's decision to make available or withhold recreational access is closely linked with the type and volume of recreation activity undertaken and government support and encouragement. The outcome rests very much with individual landholders and how they perceive the balance between the incentives and disincentives. Undoubtedly, there will remain many who value the economic functions of rural land more highly than any amenity functions it may be deemed to possess. Moreover, conflict between these primary functions would seem most probable in the urban-rural fringe where the economic value of the countryside is highest and pressure for amenity and recreation space is greatest. It is here too, that most problems and disputes over accessibility can be expected to arise.

Accessibility to Recreation Space

Accessibility has several dimensions, among them technical, behavioural and sociocultural. According to Moseley (1979), the concept cannot be divorced from the nature of the desired destination or experience. Certainly, much more than mere mobility is implied. Mobility, or the capacity to overcome space, is a technical and mechanistic condition derived from such factors as vehicle ownership, travel time and costs, and individual physical attributes. Accessibility on the other hand, is a broader concept reflecting the opportunities perceived as available for travel. It is related to the behavioural notion of 'psychic space' or 'movement space', that restricted area in which the potential trip makers react to stimuli within the constraints of their value systems, experience and perceived environmental opportunities (Eliot-Hurst, 1972). Moreover, the dimensions of a person's movement space are also, in part, a function of social and legal conventions — the institutional and organisational 'rules of the game' to which an individual is exposed.

Thus, accessibility has many facets and use of recreation space can effectively be denied in a variety of circumstances. Examples include cost of travel, equipment and licence fees; lack of time, especially blocks of suitable time; inadequate information on recreation opportunities; ineligibility to participate on the basis of age, sex, qualifications, membership of group or social class; unavailability of transport; and special problems for disadvantaged groups (see Chapter 2). In the recreational use of countryside these circumstances may be compounded by the sheer difficulty of physical access; many sites are effectively closed off because of a lack of appropriate vehicles, equipment, stamina, or expertise.

Consideration of accessibility too, can be complicated by disputes over property rights and institutional and legal constraints on movement into and through recreation space.

Property rights

Central to the question of access and availability of private rural land for recreation is the issue of rights to property and the privileges and responsibilities which ownership and control over land bestow. To some, property ownership, in a legal or economic sense, is the proprietorship of a bundle of rights (Wunderlich, 1979). Others go further and question the concept of private property altogether, stressing that property should not be thought of as *things* but as *rights*, the ownership of which is circumscribed (Dales, 1972). In this view, ownership consists of a set of legally defined rights to use property in certain ways and a set of negative rights or prohibitions which prevent its use in other ways; a proprietor never *owns* physical assets but only the rights to *use* them.

In the context of countryside access for recreation ownership of the land itself is of no particular relevance. The crucial issue is ownership (and exercise) of the right to exclude others from use (Thomson and Whitby, 1976). Difficulties arise because landholders are only one among several groups with an interest in how the resource is to be utilised. The multiplicity of functions referred to above suggests a number of potential beneficiaries who may value the land for specific purposes. This would include the occupiers and would-be recreationists, but may also cover neighbours, passers-by and conservationists at large (Phillips and Roberts, 1973). In economic and legalistic terms the access issue can be seen as one of allocating among these interested parties the various rights over land in such a way as to maximise social welfare (Thomson and Whitby, 1976). It could be that, where a landholder wishes to retain exclusive rights to recreational resources, whether they be stream, beachfront, or spectacular scenic views, purchasing such rights over and above the price of the land should be made mandatory; that is, the privilege of excluding the public would become taxable. However, others would deny that it is ever equitable to permit the holders of land to alienate recreation space to themselves.

A finer definition of rights to property would certainly seem desirable to identify those which accrue to the property holder, to the State and to society. It could be held that private ownership rights become merely the residue after public or communal rights to property are exhausted (Morris, 1975). It could be argued further that ownership rights should not apply to the aesthetic component of the resource base or extend to exclusive access to assets such as wildlife or fish to be found within a property. The landholder when taking up occupation also takes up effective control of countryside resources which may be valued by the wider community for recreation. This privilege, in turn, should imply a responsibility for making those resources available to society.

It seems that few landholders are prepared to acknowledge this responsibility. The pervasive attitude is summed up in a submission to a study made by the Ontario Trails Council in Canada:

> It is as reasonable to expect the country owner to allow the public use of his land as it would be to expect the urban owner to allow them to use his swimming pool and picnic on his lawn. The only reasonable place for public trails is publicly-owned land (Cullington, 1981: 36).

However, access even to public lands is not always guaranteed. In the United States, the Third Nationwide Outdoor Recreation Plan reported that many Bureau of Land Management and Forest Service lands are blocked off by private landholdings (US Heritage Conservation and Recreation Service, 1979). The origin of some of these access problems was the railroad land grant acts of the nineteenth century which allocated alternative allotments to the railroad and to the government. Consequently, access is often restricted by private landholders who may even charge fees as a condition for allowing recreationists across their property to reach parcels of public land.

Recreational Use of Private Land

Despite the constraints and disincentives noted, much private land *is* available for outdoor recreation with either the tacit or the explicit consent of the landholder. In England and Wales, for example, individuals and groups have long enjoyed access to designated parts of the rural environment, although even there recreationists in large numbers are unwelcome. In parts of Scandinavia recreation on private land is accepted and expected under a law known as 'Every Man's Right' (Cullington, 1981). Cullington also reports that there are indications that recreational use of private land is becoming more acceptable in Canada and the United States where the US Department of Agriculture has funded a 'Public Access Program'.

The opening up of private recreational land for *revenue* purposes is more common in Britain and North America where amenity agriculture can be a paying proposition especially in the urban fringe. The concept implies deliberate management of the farm environment and habitat to provide recreational services or opportunities for visitors. Hunting, for example, remains a popular recreational pursuit on rural lands, despite growing evidence of anti-hunting sentiment. In 1974 there were 16.4 million licensed hunters in USA, a 16 per cent increase since 1961 (Hendee and Potter, 1976). In the United Kingdom the sale of hunting rights can be a lucrative source of revenue. Up to $US 1500 per day has been paid for shooting on quality grouse moorland in the Scottish highlands where income from game sports, directly and indirectly, can comprise between 25 per cent and 75 per cent of total income from land (Cullington, 1981).

Since the early sixties the commercialisation of rural recreation has been encouraged by the United States Department of Agriculture with limited success. In the more populated states development of recreation facilities such as hunting lodges, riding stables, fishing ponds, camp grounds and zoos was seen as a means of increasing farm income and fostering efficient multiple use of rural resources. More recently, these government assistance programmes have been questioned and encouragement of small enterprises on private lands is seen as a mistake (Cordell *et al.*, 1980). Rather than promote developments which degrade rural environments, it is suggested that the emphasis should be on the visual beauty and rustic attractiveness of an uncluttered countryside. Despite this scepticism, farm tourism is a successful economic activity in Britain. Open days and demonstration farms with facilities for observing farm operations are actively promoted as a means of introducing visitors to the features and problems of modern agriculture (Countryside Commission, 1981a).

Access by agreement or public rights-of-way has few counterparts in Australia although cycleways and walking tracks on public land are gaining popularity. However, in New Zealand a programme is under way to provide a national walkway network over public and private land:

> . . . so that the people of New Zealand shall have safer, unimpeded foot access to the countryside for the benefit of physical recreation as well as for the enjoyment of the outdoor environment . . . (New Zealand Walkway Commission, 1979: 13).

The walkway system is seen as one way of bridging the gap between farmers and townsfolk. The goodwill of landholders is crucial to the success of the programme and there is no power to acquire walking rights other than by negotiation or gift. The whole scheme is embodied in an Act of the New Zealand Parliament under which the rights of property owners are fully protected with heavy penalties for offences or damage by walking users.

In USA, growing interest in linear forms of outdoor recreation has created a demand for trails to provide for hiking, bicycling, horseback riding, motorcycling, snowmobiling, snowshoeing and cross-country skiing (US Bureau of Outdoor Recreation, 1975a). Much of this need has been met by making use of linear open space held in transportation and utility rights-of-way, thereby eliminating the difficulty and expense of acquiring new land and freeing funds and manpower for development of other facilities. Realisation of the recreation potential of abandoned railroads, service corridors and canals represents more effective utilisation of these features' whose original resource function has become redundant. On a larger scale, the US Congress in 1968 enacted legislation establishing a National Trails System and this was amended in 1980 to include a new category of National Historic Trails (US Congress, 1980).

In Britain public pathways are part of the heritage and an ancient network of long distance footpaths and bridleways stretches for over 100,000 miles (approx. 160,000 km) across the English and Welsh countryside. These 'folk routes', previously neglected and overgrown are gradually being redefined, marked, and maintained to guarantee greater public access to rural lands. The Countryside Commission (1981b) actively supports the provision and upkeep of recreational paths and also encourages the establishment of farm trails in co-operation with landholders to give the public opportunities to learn about modern farming methods.

Access Problems

Clearly, the establishment of trails and other means of facilitating recreational use of private rural land is an indication of some relaxation of the access situation. In many cases however, countryside recreation remains inhibited by the prevailing attitude of particular landholders who fear, with some justification, the consequences of thoughtless negligence or deliberate vandalism by visitors. Their experience suggests that, in many circumstances, recreation is simply incompatible with other uses of countryside by virtue of its concentration in time and space as well as problems of trespass, litter, property damage and general nuisance.

These problems have been well documented in the United Kingdom where visitor pressure on landholders can be extreme. Cullington (1981) reports that farmers in Dartmoor National Park (see Chapter 7) were trying to farm with 65,000 visitors per day in the peak season of 1971. These figures were expected to rise to 95,000 per day by 1981. Even in remote upland grazing areas, disturbance to stock and damage to stone walls, gates and other farm installations can seriously disadvantage already low-income farmers whose opportunities to profit otherwise from visitors are few.

As noted earlier conflict is most likely closer to towns where fringe landholders face higher levels of trespass damage to the extent that some form of boundary protection may become necessary. In extreme cases the actions of visitors may lead to drastic modification of farming practices or the abandonment of arable farming altogether. A British Ministry for Agriculture survey of 100 farms in the Thames Valley near Slough, west of London, reported that two-thirds of respondents have been troubled by some form of trespass over the previous three years (UK Ministry for Agriculture, 1973). Similar problems, identified in Central Scotland are differentiated according to type of recreation activity in Table 6.1.

With impacts on this scale the negative attitude of rural communities to recreational use of private land can be better understood. Continuing invasion of the countryside by urban dwellers seeking diversion, set against a background of rapid changes in farming is leading to a situation in Britain where there is perhaps a greater degree of antipathy between farmers and visitors than ever before (Phillips and Roberts, 1973).

In Australia too, the lines are fairly clearly drawn between town and country and the concept of inviolate rights of property ownership is widespread and generally accepted. The landholders' attitude is typified by the following statement:

Table 6.1: Problems Arising from the Recreational Use of Rural Land in Scotland

	Rights of way	Problems arising from:		Car parking
		Walking	Picknicking	
		(Percentage of all problems notified)		
Disturbance and damage to stock	20	27	28	18
Gates left open	14	12	7	5
Litter/rubbish	14	18	27	30
Damage to dykes/fences	9	8	15	—
Vandalism	7	9	2	—
Damage to crops/grazing	8	6	—	4
Poaching/theft	10	7	4	15
Fire/arson	4	8	10	7
Noise	3	—	—	—
Trespass	2	2	2	—
Damage to trees	2	2	—	2
Access roads blocked	2	3	—	16

Source: Duffield and Owen, 1970: 138, 146.

Access to private land for sport or recreation is a privilege and privilege is not a birthright but something that can be earned by good behaviour and responsibility. This Association will not consent to accept the entry upon private land, without the permission of owners or occupiers, of any persons who are not performing a statutory function, as other than trespass (Graziers Association of New South Wales, 1975: 3).

This attitude is translated into real terms by means of a proliferation of cautionary signs at property boundaries and warning notices in the rural press advising that all permits to enter land have been cancelled and that trespassers will be prosecuted or face other dire consequences.

Thus, for many Australians, recreational contact with the countryside remains restricted and is often confined to illicit and fleeting entry of private land or viewing from a moving vehicle. Moreover, there seems little prospect of landholders being willing or able to divert resources voluntarily from what are seen as the land's primary functions — agriculture, and the like — to provision of recreation space for city dwellers.

Water-based Recreation

The presence of water is often regarded as a fundamental requirement for outdoor recreation, either as a medium for the activity itself or to enhance the appeal of a recreational setting. Water provides for a diversity of recreation experiences, some requiring direct use of the water itself (with or without body contact) and others merely requiring the presence of water for passive appreciation and to add to the scenic quality of the surroundings. The more active types of water-based recreation range over boating (sailing, power-boating, rowing, canoeing), fishing in all its different forms and swimming, including sub-aqua diving, water-skiing and surfing. Some of these, such as the last activity mentioned, are associated directly with coastal waters while others are concentrated on rivers and inland waterbodies. All in common have experienced a remarkable upsurge in participation during the past two or three decades. In some cases this has strained the capacity of the resource base to meet the growth in demand and, in turn, has generated conflict between users and uses of water resources.

Figures for specific types of water-based recreation are impressive. In the United States in 1975, for example, nearly 54 million Americans participated in fishing, involving more than 1.3 billion days for an average of 24.5 days per angler. The fishermen (and women − 16.7 million or 31 per cent were female) spent $US 15.2 billion on fishing activities, or an average of $US 282 per angler (US Fish and Wildlife Service, 1977). In England and Wales in the same year, the total number of anglers was estimated at around three million; swimming was the most popular outdoor sport with over eight million participants; and the number of pleasure craft more than doubled in the previous decade (Yates, 1977). Recreational travel on the Colorado River through the Grand Canyon increased from just seven in 1950 to 16,432 in 1972, when a quota system of river management had to be introduced (Nash, 1977).

With the emergence of new forms of water-based recreation and more sophisticated equipment these trends seem likely to continue despite energy constraints and some levelling off in population (Leatherberry *et al.*, 1980). As a consequence, many managerial problems, both social and environmental, have been created.

Some streams have become health hazards because of pollution. Others are threatened by accelerated and unregulated shoreline development. Increased recreation use can adversely affect plants, animals and soils along rivers. Erosion of banks, campsites and landings is a common problem. Growing use has resulted in more littering and vandalism to public and private property along rivers. Problems of maintenance and law enforcement have increased. There also is evidence that crowding, a variety of user-related conflicts and the impacts of recreation use on the environment have substantially decreased the quality of the experience for many recreationists (Hecock *et al.*, 1976. 2).

It should be remembered too, that waterbodies serve many important functions in addition to their role as recreation resources, among them domestic water supply, irrigation, hydro-electric power generation, navigation, flood control and waste disposal. Some of these lend themselves to multiple use in tandem with recreation, others are incompatible or involve use of the resource in such a way as to detract from its suitability for recreation.

Clearly then, there is ample scope for conflict over use of water for outdoor recreation and competition can become intense where water resources are in short supply. Conflict can occur between:

*Recreation and other resource uses such as control structures within the river system or agricultural practices and other land uses within a drainage basin.
*Incompatible recreation activities of which power-boating and water-skiing probably arouse most opposition from less aggressive forms of recreation.
*Recreationists and the environmental resources exposed to use including the water and shoreline, the flora and fauna and human settlements and communities nearby.

Conflicts are not confined merely to the water surface but can occur at access and egress points over ancillary facilities such as boat ramps, parking, campsites, access roads and the like. Even within the one specific recreation activity excess usage can generate conflict over space at peak periods. Part of the problem is the inability of all waterbodies to satisfy the requirements for particular forms of water-based recreation. At least two aspects are critical (Mattyasovsky, 1967):

*The 'form' or nature of the water and associated features. Certain wave conditions are an obvious pre-requisite for surfing; 'White' water is ideal for wild river-running; and relatively static waterbodies may be preferred for water-skiing, sailing and rowing. Features of the shoreline and beneath the water surface can be important as are the quantity, permanency and seasonal distribution of the waterbody. Boating enthusiasts who have to carry or drag their craft some distance to the water line from a poorly sited boat ramp can vouch for the problems caused by water level fluctuations and drawdown of reservoirs in dry weather or after large releases of water.

*The quality of water appropriate for different recreational uses particularly in regard to aspects such as clarity, purity and temperature. Water quality often has to be a compromise so that minimum criteria are stipulated rather than 'ideal' standards. For some types of recreation, even low levels of pollution can be tolerated depending upon the pollutants and the activity in question.

With sport-fishing water quantity and quality are both significant, and for some species temperature can also be a critical aspect of the fishing environment. It is important to consider fishing conditions for anglers as well as the fish habitat in physical and ecological terms. Habitat requirements vary and almost certainly will deteriorate with increased use. Management of the resource may require attention to the form of streams, e.g. construction of fish ladders, remedying pollution and other deficiences in the condition of waterbodies as well as control of undesirable species. The quality of water is a less important consideration with recreational boating; more important are the size of the waterbody, depth, subsurface features such as rocks, any aquatic vegetation present and compatibility with other users and uses (Mattyasovsky, 1967). Boating of any kind is space-demanding and power-boating, in particular, can cause interference and danger to others as well as water pollution and bank erosion. In addition marinas, service facilities and boat launching ramps are often necessary. Provision of sufficient on-water mooring space can be a particular problem in popular, crowded waterways. An example is Sydney Harbour, Australia where opposition to proposals for more efficient multiple mooring in marinas is strong, on the grounds of aesthetics, pollution and the need for ancillary on-shore facilities including car-parking. Once again it becomes a question of capacity, either of the water surface or shoreline, to accommodate simultaneously a number of competing uses.

Research in North America suggests that the spatial requirements for boating vary from three acres (approx. 1.2 ha) per boat for general purposes, up to 40 acres (approx. 16 ha) per boat for water-skiing

(Jaakson, 1970). An overall standard of ten acres (approx. 4 ha) per boat is recommended and this agrees with Tanner's (1973) suggested figure for boating on enclosed waters. Universal applicability of such standards is seldom possible, but awareness of spatial limits should alert resource managers to the likelihood of congestion if such figures are approached.

An obvious reaction to pressure on capacity is to create new water space. In Britain, for example, increments from the flooding of mineral workings, canal restoration and new reservoirs are expected to amount to a total increase of 20 per cent in available water for recreation by the end of the century (Yates, 1977). One of the most impressive projects is Holme Pierrepont on the River Trent near Nottingham which is one of the largest water parks in the country covering over 600 acres (approx. 240 ha) with facilities for rowing, water-skiing, canoeing and angling (Seeley, 1973). Since 1974 Regional Water Authorities in Britain have also had a statutory obligation to build provision for recreation into all new water projects (Tanner, 1973). In Australia the Penrith Lake Scheme, costing over A$ 300 million, will be developed over the next 20 years west of Sydney. The scheme provides for extraction of some 200 million tons of sand and gravel from the site and its progressive restoration and conversion to a series of lakes rivalling the size of Sydney Harbour and allowing for boating, fishing, swimming and other water-based recreation activities (Lewis, 1977).

Perhaps the most important resources which remain relatively unused for recreation are water supply reservoirs. Studies carried out in North America, Britain and Australia have brought out the recreation potential of domestic water storages in particular, because of their usual proximity to the population centres they service (Dunn, 1981). Although considerable regional variations exist in the extent to which water controlling authorities permit recreation, it is clear that there is a much more sympathetic attitude to the question in North America and Britain than in Australia (Table 6.2). Increasingly, provision for recreation is being incorporated into the design and management of irrigation and power generation storages in Australia as part of a policy of multiple use. However, there remains a general reluctance to permit recreation activities on or adjacent to domestic water supplies because of the risk of contamination.

Although the primary concern must be provision of an adequate quantity of clean water of suitable quality, modern treatment facilities make many forms of water recreation compatible with this aim. Where recreation is permitted bank and shoreline activities, as well as fishing

Table 6.2: Recreational Use of Domestic Water Supply Reservoirs in USA, Great Britain and New South Wales

Extent of use of reservoir	USA		Great Britain		New South Wales	
	No.	%	No.	%	No.	%
Water-based recreation permitted	181	68%	344	64%	10	17%
Water-based recreation prohibited	88	32%	191	36%	49	83%
Total	269 communities		535 reservoirs		59 reservoirs	

Source: Dunn, 1981: 109.

and non-powered boating, are usually accepted without question. However, even body-contact forms of recreation could be permitted where water treatment is of a high standard. In any case, there are often many other 'natural' sources of water pollution present from agriculture, native birds and animals and contaminated precipitation, as a study in northern New South Wales demonstrated (Burton, 1975). In inland Australia, water for any purpose is generally in short supply and recreational water space is severely restricted away from perennial streams. In this context, opposition to recreational use of domestic water supply storages is coming under increasing scrutiny and there are indications that a more reasonable attitude to the issue may eventually emerge.

Essential to the process of sound management of water-based recreation is adequate knowledge of available water resources. A good deal of effort in recent years has been directed towards detailed inventory, classification and evaluation of streams and other waterbodies with recreation potential (see Chapter 3). In the United States, the Heritage Conservation and Recreation Service (1980) has completed the first phase of an inventory of the nation's river resources. The inventory is designed to identify those outstanding rivers and river segments still remaining in a natural relatively undeveloped condition, which could serve as the principal elements of a nationwide system of protected rivers. In this first phase more than 700 rivers in the northwestern states of Washington, Oregon and Idaho were examined and of these, 85 were selected for further study. A method has also been developed for assessing instream flows for recreation (US Fish and Wildlife

Service, 1978). Use of such techniques should help ensure that sufficient water is maintained in designated streams to support recreational opportunities and environmental values in the face of competing demands from water diversions for other purposes. However, a specific shortcoming in many of these surveys is to overlook the legal and institutional attributes of streams and waterbodies which can restrict access and thus impair or negate their recreation potential.

Access to Water-based Recreation Sites

As far back as 1962, the Outdoor Recreation Resources Review Commission recognised the issue of access as a basic limitation on recreational use of water in the United States, whether on streams, enclosed waterbodies or in the coastal zone (ORRRC, 1962b). Nor has the access situation changed markedly for the better in recent times. Nebraska's State Comprehensive Outdoor Recreation Plan reported that the state's riparian land is virtually all in private ownership and that access to rivers for fishing, canoeing and other water-orientated activities is extremely limited (Nebraska Game and Parks Commission, 1980).

The Plan sees this as one of the challenges to be dealt with in meeting Nebraska's current and projected needs for water-based recreation and recommends a programme of public acquisition of access sites at strategic locations. In the state of Texas too, rapidly increasing demand for recreational use of waterbodies is resulting in growing conflict between riparian landholders and the public (Templer, 1980). The question of public access is one of the most poorly defined and understood areas of Texas water and property law and there is almost no reliable information to aid the recreation-seeking public.

Elsewhere in the United States, the coastal zone has been designated by the US Bureau of Outdoor Recreation (1973) as one of the areas of critical concern for protection of recreational opportunities. Not only is population becoming concentrated close to the seashore, but access to the shoreline is being lost to development and alienation by exclusive private interests. Nearly one-third of the US shoreline including Alaska is in private ownership (Figure 6.2). Some of the strongest initiatives for improving public access to coastal waters and ocean beaches have been taken in the western states of California and Oregon. Since 1913, Oregon's beaches have been designated as public highways and a chain of 36 state parks extends along much of the coast (Smith, 1981). Following the relocation of Highway 101 some distance inland, a series

Figure 6.2: United States Shoreline Ownership by Regions

Source: United States Bureau of Outdoor Recreation, 1973: 34.

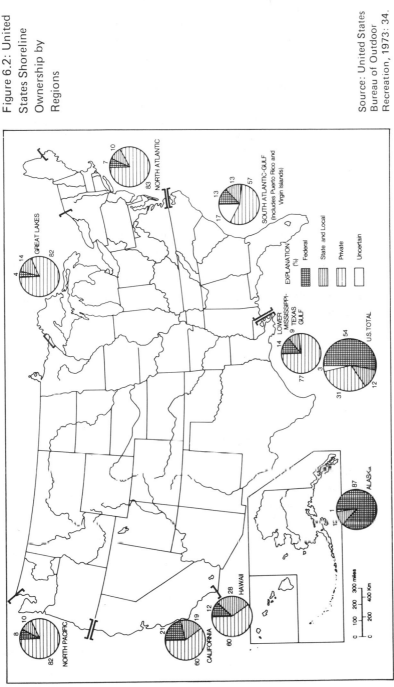

of access corridors has been established to connect the modern highway with the already public shoreline zone. Providing coastal access in the more highly urbanised state of California has been more difficult. Attempts are being made to develop vertical and lateral accessways to the shoreline, but these are resented and resisted by adjacent property owners, some of whom obstruct the corridors and harass those who use them. In an attempt to promote public awareness of coastal access opportunities a comprehensive coastal access guide has been prepared by the California Coastal Commission (1981) which describes conditions of access along 1100 miles (approx. 1760 km) of coastline and estuaries including San Francisco Bay.

As noted earlier in this chapter, Britain has long enjoyed comparative ease of access to rural lands for recreation. In regard to water-based recreation England and Wales are fortunate in possessing a fairly even distribution of rivers ranging from small streams to broad estuaries (Figure 6.3). Although angling remains a most popular recreational pursuit, opportunities for fishing non-coastal waters are heavily restricted. Fishing rights are commonly reserved for the use of landowners and their friends, or sometimes let or sold to individuals, hotels and angling associations. Game fishing for salmon and trout is a particularly valuable and closely-guarded resource commanding high rents with a capital value measured in tens of thousands of dollars per kilometre (Coppock and Duffield, 1975).

As an island nation the coastline must be considered one of Britain's most important recreational resources. No part of England and Wales is more than 75 miles (approx. 120 km) from tide-water and a good rail and road communications network puts the coast within reach of most of the population. Yet even there, there is evidence that the more popular areas are rapidly reaching saturation point. One observer puts it this way:

> Of a total, in England and Wales, of some 4,400 km (2742 miles) of coast there is at the present time an available length of only 8.89 cm (3½ in.) per person. And for spots with amenity value the length works out at about an inch each! (Robinson, 1976: 204).

Robinson points out that something of the order of six miles (approx. 10 km) of the coastal zone are becoming built-up each year and much of the undeveloped coastline is relatively remote and inaccessible in the west of Scotland. The Countryside Commission recognised the pressure on remaining unspoiled stretches of coastline

Figure 6.3: The Recreational Use of Coastal and Inland Waters in England and Wales

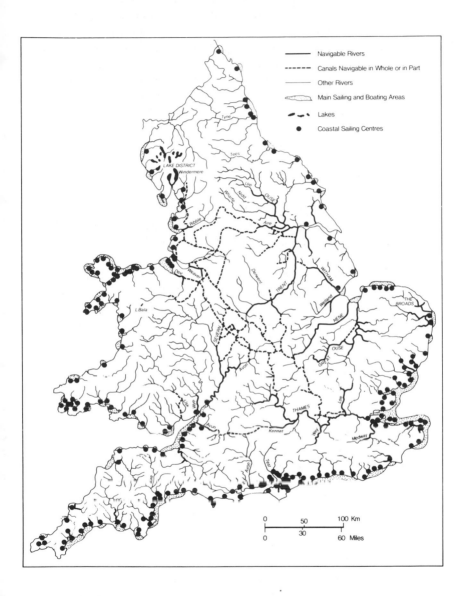

Source: Parker, 1975: 194.

and has proposed the creation of specially protected Heritage Coasts. These areas include a wide variety of coastal environments and contain some of the most impressive scenery in the country.

In Australia the attraction of the coastal zone is again very much in evidence with well over 90 per cent of the population living within a half-day drive of the sea. Many people from other countries picture Australia as a land of sunny skies, warm weather and vast expanses of sandy beaches. Whereas this scene is true for much of the country some of the time, there is cause for concern regarding the availability for coastal recreation resources to the general public. Although private beaches as such do not exist, many obstacles can obstruct free passage to the supposedly public shoreline. It has been estimated that only about one-quarter of the coastline in the state of Victoria, for example, is open to the public (Mercer, 1972). The remainder is sealed off by remoteness, by rugged terrain or by private landholdings.

The city of Sydney, with its harbour and nearby waterways, has one of the finest settings for water-based recreation in the world. Yet, to a large degree, these opportunities are lost because of limited access to the water's edge. Shortsighted policies in the past gave magnificent views over the harbour and sole access to the shoreline to a few fortunate property owners. Efforts are now being made to win back some of this access land though the establishment of Sydney Harbour National Park. Elsewhere along the coast similar proposals have been made to conserve landscape values and open up public access by way of a Coastal Lands Protection Scheme and the declaration of National Shorelines (New South Wales State Planning Authority, 1973).

In inland Australia the question of access to water-based recreation sites within privately owned land remains complex and the situation is made worse by problems of bank definition and changes in the course of streams and stream flow. In most cases visitors are unaware of property boundaries or title details and can only gain access with the permission of the landholder. It could be argued of course, that because recreation space appears relatively ubiquitous in countries like North America and Australia and agitation for improved access to country-side and water is not as great an issue as it is, for example in Britain, few problems or conflicts exist. However, demand for outdoor recreation is very much a function of the supply of opportunities (see Chapter 2). Revealed behaviour is just one subset of possible behaviours which would constitute preferred options in the absence of inequalities, structural barriers and institutional constraints. To paraphrase Moseley (1979), the challenge of rural accessibility planning is to expand the supply of opportunities by enlarging the space-time prisms available for outdoor recreation. Perhaps access to countryside and to water is a good point at which to begin.

Forests and Outdoor Recreation

Forests are an important component of the resource base for rural recreation. Whereas the essential role which water plays in outdoor recreation is clearly established, the contribution of forests is not so well-documented. Yet, forests have been providing recreational opportunities for a considerable length of time. Historically, the forests of Britain and Europe were valued more for recreation than timber production and foresters were employed by the nobility to maintain a suitable habitat for game animals and to guard against poaching.

Forests have long since ceased to be the preserve of a small select segment of the community. Just as timber production and other uses have emerged, forest recreation for the masses is now not only condoned, but promoted as a useful supplement to other resource-based recreation areas which are coming under pressure in many countries. An important element in this process is the suitability of recreation for incorporation into multiple use programmes of forest management. Forested areas can provide a full range of outdoor recreation opportunities, hiking, riding, cross-country skiing, snowmobiling, camping, hunting, orienteering, fishing and other water-orientated activities (Goodall and Whittow, 1975). Many of these pursuits are compatible to some degree with other forest resource functions such as provision of wildlife habitats and watershed protection. Many forms of timber production can also be practised in harmony with forest recreation. Of course none of the activities listed, except perhaps orienteering, is exclusive to the forest environment. However, forests probably form the largest part of rural non-agricultural land and a scenic background of trees can make a positive contribution to the recreation experience for both passive and active pursuits. Forests can also provide a suitable venue for the more noisy or visually unattractive types of recreation.

Recreational use of public and private forests is increasing in the developed world and this is by no means confined to native tree species. Cooper (1976) reviewed the use of exotic production forests for recreation in Britain, parts of Europe and USA. He contrasted this with the situation in New Zealand forests where action has been taken only recently to ease public entry. In Britain, plantation forestry dates from

1919 with the establishment of the Forestry Commission. Together with the private sector, the forest estate in England, Wales and Scotland now covers nearly two million hectares (approx. 5 million acres) or some eight per cent of the land cover (Sidaway, 1976). In the early years the accent was on the reservation and production of timber and recreation was discouraged principally because of the perceived fire hazard. Timber production remains the primary aim of the Forestry Commission, but forest recreation has seen significant growth since the designation of the first forest park in 1935. There are now seven forest parks, mostly in the more attractive upland plantations. Whereas much of the forest recreational use is concentrated in these areas, it is estimated that overall Forestry Commission land accounts for about ten per cent of the total number of day visits to the countryside (Goodall, 1975).

A number of specialist recreation activities are catered for in the 248 Forestry Commission forests. In addition, facilities are provided for other day visitors and campers and a network of forest trails has been developed. The trails are designed for foot access only and the Commission's policy is to restrict vehicles to peripheral car parks. Only six scenic drives have been developed and recreational use of the 10,000 miles (approx. 16,000 km) of forest roads is limited to a number of commercially sponsored car rallies each year. It has been suggested that 95 per cent of the public do not visit Commission forests at *all* because they cannot drive through them (Hall, 1974).

In the Netherlands the term forest is almost synonymous with recreation. Conifers and other exotic species are valued because of their quick growth to provide a vertical dimension in a landscape largely devoid of physical relief. Some Dutch forests have been planted specifically for recreation, e.g. *Utrechtse Heuvelrug* southeast of Amsterdam and contain 'mass recreation areas' with man-made lakes and beaches for swimming, restaurants and sporting facilities. In Denmark and Bavaria public forest lands are coming under increasing pressure for recreational use. Cooper (1976) reports that in both countries, people use private as well as state forests for recreation. Vehicles are not normally permitted to enter and owners often close off parts of their forests during logging operations when the fire hazard is high and for regeneration purposes. In Bavaria some intensively used sections of forest close to cities are designated as *Naturparken* and provide a major recreation outlet for urban populations.

Urban and near-urban forests are also highly regarded as recreation resources in the United States where the first national urban forestry conference was held in 1978 (College of Environmental Science and Forestry, 1978). Urban forests certainly provide valuable close-to-home opportunities for outdoor recreation in multiple use with other vital forest resource functions. However, outside the cities and the urban fringe, the responsibility for forest administration and management rests largely with the US Forest Service. The first Forest Reserve, Shoshone National Forest, Wyoming was established in 1891 and the Forest Service itself was set up in 1905.

The role of the Forest Service in managing its lands for recreation apparently began as a reaction against the threat of fire, pollution and other hazards caused by the presence of recreationists in the forests (Jensen, 1977). In 1915 the US Congress first recognised forest recreation when it gave the Service authority to lease forest land to private persons and organisations for the construction of summer homes, hotels, stores and other recreation-related facilities (Robinson, 1975). Once having become involved the policy of the Service gradually changed to one of enthusiastic encouragement of the recreational use of the forests. The important place given to recreation was confirmed in the Multiple-Use-Sustained Yield Act of 1960 in which Congress recognised five basic uses for the national forests — outdoor recreation, timber, range, watersheds and wildlife and fish.

The National Forest system now occupies an area of 188 million acres (approx. 76 million ha), or eight per cent of the area of the United States (Chubb and Chubb, 1981). This equals the area of France and the United Kingdom together and the Forest Service is represented in 44 states. The vast area and wide distribution of the national forest system provide a broad spectrum of recreational opportunities and some 200 million people visit the forests for recreational purposes each year. Figures for 1976 quoted by Jensen (1977) tell their own story. Camping is the most popular activity and there are around 5,500 developed camps and picnic areas in the forests, along with 203 developed ski areas, over 400 resorts and 18,500 summer homes. Pleasure driving is another prominent activity and the forests contain 152,000 miles (approx. 25,000 km) of scenic roads. About 17 million visitor-days of fishing occurred in the 83,000 miles (approx. 134,000 km) of streams and nearly two million acres (approx. 800,000 ha) of lakes. As well the Forest Service provides most of the wilderness areas in the nation. The National forests have truly become 'America's Playgrounds'.

In general, Australian forest management agencies have followed the trend in other countries — from questioning the role of recreation in the forests to tolerating and accepting it, and finally to welcoming recreationists and catering for their needs. This implies deliberate management of the forest landscape to create and enhance recreational opportunities. In the past, many Australians, through ignorance and uncertainty as to their welcome, regarded forests as hostile alien environments to be avoided if possible. This attitude has been countered by positive programmes by State forestry services to encourage and promote recreational use of the forests. A wide range of visitor facilities and services is now provided. Roads and forest trails have been opened up; camp sites, and in some cases visitor centres have been established. Maps, brochures, and other educational and interpretative material are also available to improve information sources and awareness levels of what the forests have to offer.

Despite all these positive indications of the acknowledgement of the growing significance of forest recreation, some scepticism continues on the part of Australian professional foresters and some hesitancy is shown by forestry authorities in some states to get too heavily involved in recreation because of the difficulty of recovering the costs entailed (Phillis, 1977). A further consideration is the resentment aroused by the vigorous campaigns conducted by environmental groups against the logging of natural forests. Particular concern has been expressed about 'disappearing' rainforests, despite the discovery that 120,000 hectares (approx. 300,000 acres) of this forest type remain in New South Wales alone, (Gordon, 1982). The protests, which have erupted into violence on occasions, are ostensibly based on a desire to preserve the forest ecosystems and permit limited recreation. The opponents of logging appear to ignore the potential for rapid regrowth of selectively logged forests, even rainforest. They ignore, also, the opportunities for multiple use of forests to include recreation *and* timber production and seem to have scant regard for the socioeconomic implications for rural communities and employment if all logging was eliminated (Green, 1978). At the same time, additional plantings of exotic species are opposed by some people on the grounds that they are unnecessary, unsuitable as habitat for wildlife and birds and do not have the recreation potential of native forests.

Clearly, a good   deal of research is required into visitor perception and behaviour, carrying capacity and evaluation of forest landscapes before this last proposition can be supported. Reference was made earlier to the work of the US Forest Service in landscape character analysis and visual management of the forest resource. In Britain too, attempts have been made to identify the attributes of a forest which contribute to its recreation potential (Goodall, 1975). The techniques have been adapted and applied with some success in Australia (Grist, 1976; How, 1982).

The evaluation method assumes that the suitability of forest environments for recreation is basically a function of:

*Topography and physical site conditions (space, slope, dissection, ground texture, accessibility and the presence of water).

*Mantle characteristics (age/height of trees, internal forest layout, tree spacing, forest routeway network).

Goodall (1975) suggests that the relative quality of forest environments in terms of their recreation supply capability or potential may be compared by means of an index based on these two groups of characteristics. Values are established for each characteristic, e.g. the proportion of slopes of various gradients, or of different tree types/heights/spacing. These are then weighted according to relative importance and combined to construct an index or yardstick against which the character of any forest can be measured to reveal its recreation potential.

The resulting Recreation Potential Index, ranked on a scale from 0 to 100, takes the form:

$$P_r = P_1 + P_2 - P_3$$

Where P_1 is a measure of topographic suitability, P_2 is a measure of mantle suitability and P_3 is a measure of accessibility.

Thus a low P_r score suggests a forest with steep slopes, young trees and poor intra-forest accessibility, with its recreation potential confined to perhaps a few linear routeways. A high P_r score, on the other hand, probably means few really steep slopes, a large number of mature trees and possibly some open land and, therefore, a wider range of recreation opportunities.

Forest characteristics are dynamic in nature, changing as the forest matures and with management practices. It follows that the P_i score for any forest will change over time especially the P_2 mantle factor as timber harvesting occurs (Figure 6.4). In addition, the Recreation Potential Index gives only a general indication of comparative inter-forest recreation suitability. It does not identify the potential of particular sites or areas, although it may be possible to derive this by selective application of the index on a grid basis within a forest. It needs also to be borne in mind that certain recreation activities have greater degrees of tolerance and flexibility in their use of a forest environment and hence, can make do with a lower P_r score. Finally, as with all evaluation techniques, care is needed in application outside the country of origin. Australian native forests, for example, are quite different from the broadleaf deciduous woodlands of Britain where the formula was originally tested.

Figure 6.4: Trends over Time in the Index of Forest Recreation Potential.

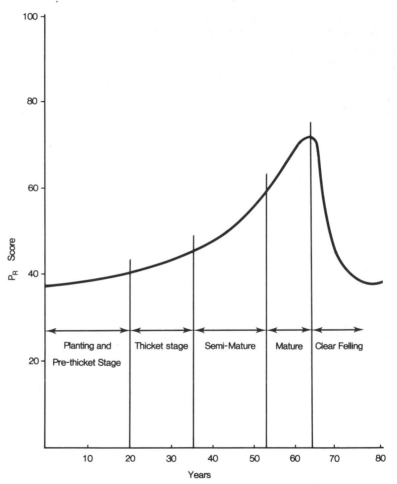

Source: Goodall, 1975: 31

Inventory and appraisal of resources are essential pre-requisites to sound management for recreational use and forests are no exception. In the first place, forests are not all equally suitable for recreation and evaluation of their recreation potential can indicate where resource development should best be directed. Secondly, some forests and some sections of forests are more suited to certain types of recreation. Again, this should be revealed by systematic survey. Finally all forests are amenable to management, and proper assessment of the resource base should reveal the scope for design measures and management strategies which will enable the full recreation potential of the forest to be realised.

Notes

1.The term 'countryside' is used here to refer to non-urban landscapes, in which man has become an important environmental agent, but which retain their rural character and appeal.

NATIONAL PARKS AND WILDERNESS

What is a national park? Is there a need for more of them and are they given sufficient priority in land use planning?

These are difficult questions to answer in a world where dollar values are often the only ones that count and tend to overshadow other considerations not so immediately obvious. National parks, of course, do generate economic benefits and considerable efforts have been made to demonstrate the magnitude of these effects (Beyers, 1970; Canadian Outdoor Recreation Research Committee, 1975). They also involve costs of at least two kinds — *direct* expenditure on establishment and maintenance, and the *indirect* or opportunity costs of commercial exploitation of resources usually foregone as the result of the park being created. The fact that governments and the community are prepared to accept these costs and support the public funding of national parks suggests that many people continue to regard them as worthwhile.

A range of values has been claimed for national parks but it seems their primary justification rests with the inherent nature of our society and the demands which expanding populations and technological progress place on the natural environment. Without this pressure large tracts of country would remain underdeveloped and there would be little reason for national parks and nature reserves. Thus, for many people the greatest value of the parks lies in their ecological role in protecting areas and features of outstanding scenic and historical worth and preserving distinctive ecosystems essentially unimpaired for future generations. For others, provision of recreational opportunities is preeminent with the parks seen as the means of physical and spiritual refreshment in a natural outdoor setting. Some would pursue this function further and suggest that national parks can become 'the engine' of regional development through exploitation of their tourist potential. A more limited segment of the population regards national parks as the vehicle for scientific research, retention of genetic diversity and the study of natural phenomena in undisturbed surroundings.

Whatever point of view is favoured there is obviously widespread appreciation of national parks and considerable support for the development and expansion of parks systems. Yet the concept of a national park is a relatively recent phenomenon. The first true national park was established at Yellowstone in USA in 1872. This was followed shortly afterwards by Royal National Park on the southern outskirts of the city of Sydney, Australia. Since these beginnings just over 100 years ago the modern parks movement has grown to worldwide dimensions with national parks to be found in all continents and under all economic and political systems.

The evolution of present-day national parks owes much to the American park movement of the nineteenth century and efforts of conservationists such as Olmstead and Muir. This movement was motivated by regard for nature and the revitalising powers of wild landscapes in an increasingly complex society. The dominant themes were the preservation and protection of the resources of nature and the opening up of these resources for the recreational needs of the nation. This movement culminated in the reservation of the first extensive area of wild land primarily for public recreation in the United States, the Yosemite Grant, in 1864 (Brockman *et al.*, 1973). This was followed by Yellowstone National Park eight years later and the Niagara Falls Reservation in 1885.

National Park Concepts

Although America was the first to establish a national park, the concept of reserving significant areas of outstanding natural landscape in the public interest evolved independently elsewhere as settlement spread in countries of the new world in the nineteenth and twentieth centuries. The result is that, despite some common features, there are as many variations of the national park theme as there are park authorities. Add to this the many state and regional parks and the picture becomes even more confused.

In 1969 the International Union for the Conservation of Nature (IUCN) attempted to clarify the concept of a national park by adopting a standardised definition. Under this terminology a national park was defined as a relatively large area.

a. Where one or several ecosystems are not materially altered by human exploitation and occupation, where plant and animal species, geomorphological sites and habitats are of special scientific, educative and recreative interest, or which contain a natural landscape of great beauty.

b. Where the highest competent authority of the country has taken steps to prevent or to eliminate as soon as possible exploitation or occupation in the whole area and to enforce effectively the respect of ecological, geomorphological or aesthetic features which have led to its establishment.

c. Where visitors are allowed to enter, under special conditions, for inspirational, educative, cultural and recreative purposes (IUCN, 1970: 156).

As could be expected, the rather restrictive and even controversial tone of the definition provoked some reaction. The clear bias towards preservation of ecosystems and the implicit limitations on human use meant that many so-called national parks in some countries would not qualify. Any exploitation of natural resources (including hunting and fishing), all construction (including water impoundments, roads and amenities) and strictly speaking, all means of transport and communication are excluded. In practice, of course, many of these land uses and facilities are permitted if only to provide the necessary infrastructure to allow the park to function. In most cases recreational pursuits such as sport-fishing, and even hunting under certain conditions, are accepted, along with non-consumptive resource uses such as hiking, boating, viewing, mountain climbing and scientific research. As noted below, active recreation is provided for and encouraged in many North American parks. Tourist amenities are accepted (but controlled) even within the park boundaries under the operation of the management authority, and many observers would argue that man-made bodies of water can enhance a park landscape.

Subsequent modifications of the IUCN definition did expand the function of national parks to include protection of man's cultural heritage as well as the conservation of nature and conceded that some facilities for visitors and administration were necessary for the management and enjoyment of a national park. However, the definition obviously still fits best parks in Africa, North America and Australia. Few parks would qualify in the Old World where very little unaltered natural landscape remains.

Attempts at generalisation are not helped by somewhat loose application of the labels 'national' and 'state' to similar areas of parkland. Some of the *state* parks of USA could well fit the national parks definition in terms of size, natural features and lack of development. Several parks established in the Canadian provinces also resemble national parks in scope, resources and management. The largest unit in the British Columbia system, Tweedsmuir Provincial Park, is a little larger than

Yellowstone and contains a wide range of mountain, forest and water environments (Chubb and Cubb, 1981). Whereas Australia's Royal National Park was the first to make specific reference to the term 'national park' in the supporting legislation, it and all subsequent 'national' parks in Australia have until recently been *state* responsibilities. Only since 1975 has an *Australian* National Parks and Wildlife Service functioned and specifically *national* parks been established alongside the state systems (see below).

The problems of generalising regarding the concept of national parks can best be illustrated by reference to representative park systems across the world.

National Parks in the United States

The US national park system encompasses nearly 300 different areas of diverse sizes and types totalling some 32 million acres (approx. 13 million ha). National parks are the best known units within the system but the Parks Service is also responsible for several other areas with designations such as national monuments and national memorials (only a few of which are actually statuary or historic buildings), national historic sites (especially those associated with American military history), national lakeshores, seashores, parkways and wild and scenic rivers. As well the Service administers a large number of lands and buildings in and around the national capital, Washington DC. The size and complexity of the American parks service make comparison with other national systems difficult. Yet many of its features, in particular the approach to national park management, have been adopted in other newly settled countries.

National parks within the US system are predominantly large natural areas containing a variety of resources and one or more distinctive attributes or features of such scenic quality and scientific value as to be worthy of special efforts at preservation and protection. In a sense, the American national parks are regarded as 'outdoor museums' displaying geological history, imposing land forms and habitats of interesting and rare fauna and flora. In 1979 there were 37 national parks in USA most of them in the western states (Figure 7.1), with a total area of nearly 16 million acres (approx. 6.5 million ha). The better known national parks such as Yellowstone, Yosemite and Grand Canyon contain some of the most spectacular scenery in the world and justifiably attract vast numbers of visitors both from North America and foreign countries. Indeed, the problem of numbers wishing to visit the parks in peak periods has led to concern for the natural resource base and has prompted a review of park philosophy and management principles in the US parks system.

Figure 7.1: National Parks in the United States

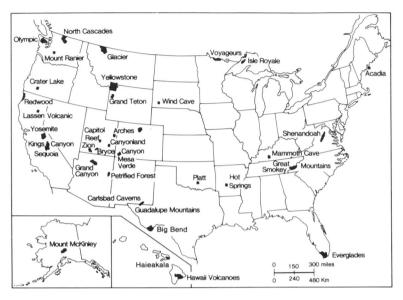

Reservation of park land for recreational purposes was a potent force, if not the primary one, in the early days of the US national parks. This initial viewpoint is interesting in view of the later change in emphasis to the conservation of nature. In the early decision-making years the attitude of park authorities was one of active encouragement of visitation by the public (Fitzsimmons, 1976). Part of the rationale for these efforts was that exposure to nature would prompt visitors to appreciate and support the parks. Broad popular support was also seen as a means of counteracting political and economic interests hostile to the national park concept. If enough visitors could be attracted parks would become self-supporting and provide the income needed for their role in the preservation of natural species and landscapes.

These efforts at 'popularisation' of the parks read a little strangely in view of latter-day problems in North America from visitor pressure, congestion and fears of deterioration of park landscapes. However, the historical context should be borne in mind. The first parks were remote and difficult of access; transport was relatively slow and primitive and public funds for park development were short. While patronage remained low there must have seemed little contradiction between use and preservation or any need for managment plans to maintain ecological values. The major problem, presumably, was how to boost attendance and justify the viability and continued existence of the parks. Funds generated by publicity programmes 'were in turn used to provide more recreational attractions and visitor services in a spiralling development cycle' (Forster, 1973: 17). The preservation responsibilities of the US National Park Service did receive some impetus from the 1935 Historic Sites and Buildings Act which called for the protection of historical sites, buildings, objects and antiquities of national importance (Doell and Twardzik, 1979). However, in many cases, these activities merely added to the attractiveness of the parks by appealing to national pride and public interest in history and tradition.

Following the end of World War II all the features of the modern outdoor recreation phenomenon emerged to bring unprecedented pressure on national parks and similar resource-based areas. Rapid rises in population coupled with economic expansion, increased affluence, leisure and mobility brought new waves of visitors to the parks seeking more diverse and sophisticated forms of amusement, not all of which were compatible with park values. Forster (1973) is most critical of what he calls 'adjustment planning' during this period. Changes were made and facilities and services provided merely to match anticipated use figures with little regard for saturation or the capacity of natural areas to absorb development or recover from wear and tear.

During the 1960s increasing public concern over the impact of rapidly accelerating use and modern technology led to greater awareness and acceptance of the need for positive steps to be taken to contain visitor activity and restore park environments. The balance in park management philosophy and practice tipped in favour of restoration and preservation of the resource base. In the opinion of the Leopold Committee (1963) the goal of park management became to preserve and where necessary, recreate the ecological scene as viewed by the first European visitor. Clearly, the protective function of national parks and the obligation to maintain the natural heritage 'unimpaired for the enjoyment of future generations' was now to receive priority. Although provision for public enjoyment and recreation remained an objective, it tended to become subservient to preservation of natural features and ecological vlaues.

Some recent management decisions of the US National Parks Service confirm this re-orientation. It is now park policy to consider new road construction as a last resort in seeking solutions to park access (Stewart, 1979); public recreational use of the Grand Canyon has been curtailed because of environmental damage and user conflicts; access to Mount McKinley National Park in Alaska is restricted; motor vehicles have been excluded from some park areas to be replaced by shuttle buses and mini-trains; and speed restrictions, one-way traffic systems and limited parking facilities have been introduced to dampen visitor use. The regulation programme has apparently received public acceptance and is enjoying some success. Visitor transportation systems now operate in 35 park areas in the United States. The first mini-train system was introduced in 1971 at Yosemite National Park and during 1977 more than eight million park visitors made use of the system there and in other US parks.

The new approach is well motivated, and grounded in the belief that more roads and easier access will only perpetuate present high levels of visitation with associated dangers of ecological degradation, scarring and erosion of the landscape and disturbance to wildlife. As a senior park administrator sees it: 'If the park experience is to keep its distinctive quality, the numbers of people and their methods of access and circulation will necessarily have to be more closely controlled' (Stewart, 1979: 16).

Despite these initiatives the strict goal of preservation is obviously unattainable in the absolute sense, while *any* level of usage is permitted. The implications of this use/preservation dilemma are discussed later in this chapter. It seems however, that for the present, at least in developed countries, perpetuation of the natural heritage and historical features is now recognised as the prime function of national parks. How long the notion of national parks as predominantly nature reserves can be maintained is open to question if community support is alienated in the process and public funding is cut back. The expectation that national parks will be generally accessible to the community is widely held. The further assumption that they will be, to a degree, self-supporting is also important in the development and expansion of the national parks system and especially so in the case of developing countries.

National Parks in Developing Countries

Many problems are associated with the establishment and management of national parks in developing countries. Park proposals are often looked at primarily in the context of potential economic and social benefits. Ecological considerations and the desirability of preserving unique ecosystems are certainly recognised, notably in the selection of environments and landscapes for inclusion in the parks system. However, in the hard practical negotiations over land acquisition and future park operation and management it is of fundamental importance that the government authority be able to demonstrate specific benefits especially for the local people.

National parks are now a reality in all corners of the developing world from Latin America, Africa and Asia to the Pacific Islands. Even in Iran before the recent upheavals there were eleven national parks with a total area of 1,500,000 acres (approx. 600,000 ha) (Köpp and Yachkaschi, 1978). In Africa, some of the parks and reserves originated from western attempts to protect wildlife and the natural landscape for recreational, conservation and scientific purposes (Nelson and Butler, 1974). However, several national parks in East Africa have been established since the end of the colonial regimes and potentially large economic returns from tourism appear to have influenced their creation (Ouma, 1970). Despite the disruption caused by hostilities associated with independence movements, tourism ranks prominently as a source of foreign funds in countries like Kenya and Tanzania and is experiencing a revival in Zimbabwe (formerly Rhodesia).

Most of the stimulus for this tourist activity comes from worldwide interest in viewing the large and varied species of wildlife to be found in national parks such as Tsavo and Nairobi in Kenya, Kiliminjaro and Serengeti in Tanzania, Wankie and Matopos in Zimbabwe and Kruger in South Africa. Kruger National Park covers nearly five million acres (approx. two million ha) and is visited by almost 400,000 people annually, 25 per cent of them from overseas (Chubb and Chubb, 1981). Similarly, in the less-developed African nations, most of the park visitors are from abroad. Whereas some newly-emerging nations regard the parks as undesirable vestiges of colonial rule, they are tolerated because of their vital role in providing local employment and attracting tourists and foreign currency.

National parks are also being established in Asia and the Pacific Island nations. However, considerable difficulties remain to be overcome. In some countries like Indonesia and Papua New Guinea, the governments have apparently accepted the notion of national parks and are convinced of the role they can play in the development of the nation (Gorio, 1978; Sumardja, 1981). Such conviction cannot always be assumed in societies where wilderness is still considered an obstacle to progress and the need for conservation is not immediately clear. There may well be difficulty in diverting money and manpower to the development of parks and a reluctance to take land out of what is considered more productive use. However, even in situations where the authorities do display enthusiasm and an awareness of the value of parks, obstacles may still surface in translating the concept to the actual park situation. A particular problem can occur in areas of prior human habitation, especially where land is in communal ownership (Dasmann *et al.*, 1973).

A particular problem in less-developed countries is the system of shifting agriculture known as slash-burn, or *milpa*, which is highly destructive of the environment. When the practice spreads into parks and reserves, as it has done in many Latin American countries, it rapidly destroys habitat and unique natural areas (Meganck and Goebel, 1979). When La Macarena National Park was established in Colombia in 1948 it covered more than 3,200,000 acres (approx. 1.3 million ha). The practice of *milpa*, plus firewood cutting and poaching, have reduced the area to less than half its original size and the lands which are lost are very difficult to restore. Adjustment of park boundaries to exclude affected areas has only a short-term effect in a culture where 'spontaneous settlement', or squatting has always been used as a device to establish rights of ownership. The problem can only be met by raising standards of living above the subsistence levels which necessitate this rapacious form of land use. If the indigenous population can receive some tangible benefit from the presence of a park, then it may be more prepared to respect the integrity of its boundaries.

The problem of people in parks is, of course, not confined to developing countries. Even the North American parks contain pockets of land in private ownership and national parks in Britain and parts of Europe are deliberately planned to incorporate inhabited areas and functioning communities (see below). Superficially therefore, it would seem good sense for the developing countries to learn from experience in the United States and elsewhere. However, the situations do not really compare and it is not easy to relate the two sets of park management practices. Moreover, there is always the possibility of resentment if recommendations for a more environmentally compatible, but less commercially rewarding type of park system, are imposed on less affluent societies.

Canadian National Parks

Not surprisingly, the parks system in Canada has some features in common with the United States; in fact, there is some shared responsibility for certain natural and historic sites along their common border. The most recently expressed objective for national parks in Canada has a familiar ring:

> To protect for all time representative natural areas of Canadian significance in a system of national parks and to encourage public understanding, appreciation and enjoyment of this natural heritage so as to leave it unimpaired for future generations (Parks Canada, 1979: 38).

However, it was not always so. As with the parks of the western United States, recreational opportunities as well as commercial considerations, were of prime concern in the early years. Interest in the first Canadian national park at Banff dates from the discovery of hot mineral springs in the 1880s. Curious as it may seem in the light of the magnificent Rocky Mountain scenery in the area, the original reason given for the reservation of land at this site was the 'sanitary advantage' of these waters and the need to protect them from commercial exploitation and control them for the benefit of the public (Scharff, 1972). In 1887, Banff Hot Springs Reserve, enlarged to an area of 260 square miles (approx. 670 km²), officially became Rocky Mountains National Park, Canada's first. The name was later changed to Banff National Park and the Canadian government and the railroads combined to develop hotels and facilities for visitors to the area.

It is worth noting that the Rocky Mountains Park Act of 1887 specifically reserved the area as 'a public park and pleasure ground for the benefit, advantage and enjoyment of the people of Canada'. This wording is almost identical with that proclaiming Yellowstone National Park. The Act went on to spell out also the protective aspect, emphasising however that no development was to be permitted that could 'impair the usefulness of the park for the purposes of public enjoyment and recreation'.

As more and more parks were added to the Canadian system transport networks were developed, all manner of visitor facilities were provided and entrepreneurs were encouraged to maintain a high level of service to promote patronage. In some cases, the recreation facilities at sites like Banff and Lake Louise themselves became major tourist attractions to complement the scenic grandeur in the surrounding park landscape. As with the American parks, concern for nature preservation was to come later as visitor pressure mounted on the park environments and the depredations brought about by indiscriminate hunting, mining and timber-getting became obvious. According to Nelson and Butler (1974) it is only in the period since World War II that a strong preservationist movement has emerged in Canada. The traditional view of tourism and recreation as fundamental underpinnings for parks was increasingly brought into question and ultimately the preservation and protection of park landscapes came to be regarded as first priority.

There are now 29 national parks in the Canadian system, plus more than 20 national historical parks and sites most of which are in the longer settled eastern provinces. Apart from Banff, some of the better known national parks such as Jasper, Kootenay and Glacier also straddle the spectacular Rocky Mountains of Alberta and British Columbia. In 1979-80 Canadian national park visits totalled 20.7 million, an increase of 322 per cent over 1960-61 (Travel and Tourism Research Association, 1981).

The policy announced by Parks Canada in 1979 continued the increased emphasis on protection of the natural and historic heritage, interpretation and educational activities and professional planning. Natural resources are now given the highest degree of protection to ensure the perpetuation of the natural environment essentially unaltered by human activity. A system of zoning is used to implement this policy and three new parks initiatives have been undertaken — Canadian Landmarks, Canadian Heritage River and Heritage Buildings. In proposals for new national parks and reserves in the Yukon and the Northwest Territories particular attention is being given to maintaining a balance between the need to protect wilderness values and the rights of local native people to continue traditional extractive activities, such as hunting, fishing and trapping in areas like Baffin Island (Gardner and Nelson, 1980). In many respects this problem resembles that of accommodating traditional subsistence resource uses within parks in developing countries.

National Parks in Britain

Prior human habitation in parks represents a problem of a different kind in the older, more densely peopled nations of Europe. Coppock (1974) has pointed out how inappropriate the IUCN definition of national parks is for a country like Britain with a long history of human settlement and no great reserves of unoccupied lands left in which to create national parks in the North American mould. Moreover, by the time the first moves were made in Britain at the end of the Second World War to establish national parks, widespread acquisition of private land would have been prohibitively expensive and politically unacceptable.

The result is that areas designated as 'national parks' remain almost entirely in private ownership and productive use. In fact, all national parks in Britain could more accurately be labelled 'national reserves' with many similar features to those set up in the United States (see Chapter 6). Agricultural holdings, fenced pastures, forestry plantations, quarries, farm structures, transport routeways and even villages and towns are all found inside the park boundaries. Management plans administered by local committees endeavour to reconcile conflicting interests between landholders and park visitors. At the same time, attempts are made to maintain and enhance the scenic quality and appearance of the landscape by controls over the location and nature of new facilities and proposals to alter existing structures.

A National Parks Commission (later Countryside Commission) was set up in Britain in 1949 and the first park, Peak District National Park, became a reality in 1951. Since then a total of ten national parks has been created, seven in England and three in Wales (Figure 7.2).The ten parks occupy an area of 3.4 million acres (approx. 1.4 million ha) or a little over one-sixth the size of Yellowstone National Park.

Interestingly, there are no national parks in Scotland. Although proposals were made in 1945 for five national parks pressures on the countryside were much less than those in England and the idea lapsed. The Countryside Commission for Scotland set up in 1967 has established some quite small country parks for intensive recreational use and has proposed a new parks system which will encompass urban parks, country parks, regional parks, special parks and national scenic areas. National parks were felt inappropriate in a Scottish context because, under internationally accepted standards, 'conservation must always take precedence over recreation and other land uses' (Foster, 1979, 4). Such an approach was seen as lacking flexibility and inhibiting retention of desired characteristics in 'a living, in-use way rather than in a museum sense'.

The concept and purpose of national parks in Britain were reviewed in 1974 and more emphasis was given to management procedures to ensure that recreational use did not threaten the scenic beauty and

Figure 7.2: National Parks in England and Wales

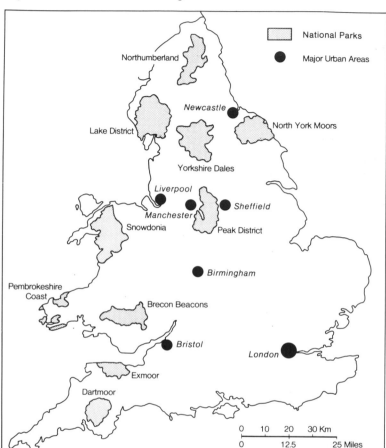

wildlife and that forestry and agriculture within the parks did not detract from the appearance of the landscape. Concern was also expressed about quarrying, the design and construction of reservoirs, housing and recreational facilities and visitor pressure on roads not designed for heavy traffic (Department of the Environment, 1974). Clearly, problems will always remain where privately owned resources play the major role in providing recreational opportunites for park users and where private interests may conflict with national priorities in conserving the natural beauty and amenity of the countryside.

The national parks of England and Wales were a product of the times and circumstances. As these change management has had to adjust. As

Coppock (1974) suggests, few would argue for the abolition of the parks, but their character may change and different solutions may have to be found to attain the objectives for which they were established. The designation of Country Parks is a move in this direction (Park, 1981). The main purpose of Country Parks is the provision of recreational facilities in an outdoor setting and in many ways they are the antithesis of national parks (Gilg, 1978). By 1976, more than 130 Country Parks had been recognised and they act as 'honeypots', providing readily accessible recreation outlets for large numbers of rural users where existing, more natural areas are under threat from over-use. In this way pressure on the national parks might well be relieved by provision of a greater range of alternative rural recreation opportunities accessible to large centres of population. Park boundaries and features need also to be reassessed to identify areas and sites where management controls may be eased, or in other cases, tightened. Whenever people are intimately involved, as they are in the British parks, more concern must be shown for *their* attitudes and welfare. The continued support and endorsement of the park concept by the inhabitants are vital for their continued success.

The Netherlands Parks System

The Netherlands shares with Britain and much of the rest of Europe the problem of developing a functioning park system within a landscape which has evolved over centuries of human use. This task is made even more difficult in the Netherlands, a country with one of the highest population densities in the world and where a good proportion of the countryside is the direct product of man's efforts to reclaim land from the sea. Yet even there 13 per cent of the country is still said to be in a more or less natural state − dunes, wetlands, woods, or uncultivated areas − and three national parks have been created (Boer, 1978). A national park in the Netherlands is defined as:

> An uninterrupted stretch of land of at least 1000 hectares (approx. 2500 acres) consisting of areas of natural beauty, lakes, ponds and water courses and/or forest with a special character as regards nature and landscape, and a special plant and animal life. (Netherlands Ministry of Cultural Affairs, 1976: 2).

The Dutch Government is endeavouring to meet the requirements laid down in the 1969 IUCN definition and to date 22 areas have been selected which meet the criteria of size, quality and integrity of area and management. It is worth noting that in the Netherlands 1000 hectares is considered sufficiently large for a national park. This compares with around 4.5 million hectares (approx. 17,300 square miles) in the world's largest national park, Wood Buffalo in Canada.

In addition to national parks the Netherlands is developing an experimental system of National Landscape Parks, which are closely related to the National Reserves in USA, the National Parks of Britain, the Regional Parks of France and the *Naturparken* in West Germany. The concept has much in common, too, with the idea of 'countryside parks' proposed for Australia later in this chapter.

With this type of park the concern is not with purely natural areas, but with areas shaped by *man and nature together* over the course of many centuries. National Landscape Parks will include villages and towns, agriculture, typical architecture and other features of human activity characteristic of the Netherlands landscape. The concept envisages that landholders, in addition to working their land, should assist in the management of the landscape park and receive payment for activities concerned with its care and compensation for loss of income as a result of any limitations on farming practice. Thus, farmers no longer will supply only grain, potatoes, dairy produce and meat, but also provide the community with an attractive landscape in a healthy living environment. Moreover, they will get paid for it. In a country like the Netherlands, especially, National Landscape Parks are seen as a complement to the national parks system and an appropriate way of encouraging people living and working in settled rural areas to maintain the natural *and* cultural values of the countryside.

New Zealand National Parks

New Zealand was one of the first nations to establish a national park after Yellowstone. Tongariro National Park came into being in 1887 as the result of a gift from the Maori people of an area of volcanic peaks in the central north island. Since that time, nine additional national parks, two maritime parks, 16 forest parks and over 1000 scenic and special reserves have been added. In all, 13 per cent of New Zealand is under complete or partial protection (Devlin, 1978). National parks comprise some 5.3 million acres (approx. 2.2 million ha) or about eight per cent of the country which has a total landmass comparable only to the US State of Colorado (Figure 7.3).

Within the New Zealand parks, development of recreation facilities

Figure 7.3: National Parks in New Zealand

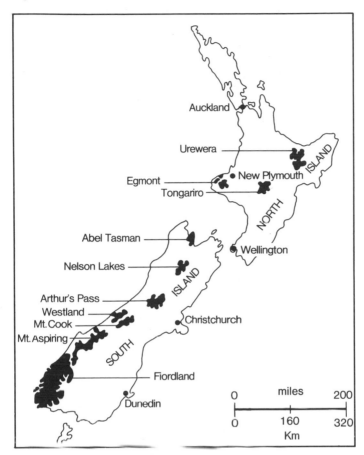

Source: Devlin, 1978: 15.

is patchy. However, one feature which has become a source of contention is the network of 'huts' used by hikers and climbers. Some of these huts were constructed as part of a culling programme to eliminate introduced species of deer, chamois, goats and pigs which cause extensive environmental damage in the parks. Others were erected as simple and rather primitive survival shelters against the risk of dangerous weather conditions in the more remote mountain areas. A lively debate is continuing over the advantages and disadvantages of the huts. Those who advocate their removal argue that their very presence negates the risk and challenge associated with a 'true' back-country experience.

They also point out that some huts are in poor condition and in hazardous locations, thus giving a misleading impression of safety. Hut sites are also said to become the focus of environmental degradation. Proponents maintain that, apart from saving lives and providing shelter and a means for informal social contact between park users, the huts are a useful management tool. Properly located and maintained, they are considered an aid to conservation and help in directing campers from alternative scattered and fragile areas. Whereas a 'no hut' policy applies in *wilderness* areas of New Zealand, it appears that the continued existence of a limited network of huts and tracks in the national parks can assist in the control and management of visitors.

Parks in Australia

As noted earlier in this chapter 'national' parks in Australia have, until recently, been the sole responsibility of the six state governments. Technically therefore, they do not qualify under the IUCN requirement that national parks be under the jurisdiction of the nation's 'highest competent authority'. However, from most other standpoints they do meet the international guidelines, national parks typically consisting of sizable areas of predominantly unspoiled landscape with the emphasis on nature conservation.

Originally, the provision of public recreational opportunities was the primary objective of national parks in Australia. The first park established, Royal National Park near Sydney, provided holiday accommodation, sporting facilities and picnic areas with the emphasis clearly on human pleasure and amusement. Since the early years the concept of a national park has broadened beyond this recreational theme.

A gradual increase in the number and area of national parks and reserves has followed the growth in environmental awareness which occurred in the 1960s and 1970s (Boden and Baines, 1981). In that period approximately 18 million acres (approx. 7 million ha) were added to the various state systems. New South Wales, the most populous state, has 59 national parks (Table 7.1), 144 nature reserves, 12 historic sites, 8 aboriginal areas, and 18 state recreation areas administered by the State National Parks and Wildlife Service (Hibberd, 1981). The total area is approximately 7.5 million acres (approx. 3 million ha) or about 3.7 per cent of the area of the state. The largest unit is Kosciusko National Park which occupies 1.6 million acres (approx. 640,000 ha) southwest of Canberra in the Australian Alps

Figure 7.4: National Parks in New South Wales, Australia

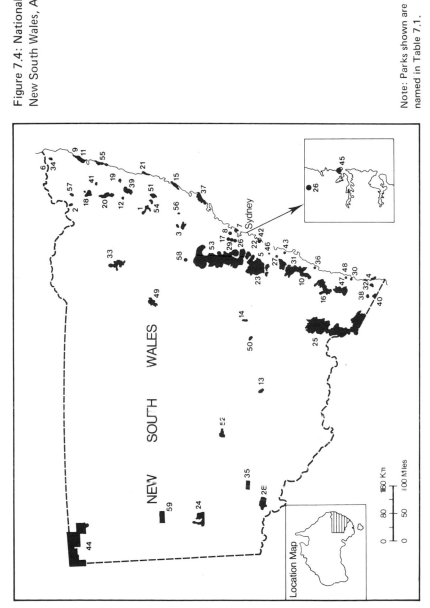

Note: Parks shown are named in Table 7.1.

Table 7.1: National Parks in New South Wales, Australia

1.	Apsley Gorge		31	Morton
2	Bald Rock		32	Mount Imlay
3	Barrington Tops		33	Mount Kaputar
4	Ben Boyd		34	Mount Warning
5	Blue Mountains		35	Mungo
6	Border Ranges		36	Murramarang
7	Bouddi		37	Myall Lakes
8	Brisbane Water		38	Nalbaugh
9	Broadwater		39	New England
10	Budawang		40	Nungatta
11	Bundjalung		41	Nymboida
12	Cathedral Rock		42	Royal
13	Cocoparra		43	Seven Mile Beach
14	Conimbla Range		44	Sturt
15	Crowdy Bay		45	Sydney Harbour
16	Deua		46	Thirlmere Lakes
17	Dharug		47	Wadbilliga
18	Dorrigo		48	Wallaga Lake
19	Gibraltar Range		49	Warrumbungle
20	Guy Fawkes		50	Weddin Mountains
21	Hat Head		51	Werrikimbe
22	Heathcote		52	Willandra
23	Kanangra-Boyd		53	Wollemi
24	Kinchega		54	Yarrowitch Gorge
25	Kosciusko		55	Yuragir
26	Ku-ring-gai Chase		56	Woko
27	Macquarie Pass		57	Boonoo Boonoo
28	Mallee Cliffs		58	Goulburn River
29	Marramarra		59	Mootwingee
30	Mimosa Rocks			

(Figure 7.4).

The Great Barrier Reef off the coast of Queensland also has a strong attraction for visitors. Following extensive lobbying by preservation-minded pressure groups the Great Barrier Reef Marine Park Authority has been set up and sections of the reef region are being successively incorporated into the marine park. Such parks, by their very nature, present unusual problems in park management. Contentious issues in this case were the question of oil exploration on the reef and the clash between the Queensland State Government and Australian Federal Government over administration of the resources of the region.

The federal body has become increasingly involved in park management since the formation of the Australian National Parks and Wildlife Service in 1975. The Service works in collaboration with the states but has sole responsibility for certain areas of nature conservation interest such as Norfolk Island and Christmas Island, as well as two national parks Uluru and Kakadu near Darwin in the Northern Territory. The Service believes that the plan of management drawn up for Kakadu may well prove a model for the development of similar parks in 'frontier' areas. Certainly, the park will have to contend with some major problems. Apart from preservation of the park environment and providing for appropriate use by visitors to a remote area, protection of Aboriginal interests, regulation of mining (uranium) in and near the park and control of feral animals may all create difficulties for park management.

Australia's largest city, Sydney, with a population approaching four million people, is fortunate in that twelve national parks are located within a radius of 100 miles (approx. 160 km). To a great extent, this situation results from the reservation of land for parks in areas where the soil and terrain were considered unsuitable for agriculture and too rugged to develop for housing. Royal National Park south of the city, Kuringai Chase National Park immediately to the north and Blue Mountains National Park to the west, are located on dissected sandstone plateaus for which no economic use was perceived at the time at the end of last century. Melbourne on the other hand, in the state of Victoria, was ringed by good agricultural land and there is now a serious dearth of parks and reserves close to the city (Mercer, 1970a).

The apparent contradiction and conflicts between outdoor recreation and nature preservation and between different types and intensities of recreational use of national parks in Australia suggest that the complexity of recreational demands should be matched by an appropriate array of recreational opportunities outside the parks. In the state of New South Wales this need is being met, in part, by the development of State Recreation Areas. These units, some of them quite large, comprise both natural areas and man-made features of scenic, historic and recreational importance. Several adjoin inland waterbodies and others occupy coastal sites. The new parks were designed to take pressure off the national parks and while haphazard destruction of their environment is obviously not allowed, they do cater for more intensive forms of outdoor recreation, even trail-bike riding and hunting may be permitted. In some, accommodation facilities have been provided while others are designed for day-visitor needs only. Provided that the recreational emphasis continues State Recreation Areas can provide a useful complement to national parks and an important additional unit in an integrated system of outdoor opportunities.

The introduction of more recreation-orientated 'peoples' parks' comes at an important stage in the development of the park system in Australia. For many years national parks have made a significant contribution to the recreation resource base. Now, in many parts of the country and for a variety of reasons, opportunities for further expansion of the national park system are becoming limited. Indeed, it could be said that Australia is entering a 'mature' phase of park development in which the initial stage of large scale land acquisition is closing, to be replaced by careful appraisal, development, and management of park resources already acquired. At the same time, consideration can now be given to alternative means of expanding the recreation opportunity spectrum of urban populations by provision of a range of different park options in accessible rural settings.

Moreover, a good deal of questioning of the role of national parks has emerged in Australia in recent years. To some, parks and wilderness areas appear as enclaves of unproductive land and havens for noxious plants and animals. Proposals to enlarge national parks on the north coast of New South Wales and to establish an additional national park in the New England region further inland have generated significant local opposition. Organisations such as 'Neighbours of National Parks' and 'The Association for the Protection of Rural Australia' are critical of the continued relevance of the North American park model to Australia and advocate the adoption of the British-European style park as well (Pigram, 1981a). The proposed new style of 'living' park environment, if developed along the lines of the National Reserves being set up in the United States, would encompass farming communities and rural settlements within distinctive scenic landscapes. The creation of 'countryside parks' in this way should not be seen as replacement for national parks, but rather as an extension of the system to allow for the introduction of a dual network of inhabited parks developed in tandem with the traditional parks.

To date however, park authorities in Australia have shown a decided reluctance to depart from the existing national parks system (Johnson, 1978). Brisbane Forest Park near the capital city of Queensland is a step in the right direction, although all land within that park is publicly owned. In the state of Victoria, the Regional Strategy Plan proposed for the Upper Yarra Valley and Dandenong Ranges on the northeastern outskirts of Melbourne encompasses many of the features of the National Reserve concept. Non-urban land in private hands comprises 23 per cent (approx. 175,000 acres or 70,000 ha) of the total land area with a further three per cent classified as urban. Approximately 105,000 people live within the region and the Strategy Plan provides for protection of the special features and rural character of the area and the maintenance of recreation opportunities on both public and private land (Upper Yarra Valley and Dandenong Ranges Authority, 1980). Apart from these initiatives a negative attitude prevails at official levels to the introduction of European-style national parks or US National Reserves in Australia. This reaction, coupled with growing resistance by rural landholders to any further acquisition of park lands of *any* kind, means that progress towards establishment of 'countryside parks' is likely to be slow. Yet, the need for innovations in parkplanning should be obvious. In a developed country like Australia, with all the pressures on resources for greater output and more efficient production methods, the transition to large scale stereotyped forms of land use can be very rapid. There is some urgency, therefore, regarding the adoption of an alternative approach to allocation of land for parks as the changing nature of agriculture and rural life acts as a disincentive for landholders to maintain the character and quality of the countryside in their keeping.

Despite scepticism and opposition from inflexible park bureaucracies, preservation-minded conservationists, and feudalistic landholders, the countryside park concept could play a useful role in Australia alongside national parks. If it can be shown, by successful pilot projects, that the economic and amenity functions of countryside can be compatible, then a range of park types can be created as and where appropriate. Given time and enlightened management, such parks have the potential to demonstrate the benefits of sharing the countryside as a living communal resource, both for ongoing productive purposes and outdoor recreation.

National Park Management

The brief canvass of park systems presented here illustrates the many ways in which the national park concept has been interpreted. This diversity gives rise to an equally complex range of park problems and approaches to the management of national parks. Despite these variations a recurring theme with all park environments is the need to strike a balance between preservation and use; how to accommodate appropriate levels of human activity, while at the same time maintaining the quality of the natural environment for which the park was established in the first place. This is the 'dilemma of development' as Fitzsimmons (1976) calls it. Use is concerned primarily with the present generation,

preservation is linked more closely with generations to come. Exped-
iency demands the satisfaction of current wants, whereas prudence
suggests limitations on such use in order to preserve park values for
future generations. Compromise is inevitable as *any* use involves some
disturbance to the park landscape and ecosystem. The aim of management should be, first, to exclude activities which are clearly inappropriate — power-boating, organised sports and entertainment centres
come to mind as ready examples. Secondly, care must be exercised to
keep unavoidable disturbance to a minimum and to recognise and
correct environmental deterioration before it becomes irreversible.

A distinction can be made between management problems which
impinge upon the park but which are externally generated and internal
problems arising essentially from visitor usage (McMichael, 1970).

External Problems

Reference has already been made to opposition from neighbouring
landholders to proposals for national parks in Australia. Conflict also
arises over what are seen as park management practices incompatible
with surrounding land uses. A case in point is the refusal of the New
South Wales Parks and Wildlife Service to allow drought relief grazing
or to carry out indiscriminate aerial and chemical poisoning of dingoes
which are considered a danger to livestock. Control measures against kan-
garoos and feral pigs are also thought not to be adequate in some parks.

Proposals for establishment and management of national parks, *do*
appear, at times, to give scant regard for resources and land use in
adjoining areas and vice versa. Manipulation of the environment outside
the park can, in effect, turn it into an island with little relationship to
surrounding ecosytems. An immediate problem is the loss of opportunity for natural checks and balances to regulate population expansion
of particular species. Dasmann *et al.* (1973) suggest that parks are most
viable when buffered by zones of extensive land use, e.g forestry.
Controlled hunting zones around parks with large wild animal populations have also been advocated to regulate the growth and movement of
herds.

A second type of conflict arises when incompatible resource uses are
imposed *inside* the park by *external* authorities. The park is seen as
relatively unused space and as public land, involves no resumption or
compensation problems. Near-urban parks especially are regarded as
'fair game' for waste disposal facilities, motorways, airport extension,
service corridors and water control structures.

Severe repercussions for park ecosystems can also be generated by the impact of fire, the entry of noxious species and externally-derived pollutants, including sewage, chemicals and industrial effluent. The fire hazard can be met partially by fuel reduction, prescribed burning and more efficient fire management programmes including detection systems and access trails (Parsons, 1977). Eradication of noxious species is another recurrent problem. In Australia's Kosciusko National Park, control measures are directed at exotic plants, introduced fish (in particular European carp) and animals such as rabbits and wild horses or brumbies (McMichael, 1970). Pollutants, such as oil spills, sewage, industrial effluents and pesticides can also affect park ecosystems and food chains especially through park drainage systems. Pollution from pesticides is most likely in parks established near zones of intensive land use. Detergent pollution may occur in parks close to the urban fringe and marine parks are obvious targets for oil pollution. Even when the source of the pollution can be pinpointed control may be difficult and would probably only succeed as part of a wider programme to combat pollution generally.

Internal Problems

Inside a park the principal concern is with the impact of recreation and associated human activities on the park environment. In part, the problem is a function of visitor numbers but it is also linked to the level and sophistication of facilities which are provided. Roads, parking, toilets, accommodation, food outlets, refuse and litter and off-road vehicles are just some of the ramifications of outdoor recreation which can place pressure on ecological quality and park resources. Much of the recreational activity is seasonal and the problems are worsened during peak periods. Again, in Kosciusko National Park an on-going debate is continuing over the place of snow sports in the park and proposals for development of additional facilities and extension of access into more remote areas (Steer, 1979). A management plan has now been drawn up for the park in an attempt to segregate and control commercial development and preserve primitive alpine zones.

Manning (1979) distinguishes between strategies and tactics in the management of recreational use of national parks. Strategies are defined as basic conceptual approaches to management, setting out different paths to preservation of environmental and recreational quality. Tactics are defined as tools to carry out various management strategies. To clarify the distinction, a strategy for example, might be a decision to limit recreational use. Within this basic strategy a number of tactics or tools might be pursued, including fees, permits, or physical barriers. Some of these were examined in greater detail in Chapter 4. Manning classifies available strategies for park management into four basic approaches each with a number of distinct sub-strategies. These are summarised in Figure 7.5. Two of the strategies deal with supply and demand aspects of recreation and park lands and two focus on modifying either the character of existing use to reduce adverse impacts, or the resource itself to increase its durability.

An important supportive aspect of park planning and management, be it strategy or tactic, is the provision of an appropriate interpretation programme to communicate to park users the objectives of management and the rationale for the various measures undertaken. In the long run, a sound interpretation policy may provide the key to resolving the dilemma between park preservation and use by developing in park users a deeper regard for national parks and a desire for a meaningful role in their care and management.

Wilderness

No discussion of resource-based recreation areas would be complete without reference to what many regard as the ultimate in natural environments — wilderness. For much of history, wilderness held a negative connotation, either as waste land or some vast, hostile and dangerous place to be avoided if at all possible, or else to be tamed, controlled and exploited.

Today, people and governments have come to think more positively of wilderness as something to be valued, used and managed with care and respect and preserved for a future world in which it could become an increasingly rare phenomenon. Many people now perceive wilderness as a large natural area where animals and plants can live undisturbed and where visitors can enjoy recreational activities of a primitive and unconfined nature. Hiking and canoeing are often given as examples of the type of recreation envisaged — that for which a minimum of mechanical aids is required.

One of the main benefits of a wilderness experience is said to be the spiritual satisfaction gained. Other advantages of wilderness recreation are physical and mental stimulation, the aesthetic appreciation of beautiful scenery and the experience of conditions similar to those encountered by the first settlers of a region. Wilderness serves as a sanctuary, either temporarily or permanently, for renewal of mind and spirit (Hendee *et al.*, 1978). In modern jargon it has become a refuge for those who wish to 'drop out' momentarily into a simpler, less com-

Figure 7.5: Strategies for National Park Management

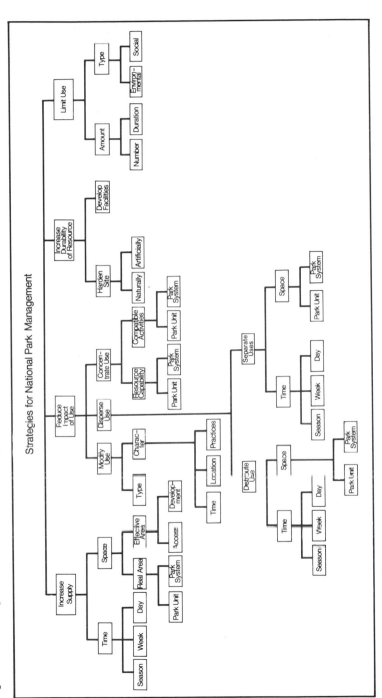

Strategies for National Park Management

Source: Manning, 1979: 14.

plicated world; a place where self-confidence can be re-established through physical challenge and reliance on self-sufficiency and subsistence skills.

Wilderness areas are also valued because of their role in nature conservation and scientific research. The size, remoteness and variety of ecosystems represented in wilderness are important for wildlife preservation, the maintenance of ecological stability and genetic diversity. Apart from being a potential source of a wide variety of useful plants and insects, wilderness also provides a reference point against which to measure changes in settled areas, in crops, forests and animal populations. Some proponents of wilderness argue that these areas also provide a buffer or safety valve against long-term disturbance of the global ecosystem resulting from large scale human interference (Australian Conservation Foundation, n.d.). Whereas this may be so it is a rather nebulous case to use as a means of persuading decision makers to close off public lands for exclusive use in scientific research. This argument has provoked a reaction in some quarters that wilderness is a selfish concept and the pursuit of a small and vocal elite. The restricted numbers and specialised forms of recreation associated with wilderness do little to destroy this impression (Sax, 1980).

A further qualification concerns the degree to which conditions in wileress areas can remain pristine. Absolutely natural conditions are impossible to find even in Antarctica. Wilderness, therefore, has to be a compromise taking in areas where there remain no permanent traces of man such as roads, buildings and modified vegetation.

The really large remaining areas of 'true' wilderness are, like the big national parks of the world, to be found in North and South America, parts of Africa and Australia, in general, areas which have not experienced heavy populaion pressure. Wilderness is not a concept generally applicable in Europe. Some limited examples of quasi-wilderness might be found in Britain, but as in Western Europe and Scandinavia, they have, with few exceptions, been extensively used by man.

Wilderness Definitions

There is no lack of definitions of wilderness. However, as its modern meaning has been in use in the United States longer than elsewhere, it is instructive to examine the definition contained in the US 1964 Wilderness Act. This Act capped a series of measures taken in the United States over some 40 years to identify and preserve the wilderness. In effect, it gave enthusiastic and permanent recognition to the concept of wilderness which had been practised by the US Forest Service since the

1920s. The Act defines wilderness as:

> An area where the earth and its community of life are untrammeled by man, where man himself is a visitor who does not remain . . . wilderness is . . . an area of underdeveloped federal land retaining its primeval character and influence, without permanent improvements or habitation, which is protected and managed so as to preserve its natural conditions and which (1) generally appears to have been affected primarily by the forces of nature, with the imprint of man's work substantially unnoticeable; (2) has outstanding opportunities for solitude or a primitive and unconfined type of recreation; (3) has at least 5000 acres of land or is of sufficient size as to make practicable its preservation and use in an unimpaired condition; and (4) may also contain ecological, geological or other features of scientific, educational, scenic, or historical value (US Congress, 1964).

In summary, wilderness as defined in the United States must be a substantially natural area over 5000 acres in size (approx. 2000 ha), that can be used for 'unconfined' recreation and perhaps with certain other features or values present. A wilderness area is not the same as a national park although some national parks may contain extensive primitive tracts of land which have wilderness characteristics. Many parts of national parks are either not primitive enough or not large enough to be regarded as wilderness. The 5000 acre minimum is really only a suggested guideline. In practice US wilderness areas are 100,000 acres (approx. 40,000 ha) or more in size.

The 1964 Act established the US National Wilderness Preservation System and provided for additional areas of wilderness to be added to the system. As of 1978, 175 areas were classified as wilderness or a total of more than 16.6 million acres (approx. 6.6 million ha). The areas are found in National Forests, National Parks, National Wildlife Refuges and on public land administered by the Bureau of Land Management. In addition, nine states in USA have wilderness policies or legislation that designates certain state properties as wilderness or primitive areas (Knudson, 1980). New York State, alone, has 16 areas totalling one million acres (approx. 405,000 ha).

Wilderness in Australia

Although wilderness movements throughout the world owe much to the American concept of wilderness, it is not possible to translate these ideas and definitions directly to other countries. Even Australia, which shares many social and historical similarities with USA has sufficient physical and ecological contrasts to raise questions regarding the application of the criteria used. Australian land surfaces are generally older and flatter than those in North America with few areas above the tree-line. There are also less physical constraints to penetration by off-road vehicles, so that in Australian wilderness areas some forms of roads and tracks may have to be accepted. Milder climatic conditions, too, mean a more even spread of user pressure over the year. At the same time, climatic extremes can create serious problems especially a fire hazard.

Recognition of wilderness values came much later in Australia than in America where the first area, Gila Wilderness, was zoned by the Forest Service in 1924. Early settlement and land use were exploitative in character with the emphasis on extraction or production of any commodity of economic value. Wilderness was not considered a discrete land use and the common practice was and is, to incorporate remnants or residual areas of wilderness into national parks. An example is the zoning of 54 per cent of Kosciusko National Park as wilderness under the 1974 Plan of Management (National Parks and Wildlife Service of New South Wales, 1974). Under the plan, wilderness was defined as large tracts of land where man's disturbance has been minimal and the landscape and vegetation are essentially in a natural condition supporting a harmonious balance of wildlife populations. A similar approach is used in New Zealand where several small wilderness zones have been declared within national parks.

Recent attempts have been made to arrive at a clear and acceptable definition of wilderness in Australia. An essential characteristic is one of size, sufficient to allow users to feel they have established contact with the wilderness, and at the same time, large enough to maintain the natural systems on which both the recreational and scientific uses of wilderness are dependent. From the recreational point of view it is suggested that the minimum width be one day's walk, or about six miles (approx. 10 km). This was the standard adopted in the first systematic survey of wilderness in Australia (Helman, *et al.* 1976). The other dimensional criteria used in that survey were a minimum core area of 25,000 hectares (approx. 62,000 acres) free of indentations and a management buffer zone surrounding the core area of about another 25,000 hectares. This was the minimum area and type of natural unit considered adequate to maintain genetic diversity and natural cycles unaltered and provide for a true wilderness type of recreation. Coastal areas were not required to meet these criteria as rigidly as inland areas because of their linear characteristics and the types of ecosystems and recreation they support.

The 1976 study and accompanying report concentrated on the eastern coast of Australia, in particular the state of New South Wales. Potential wilderness in the study area was identified from LANDSAT imagery and confirmed or eliminated through ground and aerial reconnaissance. Twenty wilderness areas were recognised; the largest, Colo-Hunter, northwest of Sydney, has a core area of 235,000 hectares (nearly 600,000 acres).

Wilderness surveys have since been conducted in the states of Tasmania and Victoria applying similar definitions to those used in the 1976 survey (Figure 7.6). Whereas that first study was carried out over largely forested country, three areas of semi-arid wilderness have been subsequently recognised in western Victoria using different dimensional criteria (Table 7.2). Other parts of Australia are yet to be surveyed systematically to delineate areas of wilderness. At the second World Wilderness Congress held in Cairns North Queensland in 1980, Cape York in its entirety was proposed for preservation as a wilderness of world importance. Despite widespread alteration to ecosystems in inland Australia from grazing and the activities of feral animals, many observers believe that large areas of the arid interior and the great deserts of Australia should also be declared wilderness, though perhaps of a special kind.

Wilderness Management

Wilderness is land which retains its natural character and is without improvements or human habitation. Simple non-mechanised forms of recreation are envisaged and to preserve wilderness values it is necessary to protect the natural ecosystems present and to maintain the topography and plant and animal populations in an undisturbed state. Thus a prime purpose of wilderness management is to keep the area as natural as possible by only allowing levels of use that are consistent with both ecological and perceptual carrying capacities. Wherever even minimal levels of recreational use are envisaged, their impact on natural systems has to be considered as well as the impact of different user groups on each other. These objectives can be solved by management techniques such as zoning, access controls and imperceptible manipulations of the environment. Human influence, both direct and indirect, has to be reduced to a minimum so that the land and the fauna and flora remain primarily the product of natural forces. In a sense, a

Figure 7.6: Wilderness Areas in South-eastern Australia

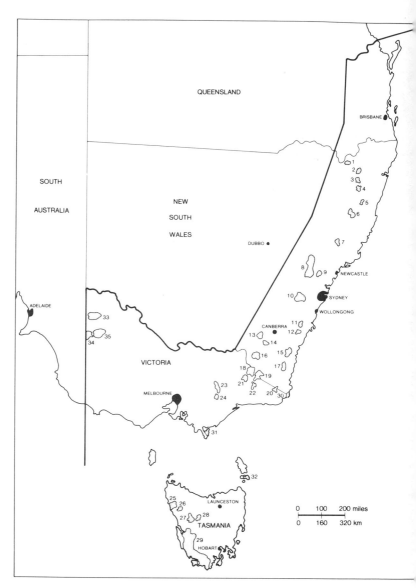

Note: Areas shown are named in Table 7.2.
Source: Smith, 1982: 102.

Table 7.2: Wilderness Areas of South-eastern Australia

	1	Binghi
	2	Washpool
	3	Mann
	4	Guy Fawkes
	5	New England
	6	Apsley
	7	Barrington
	8	Colo-Hunter
	9	Macdonald
	10	Kanangra
	11	Ettrema
	12	Budawang
	13	Fiery
Mountainous	14	Bimberi
Wilderness Areas	15	Deua
	16	Jagungal
	17	Brogo
	18	Pilot
	19	Byadbo
	20	Genoa
	21	Reedy Creek
	22	Snowy River
	23	Moroka
	24	Avon
	25	Norfolk Range
	26	Meredith Range
	27	Murchison
	28	Central Plateau
	29	South West
Coastal	30	Nadgee
Wilderness Areas	31	Vereker
	32	Cape Barren Island
Semi-arid	33	Sunset
Wilderness Areas	34	Big Desert
	35	Wyperfeld

Source: Smith, 1982: 102.

conscious decision is taken to leave the land 'unmanaged', and to exercise control only over visitors and interference from outside. The degree of intervention depends upon the size of the wilderness and the effectiveness of any buffer zone in filtering out unwanted influences.

Zoning is a common strategy employed in wilderness management.

One approach to zoning is the core/buffer concept (Figure 7.7). Here, the wilderness core is surrounded by a wilderness management zone or protective buffer. The protective function is two-way — to protect the wilderness and to protect adjacent land from disturbances such as wild-fires which might originate in the wilderness. Provision is also made for a subzone for access and minor developed facilities and separate scientific references areas within the wilderness complex are set aside with access even more restricted.

Figure 7.7: Wilderness Management Zoning

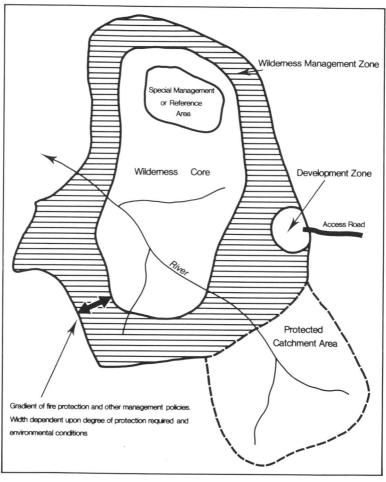

Source: Helman *et al.*, 1976: 45.

The designation of land as wilderness ia a contentious issue. A long legacy of resource exploitation brands as strange and unacceptable the sterilisation of land with potential for economic use. Even among wilderness supporters, devising management policies which will satisfy those advocating strict ecological preservation and those seeking a 'wilderness experience' is a difficult challenge to meet. Until wilderness is accepted as a legitimate form of land use and its benefits, both for outdoor recreation and nature conservation are more generally recognised, controversy will continue to surround the wilderness concept.

8 TOURISM DEVELOPMENT AND IMPACT

Tourism is an important human activity of environmental, socio-cultural and economic significance. As western societies in particular find themselves with greater leisure, relative affluence and mobility, the scale of tourism is increasing so that for many parts of the world it has become a significant generator of income and a valuable source of employment. As an agent of change tourism also has major implications for the physical and social environment.

Discussion of tourism in the context of outdoor recreation would seem to make good sense because so much tourism is 'recreational' in that tourist activities are engaged in during leisure time, commonly outdoors, for the purpose of pleasure and personal satisfaction. At the same time outdoor recreation overlaps with tourism in the distinctive characteristics and behaviour associated with each. Both involve travel, often overnight and both require extensive interaction of visitors with the resource base. Some observers assign an emphasis on economic aspects and profit-making to tourism while linking outdoor recreation primarily with non-commercial objectives (Gunn, 1979). Others make a functional distinction between tourism and recreational travel (Britton, 1979).

Such distinctions appear founded on the assumption that outdoor recreation appeals to the rugged, self-reliant element in the population, whereas tourism caters more overtly for those seeking diversion without too much discomfort. Sufficient exceptions to these generalisations can be identified to call into question any artificial gulf between tourism and outdoor recreation. Apart from emphasis on an alien environment somewhat removed form the place of residence, tourism is carried on within an essentially recreational framework. Differences then become a matter of degree and motivation with tourism calling for a more sophisticated infrastructure and tending towards the opposite end of a time-space-cost continuum to recreational travel.

This is the approach adopted in the ensuing discussion. Tourism is considered as a specialised manifestation of outdoor recreation, sharing many attributes and features of the latter, with perhaps greater potential for lasting repercussions on the landscape and the environment and thus ample scope for resource management and planning.

Tourists and Tourism

Definitions of a tourist are many and varied, but most incorporate the notions of distance travelled and duration and purpose of travel. Certainly, the term implies more than the French derivation, *tour* meaning a circular movement and *tourner,* to go around. As noted below strict tourism, or movement from place to place in sequential fashion eventually returning to the starting point, is giving way to destination tourism as a reaction to constraints on travel.

In the broadest sense, anyone who visits an area other than the place of residence is a tourist. However diversion, or the pleasure motive, is frequently seen as an essential element and allowance is usually made for the time and distance involved in travel and the duration of the visit. The picture is further confused when distinctions are made between domestic and international tourism. Thus, many countries now use the definition recommended by a United Nations conference in 1963 and since adopted by the World Tourism Organisation. For analytical and statistical purposes, a 'visitor' is described under that definition as.

. . . any person visiting a country other than that in which he has his usual place of residence, for any reason other than following an occupation remunerated from within the country visited (World Tourism Organisation, 1978: 11).

The definition covers two types of visitors, 'tourists' and 'excursionists', as follows:

Tourists: temporary visitors staying at least 24 hours (or one night) in the country visited and the purpose of whose journey can be classified under one of the following headings:
(a) leisure (recreation, holiday, health, study, religion and sport); and
(b) business, family, mission, meeting.
Excursionists: temporary visitors staying less than 24 hours (or one night) in the country visited (including travellers on cruises) (World Tourism Organisation, 1978: 11).

This definition originated in Europe some twenty years ago, so the idea that to be a tourist visitors must travel to another country is understandable. In many parts of Europe it is difficult to avoid crossing international boundaries on a trip involving some distance from home. However, what of the traveller in countries of the New World like Australia and the United States where it is possible to travel further than the distance from London to Moscow without leaving the country? Surely, the New Yorker visiting Los Angeles or the Sydney-sider visiting Perth is also a tourist in the real sense of the word.

The WTO definition does have the virtue of international recognition as the basis for statistical reporting of foreign visitors entering a country, despite the inclusion of non-discretionary travel under the tourist umbrella. Certainly, from the broad perspective of interaction with the tourism environment, distinguishing between 'pure' tourism for pleasure and other forms of short-term travel is academic. From the point of view of claims on transport, accommodation and food services, it matters little whether the visitor is on business or on a honeymoon. Moreover, as will be seen subsequently travel motivation is complex. A tourist may conduct business while on vacation, or attending a convention and the business traveller may well combine pleasure with the primary purpose of the trip. This all-inclusive approach was the one adopted in a study of the economic significance of tourism to Australia, where it was argued that the economic impact of the tourist dollar is essentially the same as that spent by the business traveller (Pigram and Cooper, 1977).

However, purpose of visit cannot be ignored. Pleasure travel is discretionary and could be expected to be more responsive to promotion and positive public initiatives than that of business personnel. Disaggregation of travel statistics on the basis of motivation is also useful for marketing strategies and to guide decisions on private investment and government assistance. Furthermore, in common usage the word 'tourist' has connotations of pleasure travel, usually of some distance and duration and excludes visits specifically for business, military, educational, therapeutic, or family purposes. In this sense, tourists and tourism become identified with discretionary travel by individuals and groups and with all the related aspects, associated activities and sustaining services (Kaiser and Helber, 1978).

The Scope of World Tourism

Over the past 30 years tourism has become one of the largest single items in world trade. Statistics tell the story. From 1950 to 1972 annual international tourist arrivals in all countries grew from 25 million to almost 200 million, an average growth rate of about 10 per cent per year. In the same period total foreign exchange earnings from tourism rose from US$ 2.1 billion to US$ 24 billion, an average annual increase of about 11 per cent. By 1976 the number of arrivals was estimated at close on 220 million, an increase of more than 90 per cent in a decade and these travellers spent in all about US$ 40 billion. Arrivals had grown to 264 million by 1978 and expenditures to around US$ 63 billion (World Tourism Organisation, 1979).

The major flows of international travel are regional and the effects are not evently spread throughout the world. The main tourist movements are between the developed countries, particularly those of Western Europe and across the North Atlantic. The United States and West Germany are by far the most important countries in terms of generating tourist movements, these two accounting for nearly 40 per cent of arrivals worldwide. A further 40 per cent is generated by another ten countries – United Kingdom, France, Canada, Belgium, Netherlands, Italy, Switzerland, Sweden, Denmark and Austria.

Tourist destinations are more widely distributed than countries of origin. Whereas Europe and North America together received almost 85 per cent of tourists in 1976, the individual countries which generate tourist flows are not always the ones which receive them. Two of the most popular countries of destination are Canada and Spain while West Germany accounts for less than 10 per cent of tourists visiting Europe (Matley, 1976). In general the flow of tourists is from the more developed, industrialised and urbanised nations, to the warmer, less densely-populated and developed countries closer to the equator. In a few states such as the Bahamas, some Caribbean islands and Spain, annual arrivals exceed the local population.

Some parts of the world receive significant financial benefits from tourism, the earnings from which make up one of the fastest growing credit items in the balance of payments for certain countries. Tourism is a major export earner in East Africa, the Mediterranean, Mexico and Ireland. In 1975, international tourist receipts as a percentage of exports were 19.6 per cent in Kenya, 28.1 per cent in Morocco, 32.7 per cent in Tunisia, 27.2 per cent in Greece, 45.3 per cent in Malta, and 44.3 per cent in Spain (World Tourism Organisation, 1978). In both Spain and Italy international tourism is a major factor offsetting trade deficits. In Mexico the four million foreign visitors in 1978 contributed US$ 2.8 billion or 50 per cent of the annual balance-of-payments income (Chubb and Chubb, 1981). In Eire, a country with an obvious comparative and competitive advantage for tourism, expenditure by foreign visitors is said to make up the largest single 'export' of the country, providing up to 15 per cent of national employment and injecting purchasing power into the economy equivalent to an additional resident population of 350,000 people (Burkart and Medlik, 1974).

Tourism is dynamic in nature and highly sensitive to changing world circumstances, e.g. energy crises, escalating travel costs and international terrorism. It seems that the rapid expansion which took place recently in world tourism may now be levelling out as the costs and uncertainties associated with international travel begin to take effect. Of necessity, this should stimulate entrepreneurs and tourist development authorities to seek out new destinations, especially in Third World countries, to attract visitors and explore fresh source areas from which tourist flows can be generated. More attention may also need to be directed towards the potential of domestic tourism to fill the empty beds. In a comment on the size of the British holiday market, Robinson (1976) reports that in 1973, some 40 million Britons took a holiday within the confines of the United Kingdom generating expenditures of over £1000 million. The United States also has a highly developed domestic tourist industry. The family vacation market there accounted for almost 49.5 million trips in 1977 with expenditures of US$ 31.3 billion (Travel and Tourism Research Association, 1981).

With foreign travel, distance and costs will always be constraints but some countries of the Pacific basin, particularly China, are emerging as potential areas for tourist development. Close by, Japan and to a lesser degree the Soviet Union, represent major new markets for international tourism. In 1962 a mere 75,000 Japanese travelled abroad. By 1972 more than 1.4 million Japanese tourists took overseas trips. This figure had reached 2.5 million by 1975 and 4.1 million by 1979 (Japan National Tourist Organisation, 1980). Already, many countries, from Australia to South America, are feeling the impact of a new and peaceful Japanese invasion.

The Resource Base for Tourism

The complex pattern of tourism across the globe reflects the diversity of environments which constitute tourist resources and the varied exeriences which travellers seek. A common element is contrast between the home region and the destination. Were there no perceived differences from place to place (natural or fabricated), tourism would not exist. Contrasts may be sought and discovered in the physical environment, the cultural and historical landscape, the people, or even artificially created attractions and world events (Matley, 1976).

Of all the factors affecting the development of tourism, the most important are physical. As noted above, some of the strongest flows of tourists are from cool, cloudy regions to places highly regarded for their warm sunny climate. For many tourists 'wanderlust' appears to take second place to 'sun-lust'. By contrast, the popularity of winter tourist resorts rests in great part on cool (though hopefully sunny) weather and the assurance of adequate and long-lasting snow cover (Pigram and Hobbs, 1975).

Another physical factor with obvious implications for tourism development is the appeal of the coast. Mercer (1972) explains the coastal location of many resorts in terms of the attraction of edges or junctions in the landscape, the coastline representing the interface between land and sea. The success of coastal resorts reflects the attraction of the beautiful setting but even away from the coast the physical terrain holds great appeal for tourists.

Matley points out that one component of the physical environment which has more limited significance for tourism is the presence of mineral springs or spas. In historical times conviction in the medicinal properties of mineral waters for drinking or bathing stimulated the earliest visitors to places like Bath and Tunbridge Wells in Britain, and Spa itself, in Belgium. Despite advances in modern medicine, 'taking the waters' at spas and similar health resorts continued to attract a considerable clientele. Increasingly however, with the development of additional facilities close by for amusement and diversion, the function of the spas became more social than therapeutic. One health resort in the United States, French Lick in southern Indiana, even became the focus for thriving illegal gambling and liquor activities in the 'prohibition' era. However, tourism for health purposes remains important for many people and clinics and sanatoria continue to attract significant numbers of gullible and wealthy patrons.

A related phenomenon with implications for tourism is the drawing power of religious shrines like Lourdes in France and Knock in Ireland, based in part, on belief in the miraculous powers of water from local springs which had their origin in visions last century. An international airport constructed at great cost is nearing completion close to Knock and is expected to bring even more visitors to that shrine. Spiritual reasons have always been a powerful stimulus to travel and large numbers of pilgrims continue to visit Mecca and other Moslem holy places annually. Religious centres such as the Vatican, Jerusalem, and

Benares also attract pilgrims in large numbers.

Many tourists are genuinely curious about foreign places and people so that aside from the physical environment, the opportunity to make contact with other people's culture and way of life is a strong influence on tourism. Matley (1976) notes the appeal of what he calls 'ethnic' tourism and the interest shown in folk-lore, strange customs and traditional architecture, crafts and foods. Not all of these are authentic and the potential of tourism for distortion of the cultural tradition of host communities is raised later in this chapter.

Interest in past cultures is also the basis for historical tourism where the primary focus is on inspecting the legacy of a bygone age. Features of historic interest have a proven fascination for tourists whether these be the magnificent homes and castles of Britain and Europe, artifacts and ruins of the ancient world, sites of military battles, picturesque villages mirroring a past lifestyle, restored railways and steamships, or the collections of miscellaneous junk which pass for museums in some small isolated settlements in outback Australia. Countries like Australia with a relatively short history, often find it more practical and rewarding from a tourism point of view, to re-create features and settlements of the past and present these in something of an outdoor museum setting. Thus, Old Sydney Town portrays life in the first European settlement in Australia and Sovereign Hill one of the early goldmining towns in the State of Victoria. Historical theme parks also flourish in the United States where attractions like Knott's Berry Farm and Disneyland in Los Angeles rely to a great extent on revivals of the past.

Clearly, tourism and nostalgia have a mutually beneficial relationship; interest in history stimulates tourism, which in turn makes historical preservation possible. 'Preservation pays', and that slogan was the theme of a recent conference organised by the Pacific Area Travel Association in San Francisco (Smith and Sherman, 1981). The choice of venue was appropriate; much of the charm of San Francisco rests on features preserved from the city's past, e.g. the Cable Cars and Ghiradelli Square. These success stories are matched by impressive efforts at preservation in the South, such as Savannah, Georgia and the old French Quarter of New Orleans. Handled correctly, preservation can certainly pay in terms of tourism. As Newcomb (1979: 232) rather poetically puts it: 'Our visible past is like a fire which . . . if we tend it carefully . . . will illuminate our pleasure and . . . touch our imagination and our hearts.'

Some of the most spectacular examples of restoration are to be found in the historic districts of urban centres. However, cities such as Paris, London and New York are major tourist destinations in their own right, notwithstanding Christaller's (1963) assertion that tourism avoids central places. In this context, tourism can be regarded as an urban resource in that it contributes to city revenues, creates employment, plays an important part in urban renewal and helps support threatened amenities (Wall and Sinnott, 1980).

This brief canvass of the resource base for tourism illustrates the diversity of settings which appeal to the pleasure traveller. Such diversity is important because it provides the very necessary element of choice to the system and acts as a continuing stimulus to fresh discovery of new tourist destinations and experiences. It also brings out the many opportunities for creation and enhancement of resource settings for tourism.

The Tourist System

Tourism, by definition, involves not only tourists but the tourist destination (including residents and the host environment) and the linkages between the two. Some writers suggest that a systems framework is the most suitable means of drawing these facets together for study.

Leiper (1979; 1981) proposes an open system of five interacting elements encompassing a dynamic human element, the *tourists*; three geographical elements, the *generating region*, the *transit route*, and *destination region*; and an economic element, the *tourist industry* (Figure 8.1). Leiper's model recognises that the central element of the system is people – the tourists themselves. They comprise the energising source and their attributes and behaviour help define the role of other elements in the system. The generating region is the origin of potential tourism demand linked by transit routes to the destination region or focus of tourist activity. Subsumed within these three geographical elements are the industrial component and service infrastructure of tourism, comprising all the firms, organisations and facilities intended to serve the specific needs and wants of tourists, before departure, en-route and at the destination(s).

Leiper's model can be criticised in that it might be argued that the destination region and its distinguishing characteristics should receive more prominence and the generating region less. Obviously, the latter is the scene for a good deal of advertising and promotional activity

Figure 8.1: The Tourist System

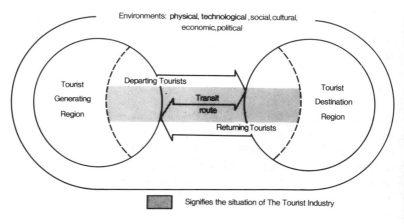

Source: Leiper, 1981: 75.

designed to stimulate tourism. Market research has also been directed towards discovering what it is about the environment at the origin which helps generate an exodus of tourists. Unfortunately however, tourists 'at home' are often indistinguishable from the rest of the population and even if they were, their presence and often hum-drum every-day existence, holds no special significance for the generating region. The destination on the other hand receives and reflects the full impact of the influx of visitors. This is where most tourism studies have been directed and rightly so. Leiper (1979) concedes that it is the destination region where the most significant and dramatic aspects of tourism occur. Its attractions and facilities are essential to the tourism process and it is the location of many of the important functional sectors of the tourist industry. To a significant degree the environment and landscape of the destination region could be said to be an index of all the positive and negative features of modern tourism.

One of the best-known attempts to portray tourism in systems terms was put forward by Gunn (1972) who also recognised five structural components of the tourism environment – *people* and *attractions*, linked and supported by *transportation, information* and *services-facilities* in a dynamic, functional system (Figure 8.2). Whereas none of these components can exist in isolation it is useful to consider the distinctive attributes of each which contribute to the viability of the overall system.

Figure 8.2: Components of the Tourism Environment

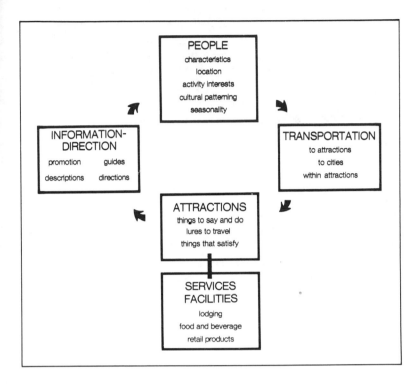

Source: Gunn, 1979: 36.

Attractions

Gunn describes these as the 'real energiser' and 'first power' of the tourist system. Features of the environment such as Niagara Falls, the Isle of Capri, the Tower of London, or Sydney Opera House, all have something in common — the capacity to attract and excite millions of visitors. Without such attractions, tourism as we know it, would not exist. It is important to recognise, too, that magnetism is not somehow an inherent quality, or that only natural features qualify as tourist attractions. The many man-made entertainment complexes often created from an unremarkable resource base (e.g. Disneyland) disprove any such supposition. In this context Gunn points out that every tourist attraction is, to some extent, created by man. Even apparently natural features such as the Swiss Alps, or historic sites such as

Hadrian's Wall, require some embellishment, if only signposting, to cater for visitor use. Despite these qualifications tourist attractions remain environmentally based, in the sense that they are tied indirectly or by association with a specific setting or location. For many attractions identification with place is so fundamental that if removed to a different site the new setting may appear incongruous. Of course, this does not always detract from the tourism function. The successful transplanting of London Bridge to Lake Havasu, Arizona, says something for human ingenuity as a tourist entrepreneur.

Services – Facilities

Tourist attractions are an amalgam of resources, services and facilities – a composite product designed to draw tourists to a destination, support them while they are there and presumably, persuade them to return. Apart from the tourists themselves, the service-facilities component is the most obvious physical manifestation of tourism; the motels, bars, restaurants and craft shops which make up the landscape of tourism and give it recognisable character. Services and facilities are essentially created amenities complementary to the natural or cultural features of the resource base. Their role is to bring tourists into beneficial contact with the attractions at the destination.

In rare cases services and facilities can develop such distinct appeal, or be deliberately designed to become attractions in their own right. More commonly, it is the environmental setting which gives them meaning and purpose. Yet, the relationship is very much two-way. An attraction of average or even mediocre quality may be enhanced by imaginative harmonious amenities. Conversely, the inherent magnetism of an outstanding natural feature can be impaired by inappropriate or poorly designed services and facilities. Only the most insensitive visitor could remain indifferent to the garish vulgarity of the approach to Niagara Falls, one of the wonders of the world. It is almost as if man has set out to mask the natural splendour of this feature with a veneer of all that is ugly in landscape design and commercial display.

This theme is taken up again in the discussion of tourism and the environment. Clearly, the development of tourist attractions calls for close attention to the setting, range and quality of supporting amenities and to the integration of these structures into attractive surroundings, compatible with the nature of the site. The reciprocal arrangement of attractions, services and facilities can make a significant contribution to, or detract from, the image and appeal of a tourist destination.

Transportation

To many observers tourism and pleasure travel are synonymous and therefore transportation becomes a basic component of the tourist system. Even the declining emphasis on *tourism* as such and the rising costs of travel do not lessen the importance of the journey as the essential linkage between tourists and their destinations. The constant efforts to reduce the duration and contain the cost of the travel component have led to all manner of innovations in mass transportation, not all of them adding to the well-being of those involved. In many instances travel has become a necessary evil of modern-day tourism and the standards of comfort aboard a jumbo jet aircraft have been compared with those of a cattle pen!

See the people strapped in their seats and fed like fowls. Watch them queue for the lavatories in flight and indulge in the futile attempt to sleep sitting upright. See them emerge tired and disoriented, clutching a bag of duty-free goodies, suitcase and passport and queuing for a customs check and baggage trolley . . . (Fitzgerald, *Sydney Morning Herald*, 26 November, 1979: 7).

Gunn (1979b) points out that tourists, as travellers, make a number of functional demands on a transportation system. A basic consideration is efficiency of movement to and from destinations and within the tourist zone. This implies convenience, dependability, safety, reasonable cost and in most cases, a speedy trip. Where possible these aspects should be complemented by a degree of comfort and pleasure.

Even in short-range systems of transportation where the characteristics of the trip may be of less consequence, Gunn (1972) sees great opportunities for creating more effective circulation corridors. For the genuine tourist, the transport system becomes more than a means of getting to a destination; the journey is an integral part of the tourist experience. Pleasure travellers thus relate to the environment through which they are passing and the routeway becomes a tourist resource in itself. Transportation planning for tourism has to be sensitive to the wishes of travellers and to the purposes for which a trip is being made. The different nature of tourist traffic also needs to be recognised in order for it to be separated from other traffic flows. Identification and mapping of tourist drives and a network of purpose-designed and built scenic routeways can provide pleasure travellers with high quality transit corridors to enhance their visit.

Information

A vital component of the tourist system is the 'image' of the tourist destination and its attractions as perceived by the visitor. It is the critical factor in choice and decision making so that considerable effort needs to be directed into providing a sound information base on which rational decisions can be made.

The image of the tourist destination is derived partly from experience and inherent beliefs or personality 'hang-ups' regarding what the trip or vacation will entail and partly from a variety of external sources and influences. It is important to distinguish between this latter 'induced image' and the former 'organic image', to separate that which is within the power of the developing agency to influence from that which is not (Gunn, 1972). This is where advertising, publicity and personal advice come in. Recommendations from others are certainly an effective form of promotion but advice from travel agents, tour operators and the media play a valuable role in stimulating tourist interest.

Creation of an attractive tourist image really amounts to giving the destination or feature a personality, an atmosphere and an easily remembered identity. The message needs to be original, simple yet exciting, up-to-date, accurate and honest. It could be counter-productive to stimulate expectations too much if disappointment and disillusionment ensue when attractions subsequently do not measure up. At the same time it is unrealistic to expect budding tourists to discover the delights of a place themselves. An information gap contributes to a credibility gap and makes it just that much more difficult to instil an induced image into the perception of potential visitors strong enough to offset the organic image which may be inhibiting their choice.

Initial contact between guest and host is critical because, ideally, reinforcement of the favourable prior image created should come during the tourist experience itself if a repeat visit is to occur and the attraction is to be recommended to others. From this point, too, lines of communication between management and the consumers need to be kept open if visitors are to get the maximum satisfaction out of the trip. Tourists at large are dependent upon maps, literature, signposting and similar information sources to direct them to what attractions are available. The quality and effectiveness of these sources determines whether the response will be positive or negative. All too often, poorly designed, dated, or indecipherable advertisements reflect apathy (or perhaps arrogance) on the part of tourist operators and management and have a predictably dampening effect on patronage.

Yet, it should be obvious that in the harsh commercial world of pleasure travel, the tourist experience is bought and sold in a competitive environment marked by close substitutes. It has been suggested that the market for various types of outdoor recreation moves through a curve or cycle from infancy to senility (Lapage, 1974). The success of an enterprise therefore, may well depend upon developing a marketing package and advertising programme appropriate to a particular stage of growth. With tourism, it should be possible to fit selected attractions and destinations to the relevant position in the cycle and adopt a marketing strategy to suit. In economic jargon, the key to success lies in product differentiation and promoting *specific* tourist experiences for *specific* market segments − from singles to pensioners and gourmets to garden-lovers.

People

The test of whether the information component is well-directed rests with the impact on people, the tourists themselves. They are the only ones who can close the circle and complete the system. A successful tourist destination is one that can attract visitors, provide for them, guide their movements and activities and send them home satisfied with the likelihood of a return visit and a recommendation to others. For this to be achieved understanding of the human dimension is essential. Insight is required into tourists and potential tourists, their decision-making processes, their expectations and their satisfaction levels.

It is no longer sufficient for management to rely on experience or intuition. Hard data are needed on which to base decisions concerning investment, development of attractions, provision of services, advertising and the like. Informed judgement is fine to a point but if carried too far, can distort proper assessment and constructive reaction. Gunn (1979) rightly points out the need for planners to divorce themselves from personal and often biased concepts of tourists. This sort of objective stance can only be achieved through systematic market research, both quantitative and qualitative. The aim should be to discover what tourists think, not what management *thinks* they think

That said, it is not always easy for tourist operators to interpret consumer preferences accurately: '. . . human behaviour is complicated. People vary in their characteristics − their habits, interests, thresholds of satisfaction, the way they spend money and priorities' (Gunn, 1979: 150).

In particular, the motivation for pleasure travel is elusive and its dynamic, multi-facted nature does not lend itself to generalisation.

Earlier in this chapter the various factors which contribute to the appeal of places as tourist destinations were discussed. However, the phenomenon of tourism cannot be satisfactorily explained on the basis of physical or cultural attractions alone. A conscious decision must be made to seek a tourist experience and the reasons for this decision and all its ancillary aspects can be as diverse as the tourist population itself (Crompton, 1979; Dichter, 1979).

The question, 'what makes tourists travel?' is no more or less difficult to answer than any other aspect of recreational behaviour, or indeed consumer behaviour generally. Gunn (1979) suggests that predisposition, or propensity to travel, has much to do with it, and a lot of effort by market researchers is put into identifying 'target' groups at which specific promotional material can be aimed. It is not sufficient to discover why people engage in tourism but also the reasons which inhibit travel, the most important of which are: expense, time constraints, physical limitations, family circumstances, lack of inclination, and psychological deterrents (Robinson, 1976). Undoubtedly, the notion of change and contrast is attached to much tourism behaviour and a person's mental state can mould positive or negative attitudes to travel. Dann (1977; 1981) believes that two twin 'push' factors predispose people to become tourists — what he calls 'anomie', or the need to break out of dull, meaningless surroundings and situations, and 'ego-enhancement', or the desire to be recognised, feel superior, or create envy as the result of undertaking a particular trip or vacation. Underlying both is a strong fantasy component so that tourism becomes a form of escape. It is not so much the tourist experience that matters but the act of getting away which counts. Research orientated towards human behaviour is important in tourism because it offers the prospect of some insight into the real workings of the consumer's collective minds. Understanding of the people component in Gunn's model is a fundamental input to proper planning and management of tourist development.

In summary, the tourist system can be seen as a joint product of resources and people with those essential elements brought together by way of the linking mechanisms of services and facilities, transportation and information. Appreciation of the place of each in the system and their interdependence is necessary if fragmentation is to be avoided and satisfying tourism environments created and maintained.

The Landscape of Tourism

Reference was made earlier to the landscape of tourism not so much in the sense of attractive scenery, but as the association of distinctive physical and cultural features characteristic of tourist development. Used in this way the term is analogous to agricultural landscapes or residential landscapes. The landscape of tourism reflects the imprint, both good and bad, of mass travel on the environment and the relationship is inescapable. The landscape makes tourism and in turn, tourism makes the landscape.

Given the diverse nature of resources and experiences which appeal to travellers, the range of recipient landscapes created for and emanating from tourism is wide. The natural beauty to be found in the west of Ireland, the glittering facade of Las Vegas, or the simulated atmosphere of the South Seas re-created in Hawaii, all represent particular landscape types orientated to tourism. Whereas it is easy to deplore the 'look-alike' landscapes spawned by mass tourism across the globe (Ekbo, 1967), it is another matter to attempt to interpret and explain their evolution from a generic point of view (Price, 1980; 1981). Some interesting work has been carried out on the townscapes of tourist resorts.

Lavery (1974) outlined the historical background to the development of holiday resorts in Western Europe, in particular, alpine resorts, spas and seaside resorts. He proposed a typological classification of resorts based on their function and the extent of their visitor hinterland. A hierarchy of eight categories was identified encompassing: capital cities; select resorts; popular resorts, minor resorts; cultural/historic centres; winter resorts; spas/watering places and day-trip resorts. Lavery concedes that the classification is subjective and obvious omissions are specifically seaside resorts, religious/spiritual centres and 'created' resorts such as Disneyland in Florida. Some resorts would also fit several categories while others have progressed from one particular orientation to another.

Undoubtedly tourist resorts, like resources in general, pass through cycles linked to fashion and tourist behaviour. The popular appeal of established destinations fluctuates as changed circumstances trigger a new set of interests and a different clientele. Innovative forms of tourism may emerge and lead to the eclipse of redundant tourist outlets and the discovery of fresh attractions and venues. Explanation of such cycles has been linked to the behavioural characteristics of travellers. Two major human polarities have been identified (Plog, 1972).

Allocentric persons —self-confident, successful, high earners and frequent travellers who prefer uncrowded destinations and exploring strange cultures.

Psychocentric persons — unsure of themselves, low earners and infrequent travellers who seek the security of tours and familiar destinations.

The great majority of people are mid-centric, falling between these two extremes and favouring budget tours, heavily used destinations, familiar food and chain-type accommodation. According to this hypothesis resorts tend to rise and fall in cycles which match their appeal to particular categories of tourists (Figure 8.3).

> They move through a continuum . . . appealing first to allocentrics and last to psychocentrics . . . As the destination becomes more popular, the mid-centric audience begins to pick it up . . . (which) leads to further development of the resort, in terms of hotels, tourist shops, scheduled activities for tourists and the usual services that are provided in a 'nature' resort area . . . continued development . . . carries with it the threat of the destruction of the area as a viable tourist resort . . . Destination areas carry with them potential seeds of their own destruction, as they allow themselves to become more commercialized and lose their qualities which originally attracted tourists (Plog, 1972: 4).

In some ways this psychographic continuum of resort development resembles the Lapage 'stages of growth' described earlier in this chapter. As with the Lapage model it is important to note that decline of a resort is not inevitable and with planning and sound management, it is possible for success to be predicted, achieved and sustained. The possibility of rejuvenation is also stressed by Butler (1980), who cites the example of the introduction of gambling casinos into Atlantic City, New Jersey as an attempt to tap a new resort market.

From the point of view of landscape it could be expected that each category of resort would develop its own recognisable blend of structures, activities and functions making up a tourist environment responsive to the requirements of the predominant type of visitors. Distinctiveness of tourist centres as special-purpose settlements is perhaps best seen in the morphology and townscape of seaside resorts especially those of Britain and Western Europe. Elements of the typical coastal resort have since diffused to parts of USA and Australia.

Figure 8.3: The Cycle of Tourist Resort Development

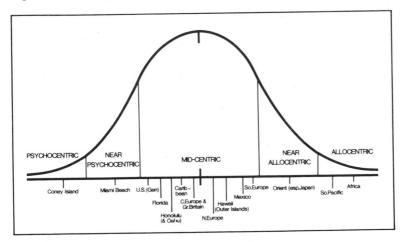

Source: Kaiser and Helber, 1978: 8 (after Plog, 1972).

In a study of English and Welsh seaside resorts Barrett (1958) identified several common morphological features or characteristics. In
particular, he noted the significance of the seafront in the structure
and location of the commercial core and a marked zonation of vacation accommodation and residential areas. Moreover, because growth
along one axis was precluded or restricted, elongation of settlement
occurred parallel to the coast. In Barrett's study the core shopping
and business district was offset symmetrically to a frontal retail and
accommodation strip which was the focus of resort activities and func-
tinally and socioeconomically distinct from the rest of the town (Figure
8.4). All these features were subject to modification because of terrain
and pre-resort transport and land use patterns.

Studies of New Jersey seashore resort towns also identified linearity
in the various functional zones in response to location of principal
routeways and proximity to the beach and recognised a specialised
frontal trading zone termed the Recreational Business District
(Stanfield, 1969; Stanfield and Rickert, 1970). This zone was spatially
and functionally distinct from the Central Business District and comprised an aggregation of seasonal retail establishments catering exclu-
sively for leisure time shopping. Stanfield nominated the boardwalk as
a uniquely American phenomenon and grouped it with the British pier
and promenade as a major contribution to the morphology of resort
settlements.

Figure 8.4: Schematic Model of an English Seaside Resort

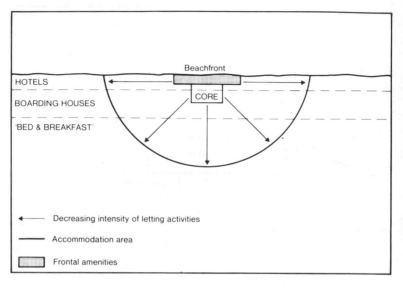

Source: Barrett, 1958: 36.

Lavery (1974) put forward a schematic representation of a 'typical' seaside resort with prime frontal locations occupied by the larger accommodation facilities with a gradation in land values and tourist-orientated functions away from the seafront, the main focus of visitor attraction. Lavery also noted the spatial and functional separation of the CBD from the RBD, and associated the latter with the main route from the public transport terminal, e.g. railway station, in contrast to the emphasis given by Stanfield to vehicular access.

In Australia an attempt was made to establish the extent to which the 'model' features found in British and North American seaside settlements were present in beach resorts on the Australian coast (Pigram, 1977). The study was carried out at the Gold Coast on the Queensland/New South Wales border which in the past twenty years, has become the focus of intensive tourist development catering for over two million visitors annually (Figure 8.5). Several interesting parallels can be drawn between the urban structure of Gold Coast settlements and that outlined above. The attraction of the coast and beaches, the role of routeways and termini, the importance of topographical features and the influence of pre-resort form and function are readily discernable.

An interesting aspect in the Australian study area was the develop-

Figure 8.5: The Gold Coast Tourist Complex, East Coast of Australia

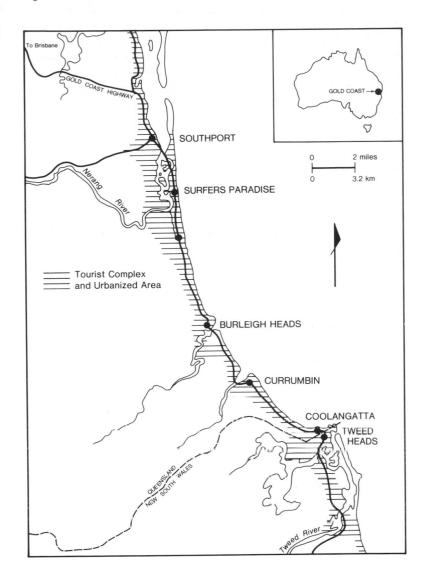

ment of paired resort nodes at either end of the Gold Coast tourist complex. At the northern extremity, Surfers Paradise dominates the amusement and entertainment scene (RBD) whereas Southport is the regional and commercial centre (CBD). In the south, Coolangatta specialises in recreational business while the Central Business District is across the border in Tweed Heads. The end result is paired beach resorts which reflect, in part, the antecedents of British settlement in Australia, yet show clearly the effects of modern forces shaping the tourism landscape.

It is interesting to speculate on the morphological implications for resort development as automobile travel becomes more expensive and difficult, more sophisticated transport systems evolve, individually-structured recreation pursuits give way to mass tourism and inflation puts many present forms of accommodation out of reach. In 1982 a resort 'boom' was reported in Australia with over A$ 3 billion worth of tourist resort projects planned (*National Times*, 13 June, 1982). It may be that the character, form and function of these new resorts will have to adjust to a more limited range of carefully programmed travel opportunities for the tourist of the 21st century.

Tourism and the Environment

The many ramifications of tourism give much scope for interaction with the environment. Some observers, while conceding beneficial spin-offs in the economic, political and cultural spheres, remain convinced that, 'in the long run, tourism, like any other industry, contributes to environmental destruction' (Cohen, 1978: 220). Others, like the author, believe that given proper planning and management, tourism can enhance the environment and be a positive influence in the process of cultural dynamics (Pigram, 1980). To confuse the picture further there is considerable disagreement as to whether the incidence and magnitude of the effects of tourism can be accurately measured. Moreover, the relationship is often expressed in terms of opposing alternatives — either protecting the environment *for* tourism, or protecting the environment *from* tourism. However, these objectives need not be mutually exclusive. There appear to be several modes of expression of the impact of tourism and the net effect may well be environmental enhancement.

Tourist development can contribute to substantial upgrading of the recreational resource base and thus add to visitor enjoyment. According to Gunn (1973) tourism can lead, for example, to an improved transportation system through advances in vehicle and routeway design which allow greater opportunity for pleasurable and meaningful participation in travel. Enhanced understanding of the resource base is another positive outcome of pleasure travel brought about by the application of innovations in communication media techniques to interpret and articulate the environment to visitors. Beneficial modifications or adaptations to climate in the form of recreational structures, clothing and equipment have also been developed in response to the stimulus from tourism. Better managed habitats for fish and wildlife, and control of pests and undesirable species have become possible through the economic support and motivation of increased usage. Further positive response can be seen in the broadening of opportunities to view and experience both the physical and cultural world. Ready examples are the opening up of forests for recreational use and increasing agitation for better access to water-based recreational resources along streams, lakes and the coastline.

On another plane, increasing cultural consciousness has stimulated restoration of historic sites and antiquities. Referring particularly to Europe, Haulot (1978) asks how this heritage — the landmarks, castles and artifacts of past eras — could be kept intact if its existence and preservation had not become the ongoing concern of a great audience of tourists resulting both in substantial financial contributions from the visitors themselves and generous state support?

Design of contemporary tourist complexes, too, appears to be benefitting from the demands of a more discerning tourist population. Whereas there remain many examples of unfortunate additions to the tourist landscape, modification of the built environment for today's tourist is marked increasingly by quality architecture, design and engineering. Higher standards of safety, sanitation and maintenance also help to reduce the potential for pollution. These advances demonstrate that tourism need not destroy natural and cultural values and in fact can contribute to an aesthetically pleasing landscape (Wimberley, 1977).

The type of enlightened development possible is exemplified in the many sophisticated tourist complexes now to be found in various countries of the world (Baud-Bovy and Lawson, 1977; International Council of Societies of Industrial Design, 1977). The ambitious Farnborough resort complex being constructed by Japanese interests near Yeppoon on the Queensland coast of Australia is a further example of the commitment of a new generation of developers to environmentally compatible forms of tourism (Figure 8.6). The project envisages:

> . . . the creation of a great park offering an international cross-
> cultural experience through a series of international villages, the
> theme of which would be reinforced by representative traditional
> architecture and landscapes (UDPA Planners, 1978: 6).

The plan calls for the preservation of existing wetlands and other
physical features and the blending of the man-made environment into
the natural scenic background. Stability of the frontal dune system is to
be maintained and development limited to necessary rehabilitation and
landscaping with boardwalk trails for beach access. A key concept
incorporated into the project is that of a 'Management and Drainage
Divide' for the containment and safe dispersal of effluent and wastes
(Figure 8.7). A system of nature reserves for flora, fauna, birdlife and
fisheries is also proposed and the plan calls for the elimination of motor
vehicle traffic within the site in favour of pedestrian pathways, shuttle
buses and water craft. Such measures can only be interpreted as positive
evidence of an attempt to ensure the creation of an exciting resort
setting in keeping with ecological constraints and with minimal environmental disturbance.

The environment, of course, also includes human resources and
tourism can affect customs, crafts, attitudes, traditional values and the
way of life generally. The Yeppoon project has received more than the
usual amount of cricitism on sociocultural grounds because of some
lingering anti-Japanese sentiment and fears that the resort would
become a foreign enclave and distort the character of the area. However
even here, wider recreational and social opportunities should result
from harmonious interaction between residents and visitors in a type of
'cultural multiplier' reaction. Contact between local inhabitants and
tourists can only lessen introspection and reciprocally broaden awareness of peoples, regions and their problems.

Although it can be conceded that tourism has much (perhaps unreal-
ised) potential for environmental enhancement, negative impacts do
occur from the predatory effects of seasonal migrations of visitors
(Young, 1973). The most obvious repercussions are likely to be in
natural areas but the built environment may also be impaired and the
social fabric of host communities can be widely disrupted.

Gunn (1973) instances pollution, both direct and indirect and in all
its forms, as a conspicuous manifestation of the detrimental effect of
tourism. However, erosion of the resource base is probably a more

Figure 8.6: Location of Proposed Farnborough Tourist Complex on the Coast of Queensland, Australia

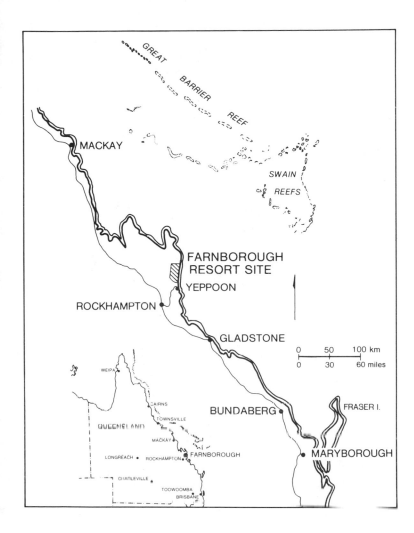

Source: UDPA Planners, 1978: 3.

Figure 8.7: Site Plan of Farnborough Resort Complex

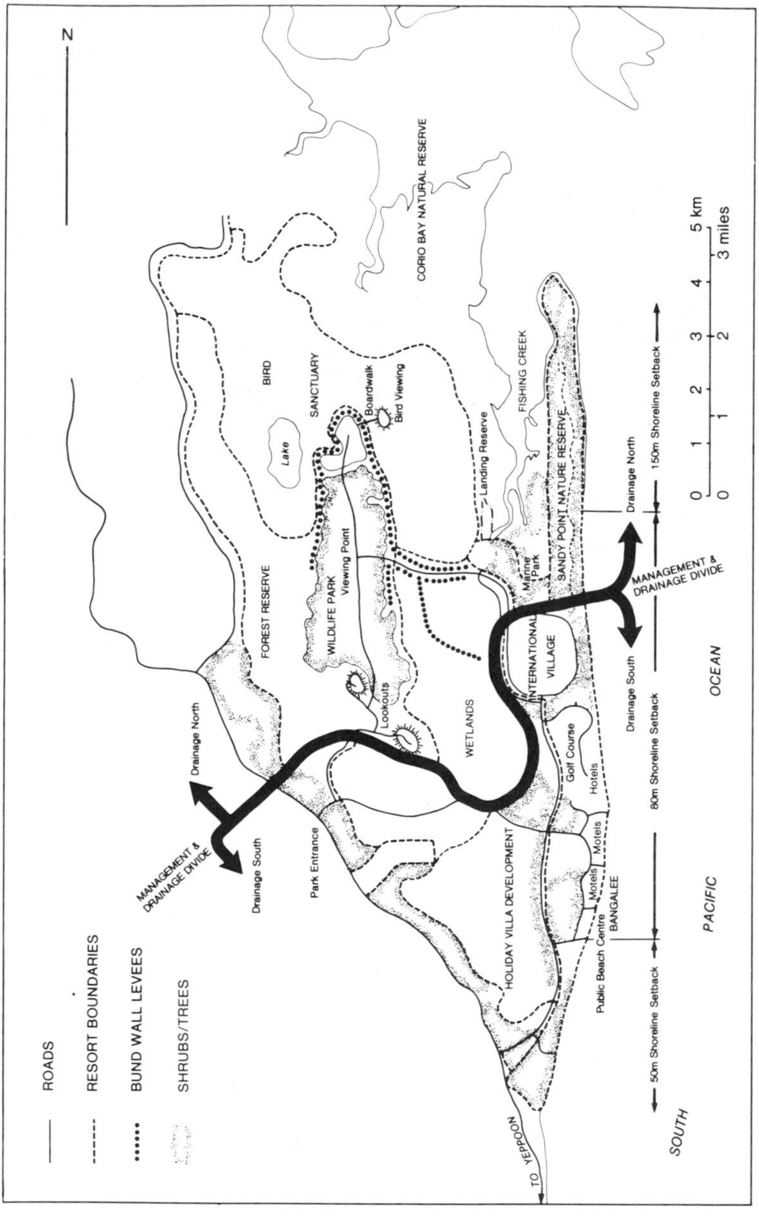

Source: UDPA Planners, 1978: 26.

serious environmental aspect. This can range from incidental wear and tear of fauna, flora and structures, to vandalism and deliberate destruction or removal of features which constitute the appeal of a setting. This erosive process is accelerated at times by use of incongruous technological innovations and by inferior design and inappropriate style in the construction of tourist facilities. It is well to remember, of course, that the strange architecture of today may become the heritage of tomorrow. However, Tangi (1977) describes some of the tourist resorts of the Mediterranean as architectural insults to the natural or historical sites where they are located. It is such circumstances which give some substance to the assertion that the 'creation of ugliness' could be one of modern tourism's greatest contributions to the environment.

In many resort areas environments must serve not only conflicting tourist uses but also the resident community, many of whom take a proprietorial attitude towards their surroundings. Congestion and overtaxing of infrastructure and basic services can generate dissension between transients and the domestic population which comes to resent the intrusion of tourism (Pearce, 1978; 1979). In a related study, Rothman (1978) listed municipal services and facilities, access to recreational sites and personal and social life, as features of the sociocultural environment seasonally curtailed by the presence of vacationers. Social interaction between residents and tourists was reported as minimal with large numbers of visitors opting for an exclusive environment which requires the least cultural adjustment on their part. In developing countries too, aspects of tourism may have long term disruptive effects on the life-styles and employment patterns of host communities (see below).

With so many variations on the theme it is difficult to generalise on the relationship between tourism and the environment. The relative importance of each factor varies with the location and situation and negative effects need to be balanced against positive impacts. Certainly, the ugly face of tourism appears to receive wider exposure and the relationship depicted in Figure 8.8a could well apply with an increase in tourism bringing about a decrease in the quality of the environment. Yet change does not necessarily equate with degradation, and tourism and environmental quality are not mutually exclusive goals. The net effect may be marginally negative (Figure 8.8b), or the two may be organised in such a way that both benefit and give each other support (Figure 8.8c).

Thus, tourism and environment are not merely interrelated, they are interdependent. According to Gunn (1972) tourism and protection of

Figure 8.8: Tourism Development and Environmental Quality

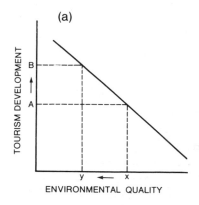

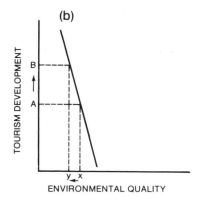

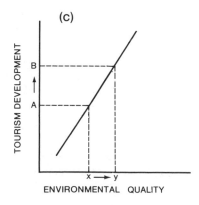

the resource base are more alike than contradictory. He maintains that the demands of tourism, instead of conflicting with conservation, actually require it. Otherwise, the very appeal which lures the visitor to a site will be eroded and with reduced satisfaction will go any chance of sustained viability for the destination.

The Economic Impact of Tourism

The role of tourism in the economy is seldom perceived clearly. Rarely are specific economic sectors focused on tourist activities and the attributes of the tourist 'industry' which would facilitate an assessment of its overall economic significance are difficult to establish. Yet, without such assessment, decisions regarding tourism at various scales, at both the public and private level, must be made in a vacuum. Allocation of resources to tourism enterprises by governments, investors, consultants, or planners, is too important to be based merely on intuition or value judgements that tourism is a good (or bad) thing. In the harsh environment of commercial risk-taking and in the disbursement of public funds economic worth must be proven, not merely inferred.

The term 'tourist industry' can be taken as a generic expression, rather than indicating a homogeneous entity (Australian Bureau of Industry Economics, 1979). As such, it includes activities which are clearly of primary importance to tourism as well as other enterprises where the degree of involvement with the travelling public is indirect or secondary. On this basis the tourism industry comprises accommodation outlets, food and catering establishments, travel agents and operators, transport services, recreation and entertainment facilities primarily for travelling and public agencies concerned with tourism. The impact of tourism at an international level has been described earlier in this chapter. However, it is on the domestic scene where the economic effects may be demonstrated most effectively, at the national scale, as well as regionally and sectorally.

The most obvious economic impact of tourism is associated with expenditures by tourists themselves becoming a source of income and employment to the recipients. Tourism can also play an important role as a means of decentralisation and of boosting employment in otherwise depressed regions. In less developed areas resources may be unproductive for agriculture or industry but can become a source of wealth through tourism. The generation of economic activity as a result may prevent further erosion of population and may also lead to a fuller utilisation of existing resources, facilities and services. As a consequence enterprises previously operating at less than capacity are able to expand production to the point where economies of scale can be realised and in so doing, can function more efficiently, as well as develop a better quality product or service. The injection of new spending, in turn, can lead to renewed growth from an expansion of economic activity generally.

From the point of view of employment tourism makes up a large segment of the service industries and requires a large, diversified and dispersed labour force. Employment generation, therefore, is an important benefit accruing from tourism. The two broad types of employment created are:

Direct Employment; including occupations created in the tourism industry such as in accommodation, travel agencies and transport operators.

Indirect Employment; or the additional jobs generated by the need to increase the service and physical infrastructure of an area to support tourism and the tourism industry, e.g. retail sales and road construction.

Research carried out in the USA has shown that in some areas up to a quarter of the local wage bill is created by tourist spending and that tourist expenditure generates more work in retail and service firms than could be provided by an equivalent amount of general expenditure (Archer, 1973a: 6).

Moreover, the travel market provides jobs for supplemental workers — part-time, casual and seasonal labour and in particular, females and the less skilled. In general, tourism is labour-intensive rather than capital-intensive and hence is a growth industry in terms of employment.

Direct or primary expenditure is not a true and complete measure of the prosperity created by tourism because the initial recipients, in turn, recirculate a certain proportion, thus generating additional income and employment. At each round of transactions some money leaks out of the system so that the income-creation effects are successively reduced and ultimately exhausted. This subsequent indirect impact of the initial tourist spending results from an important economic concept known as the 'multiplier effect'. Furthermore, as incomes rise within a region local consumption expenditure increases and this may induce an even greater impetus to the regional economy. 'Together the indirect and induced changes are called secondary effects and the multiplier is the ratio of the primary plus secondary effects to the primary direct effect alone' (Archer, 1973b: 1).

The magnitude of the multiplier depends upon the degree to which a regional economy is able to retain as income, the money spent by visitors. This, in turn, is a function of the ability of the local economy to produce the various items and services consumed by tourists. The smaller the size of the region's economic base, and the fewer intra-regional linkages, the more goods and services which have to be brought into the region. In these circumstances, the greater will be the leakage and hence, the lower the value of the multiplier.

The multiplier concept has incurred some criticism and its theoretical and practical limitations are well documented. The shortcomings rest not so much with the model itself, but in the ways in which it has been misapplied. It is especially difficult to generalise from one situation to another; the multiplier effect varies from project to project, from region to region and from one form of tourist activity to another. Despite the criticisms and deficiencies inherent in the concept, some attempt needs to be made to derive an estimate of the multiplier and to incorporate these secondary effects into an assessment of the overall economic significance of tourism. In a recent study of the travel industry in Australia, the following estimates for tourism multipliers were derived (Pigram and Cooper, 1977):

Income Multiplier = 1.25
Employment Multiplier = 1.52

These results mean that for every direct dollar generated by tourism activities, a further 25 cents would have been generated in the rest of the economy. Similarly, for every two direct jobs in tourism, one indirect job would have been created. The same study estimated that, for the 1974-5 period under review, the direct contribution of tourism to the Gross Domestic Product of Australia was A\$ 1752 million or 2.9 per cent. Direct employment as a result of tourism was estimated to be 158,600, or 2.7 per cent of the Australian total. Applying the multipliers given above to these figures, direct tourism expenditure would have generated an additional A\$ 438 million in indirect output and 82,472 extra jobs would have been created indirectly from tourism to give a total employment figure of 241,072, or 4.1 per cent of the national workforce.

The economic significance of tourism varies sectorally with the type of activity and the characteristics of travellers and host communities. It also varies spatially with the degree of regional self-sufficiency present. In these circumstances economic analysis becomes an important tool for establishing and justifying the type and direction of public investment and assistance to the industry as well as a guide for private promotional initiatives and marketing strategies. For a tourist destination like Australia such economic guidance and assistance with decision making are vital during a period when new pricing structures and advances in transportation are helping to reduce isolation and expose the country to the international travel market. For developing countries the need to clarify the role of tourism as a strategy for development is even more urgent.

Tourism and Developing Countries

According to Turner (1976) tourism seems tailor-made for the Third World and a growing number of developing countries are placing emphasis on tourism in their development plans. Reasons are not hard to find. A ready market is available for the attractions these destinations can offer; many of them have an appealing climate, combined with exotic scenery and a rich cultural and historical heritage. Land and labour costs are comparatively low and in the absence of significant mineral production or an export-orientated agricultural sector, tourism is a potential source of foreign exchange and can generate new opportunities for employment and stimulate demand for local products and industries. Tourism is also said to make possible improvements in the local infrastructure with the provision or upgrading of roads, airports, harbour facilities, accommodation, shopping, entertainment, communications, health services, power and water supplies and sanitation.

For some countries tourism appears to have fulfilled its promise and as noted earlier in this chapter, parts of the less-developed world have received significant financial benefits. In the Caribbean, for example, international travel is a prime source of foreign exchange earnings, contributing US$ 31.2 million, or about 9.4 per cent of the total to gross regional product (Peters, 1980). Yet even there, misgivings have been expressed as to whether tourism is the most appropriate form of investment for the region (Britton, 1976). Typically, the kind of questions which are raised are:

*Is tourism the best way towards economic independence and a

a better way of life for less-developed countries?
*Can, or should, economic control be in local hands?
*To what extent does the multiplier effect apply?
*Does tourism help revive and sustain cultures or does it destroy traditions?
*Does tourism promote understanding between hosts and guests or misunderstanding and prejudice?

These and other related economic, social and political questions need to be addressed before even qualified endorsement can be given to tourism as a strategy for regional development (de Kadt, 1979).

In the first place, foreign exchange earnings are offset by considerable expenditure caused by tourism on increased imports, including food and drink and on development of the necessary infrastructure for international travel. In Fiji, for example, 53 per cent of hotel food purchases, 68 per cent of standard hotel construction and outfitting requirements, and over 95 per cent of tourist shop wares were supplied from imports (Britton, 1980). A further drain on foreign exchange is attributed to repatriation of the profits of foreign-owned corporations and payment of salaries to higher-skilled personnel imported to the better-paid positions in the tourist industry. Recent figures for Fiji suggest that, at most, 45 per cent of the tourism dollar stays in the country and in some cases, leakages may go as high as 60-80 per cent (Biddlecomb, 1981). Moreover, the number of jobs open to an indigenous population lacking the appropriate skills is limited. In Fiji once again, 57 per cent of hotel management positions were filled by expatriates in 1976 (Britton, 1980).

Too great a commitment to tourism brings with it the twin dangers of loss of control over resource allocation and decision making and dependence on a fluctuating economic base. Tourism is notoriously open to pressures from inflation, fuel crises, industrial troubles, security fears and the fickle nature of resort popularity. If local populations have deserted traditional occupations for work in tourist undertakings any downturn in international travel can be doubly unfortunate. All too frequently the rate and direction of tourist development are in the hands of transnational corporations especially in the areas of transport, hotel chains, tour wholesaling and marketing. In the South Pacific, for example, no island nation owns any of the companies which operate cruise ships and few governments can afford a national airline. The extent of external control is likely to grow with the tendency towards vertical integration in the tourist industry.

Even where economic benefits can be demonstrated these must be balanced against adverse sociocultural consequences. Costs and benefits are not evenly distributed between local residents and tourists, or within host communities (UNESCO, 1976). The confinement of tourists and their expenditures to air-conditioned enclaves offering carefully programmed travel experiences can become a source of frustration and resentment and merely accentuates the gulf between affluence and poverty. Imported goods and services compete with local enterprises and conflicts can occur as commercialisation of land and resources intrudes on traditional values.

Tourism can also serve as a powerful agent of social change and disruption. The excesses of tourism and the unregulated behaviour often associated with it can act as an affront to host cultures. Biddlecomb (1981) nominates conspicuous consumption, eccentric clothing, unacceptable sexual behaviour, e.g. nude bathing and illegal activity, including use of drugs, as sources of inter-personal and inter-cultural tensions. An increase in crime and anti-social behaviour is only one of the many possible undesirable consequences of tourism, even in developed countries (Walmsley, *et al.*, 1981). According to Butler (1975), the extent to which tourism is capable of inducing change in the host society is a function of the characteristics of the visitors and of the destination. He contrasts the localised impact of say, a cruise ship, with that of large numbers of visitors on an extended stay especially where there are sharp economic and cultural differences between the tourists and indigenous people. On the other hand, a strong local culture and pronounced nationalistic outlook can act as a buffer to distortion of the social fabric.

A similar anthropological theme is to be found in the study of 'Hosts and Guests' edited by Smith (1978) where the potential of tourism to foster cultural disruption and transformation of life-styles is illustrated in individual case studies drawn from around the world. Further examples of societal strain as the result of the incursions of tourists were presented to a UNESCO Workshop on Tourism in the South Pacific (Pearce, 1980). The workshop conceded that tourism was only one factor in social change but recommended closer examination of alternative forms of tourist development which would minimise adverse effects on the islanders' way of life.

This approach is summed up in the Cook Islands Government policy emphasis on indigenous tourism:

Tourism should not be the means for us to change our way of life but an incentive to make us more aware of what we are in terms of our culture, customs and traditions. This should not be interpreted negatively to mean that all changes which affect our way of life must be avoided. Change is inevitable. Instead, a positive rate and direction of change and how we manage that change and its conflicts are more important.

The guiding principle should be: preserve that which is good, modify or destroy the bad and adopt the new to strike a balance (Okotai, 1980: 173).

Achieving this ideal and at the same time, providing pleasure and satisfaction for the many visitors seeking a genuine tourist experience in developing countries, calls for a strong commitment to planning.

Planning for Tourism

Many of the problems and undesirable features associated with tourism flow from inadequate attention to the planning and design of the tourist developments. At first sight planning for tourism might seem a contradiction in terms and likely to inhibit the spontaneity identified with pleasure travel. However, as Gunn (1979b) points out in the introduction to his book, *Tourism Planning*, covert planning of tourism has been going on for years and should be regarded as essential as the planning of other sectors of the economy. It is the absence or weakness of planning which allows the development of types of tourism incompatible with natural systems and permits the expansion of tourism into areas at a rate inconsistent with the capacity of the infrastructure and society to cope with the extra pressure.

Gunn's philosophy is that satisfying tourist settings should grow from natural forces and be complementary and compatible with them. Appropriate design of tourist facilities using local materials to blend with the environment, close attention to principles of location and site selection, the implementation of necessary management strategies and enlightened interpretation programmes to educate visitors concerning environmental values, can all help to mitigate undesirable impacts from the disordered growth of tourism. In particular, the pursuit of economies of scale through the development of ever-larger, more sophisticated tourist complexes needs to be questioned. In tourism, as in many aspects of modern society, 'small can be beautiful'.

In his earlier book, *Vacationscape*, Gunn (1972) put forward a number of broad guiding principles of landscape design in what he calls the art of creating satisfying environments for tourism. Such an approach places particular emphasis on functionalism — structural, physical and cultural/aesthetic — in tourist landscape design. All structural elements must first be able to withstand wear and the stresses of mass use. Equally importantly, the tourism-recreation environment must function physically, with adequate capacity, space and equipment for desired activities. The most critical element of all is cultural/ aesthetic functionalism — the ability to please and satisfy the users. Other essential components of the landscape design process for tourism are the importance of order, balance, scale, spatial relationships, interrelatedness and integration, areal and site clustering and the elimination of the friction of unplanned development without lapsing into uniformity, conformity and monotony. Tourist facilities must, of course, be appropriate to the site and sensitive to the topographic, ecological and sociocultural setting. The travel experience should be seen as sequential and incremental injecting a vital element of dynamic continuity into the tourist landscape. In this context, Murphy (1980) suggests that the planning and design of tourist landscapes has much in common with the layout of a retail supermarket, in that both attempt to attract, guide and ultimately satisfy the consumer's needs. Again, tourism like retailing is not a static phenomenon and change should be anticipated. Although the environmental base may offer some resource constraints and design decisions already made may pre-empt many options, development should be kept as open and flexible as possible to cope with increasing and diverse desires and needs.

To some, the art of Vacationscape may seem a Utopian ideal of no practical relevance and such a desirable state of affairs could not be expected to occur spontaneously. It will not be easy to reconcile the growth of mass tourism with the need to maintain the natural and human heritage. Substantial material interests are always involved and emotive appeals to the ethics of developers are unlikely to achieve the desired outcome. It is often difficult to demonstrate conclusively the cost over time of environmental degradation.Therefore, in the absence of coercive measures, developers may be inclined to ignore the longer term consequences, thereby deliberately excluding consideration of limitations of the resource base in the planning phase. In other cases environmental concern may be superficial or may even involve 'improvements' which are offensive and incongruous. Consequently, as with all significant development proposals, an assessment of likely environmental impacts of major tourism projects should be mandatory along with the usual physical feasibility studies and appraisal of economic costs and benefits (Inskeep, 1975; Pearce, 1981). This requirement needs to be supported by on-going monitoring of the continuing effects of tourism on natural and human systems.

Perhaps one of the more promising ways in which a higher order of compatibility can be achieved between the tourism phenomenon and the environment which nurtures it, is an acceleration in education and communication relative to environmental matters (Sprugel, 1973). This process should encompass the several components of the industry – the providers and managers of tourist attractions and the tourist participants themselves. It is not enough merely to inform these groups of the environmental consequences of resource misuse. They must somehow be instilled with a conscience and an inbuilt sense of responsibility and concern for environmental quality.

Motivation for this change of attitude can come first from improved economic understanding of environmental values in the tourist business. The educational process must also be directed towards altering a pervasive perception of the environment as a force to be overcome, made up of resources there for the taking. Equally essential is education of the tourism entrepreneur away from the narrow focus of material success to a wider appreciation of the need for social responsibility. This implies, among other things, awareness of environmental considerations in assessment of development policy alternatives. However, reconciling ethics with economics is never easy.

Tourists too, would benefit from a more enlightened appreciation of the interaction between resource use and environmental quality. Gunn (1973) would go further to suggest that the tourist experience would be immeasurably improved if education was available in the planning of pleasure travel and in participation in recreational skills. He instances boating, photography, safety procedures and even travel etiquette, as examples of areas where knowledge is lacking. Such a programme should not be pursued to the point where all spontaneity is removed from a visit or activity. Undoubtedly however, there would be fewer unwelcome travellers abroad and more satisfied visitors and hosts if tourist behaviour was more constructive and better motivated.

It is one thing to acknowledge the potential role of tourism as an instrument of environmental conservation and quite another to translate this role into practical terms acceptable to the developer, the tourist and the wider community. Nevertheless, there is evidence of increasing awareness of the need for an integrated approach to the planning and management of tourism resources which takes into account the ecological, social and economic circumstances of the host region as well as the demands of the tourist.

9 OUTDOOR RECREATION PLANNING AND THE FUTURE

From a pragmatic viewpoint, Lapage (1980) has described good planning as a two-step process — 'First you figure out what is inevitable. Then you find a way to take advantage of it.' This concluding chapter begins by trying to forecast what is likely to happen in the field of leisure and outdoor recreation to the turn of the century and then explores some of the implications of the changes predicted for planning and resource management. Towards what kind of future then, should planning be directed?

Trends in Leisure and Outdoor Recreation

The only things certain about the future are uncertainty and the inevitability of change and need for adjustment. Forecasts about possible leisure scenarios range from the fanciful prophecies of science fiction to more considered statistical predictions based on short-term projection or extrapolation of current trends. Such forecasts can only be expressed in terms of probability and without the benefit of insight into innovations, changes in social circumstances and public policy, or technological breakthroughs. Both the demand dimension (e.g. population characteristics and recreation propensities) and the supply side of the equation (e.g. futuristic possibilities regarding the availability and use of recreation space) lack definition. Moreover, any planning initiatives must be undertaken against a background of increasing environmental awareness and constraints on freedom of choice because of concern for repercussions on nature and society. The travel industry, for example, will have to grapple with specific issues such as air and noise pollution, which have to be solved regardless of cost in money or efficiency terms (Narodick, 1979). 'Consumerism', too, will impose greater demands on the recreation planner to provide quality products and experiences which will not always coincide with the anticipated trend to mass participation.

Veal (1980) conceded that by its very nature, prediction of leisure activity must be one of the more difficult areas of social forecasting. However, this did not deter him from making projections of the rates of

221

growth of leisure activities (Table 9.1). Camping, certain indoor and outdoor sports and spectator activities showed the highest rates of growth in Britain for the forecast period.

Table 9.1: Rates of Growth of Leisure Activities in England and Wales, 1973-91

Activity	Projected growth in number of participants 1973-91 (%)
Camping	33
Golf	33
Soccer	7
Cricket	21
Tennis	37
Bowls	17
Fishing	19
Swimming outdoors	25
Outdoor sport	23
Badminton/squash	59
Swimming indoors	21
Table tennis	29
Billiards/snooker	23
Darts	− 5
Indoor sport	23
All sport	21
Watching	
horse racing	10
motor racing	33
soccer	15
cricket	19
Total watching	19
Visiting parks	6
Visiting seaside	17
Visiting countryside	21
Visiting historical buildings	25
Visiting museums	25
Visiting zoos	18
Going to films	18
Going to theatre	20
Amateur music/drama	25
Going out for meal	21
Going for drink	15
Dancing	17
Bingo	− 4

Source: Veal, 1980: 54.

According to Van Doren (1981), the United States also is at a critical period in the development of leisure, recreation and travel. He presents an historical perspective of these areas in the form of an analytical summary of significant events in that country in the nineteenth and twentieth centuries (Table 9.2). Whereas it is possible to query the precise timing and duration of the eras designated and the extent to which they can be applied outside USA they do represent a broad picture of past changes in leisure life-styles and evolving patterns in the immediate future. Perhaps the strongest suggestion to emerge from the table is the implication that limits will have to be accepted on individual recreation activities and emphasis will be more on group involvement and mass participation.

Van Doren was addressing a most important conference held in the United States in 1980, the subject of which was trends in outdoor recreation. One of the contributions focused on changes in American society, institutions, economy and life-style which have special significance for outdoor recreation (Reidel, 1980). Predictably, a major factor was the so-called 'energy crisis'.

Ever since President Herbert Hoover promised to put 'a car in every garage and a chicken in every pot', Americans have carried on a love affair with their automobile(s) and American society has been geared to the presumption of car ownership and use. Awareness of this state of affairs is important in appreciating the trauma experienced when the 1973-74 OPEC oil embargo hit USA. Mobility patterns geared to almost friction-less space suddenly had to cope with very real constraints on travel. Sharp rises in gasoline prices and restricted availability forced a re-ordering of priorities in the use of the automobile with recreational trips subject to close scrutiny as to their extent and necessity.

A series of surveys since the initial emergency present a confused picture of the long-term implications of higher fuel prices and supply uncertainties. Certainly, the effect is not likely to be quite as clear-cut as Reidel would have us believe:

Pleasure driving and long-distance auto vacations will soon become genuine American Graffiti . . . we'll surely shorten the range of our recreation trips. Recreation vehicles, energy-hungry boats and ORVs may not disappear, but it's clear they will not be the playthings of the average American (Reidel, 1980: 10).

Nevertheless, results from the US Census of Transportation show that a substantially higher percentage of recreation trips in 1977 was

Table 9.2: Significant Events by Recreation/Leisure/Travel Eras, USA

Variable	High Society 1860-1920	Mass Recreation 1920-1958	Mass Mobility-Transience 1958-1974	Post-Mobility Adjustment 1974-
Population Characteristics Trends	Rural N.E. Midwest 50 million people	Rural-urban Suburbia West Coast 130 million	Urban-nucleated city 70-75% of population Sun Belt growth 200 million	Central city, small town growth, rural 242 million (1990)
Person/Societal Philosophy	Nuclear large family Puritanical work ethic Self-denial	Smaller family Leisure recreation emergent A privilege to enjoy leisure	Single-parent family Self-gratification 'me' generation Minority actions Changing role of women, ERA	Leisure recreation a right Individual awareness Self-actualisation Self-improvement
Time	60-hour workweek Sunday free	50-hour workweek Saturday free Paid vacation	40-hour workweek 3 day weekends	38-hour workweek Moonlighting Do-it-yourself home repairs
Income, Money	Hourly wages	Salaries	High disposable income Era of credit 2-income families	Inflation Zero growth Cost consciousness Electronic money
Activities and Equipment	Church-centred Bicycle, golf, tennis	Family-centred Improved equipment Boats, camping equipment, etc.	Social group Specialised activity equipment ORVs Back to nature movement	Electronic games Human energy Physical fitness High-risk sports

Political Action	Conservation preservation Leadership-management of natural resources	Environment management public use	Reactionary leadership Environmental awareness ecological ethics. congestion in parks	Public involvement leadership Localised congestion
Public/Private Organisation	Professional sports Public recreation movement City-national parks Amusement parks	Amateur sports State parks TVA-C of E Regional parks	Disneyland-theme parks Mission 66 Individualised travel	Airline deregulation Tourism caucus Package tours
Technology and Communication	Photography Movies-wireless Mass production Literature	Radio-television Plastics-super alloys Air conditioning Computers-electronics	Instant photography Satellite communication Computer management	Videophone Cottage electronics
Mobility	Coal and steam Railroad, ship, mass transportation	Automobile Airplane, small group transportation	Interstate highways RV, sub-sonic aircraft	Supersonic travel? Mass transit?
Facilities/Services	Luxury hotel/resorts Second homes wealthy Overseas travel	Motels Second homes-middle class	Private campgrounds lodging Franchises, fast foods Full service campgrounds	Family camping time sharing, cruise ships, one-stop vacations reservations to enter parks

Source: Van Doren, 1981: 4.

for shorter distances compared with 1972 (Corsi and Harvey, 1980). Moreover, there was a slight-to-moderate shift to various forms of public transportation for recreation trips and recreation vehicle sales were severely affected. Obviously, energy problems are already having a marked impact and unless significant and sustained improvements occur on the supply side the trend will continue towards closer-to-home, energy-efficient forms of recreation (Table 9.3). In the process, greater pressure is likely to be felt on recreation resources — forests, water-bodies, countryside — in near-urban areas and the need for resource management will become even more apparent.

A second group of factors identified by Reidel (1980) was that of changing life-styles which he related to alterations in demographic patterns and social vlaues. The changing age distribution of the popula-tion, postponement of marriage and children (perhaps indefinitely), liberation of women and more frequent breakdown of family relation-ships are seen as some of the important influences on leisure and outdoor recreation in the United States.

> Our rapidly aging population can be traced to the . . . 43 million children (born between 1947 and 1957) who will be middle-aged in the 1980s and 1990s . . . married couples who made up 70 per cent of households in 1970, will comprise only 55 per cent in 1999. One out of three people will live alone or with a non-relative, as compared to one in five in 1970 (Godbey, 1981. 299-300).

Coupled with sharp reductions in the hours and periods of work and a change in attitudes to work and play, these trends are helping to shape a different set of recreation patterns and demands in North America and similar developed economies. The United States also shares with Canada, Britain and increasingly with Australia, strong overtones of cultural pluralism in its population characteristics. Once again, a reaction can be discerned in leisure behaviour, as new groups of people are assimilated to a greater or lesser degree into the population as a whole (Table 9.4). A heterogeneous society offers a richer spectrum of recreation opportunities, but at the same time generates difficulties for governments in providing a sufficiently diverse array of recreation experiences.

Overshadowing all of these factors are economic considerations. As inflation, unemployment, deepening recession and outright poverty continue to bite into the scope for individual decision making, recrea-tion opportunities must contact. Chubb and Chubb (1981) detail the

Table 9.3: Gasoline Prices/Availability and Outdoor Recreation

Type of Adjustment Package	Attribute	Present	Future
1. Activity Space Reduction:	Shape	Shrinking	Optimal Compact Shape
	Tendency	Intervening Opportunities	Distance Decay
	General Pattern	National/Regional Sites	Regional/Local Sites
	Mode Efficiency	Increasing Importance of Fuel-Efficient Cars	Further Increases in Fuel-Efficient Cars/Technological Breakthroughs
2. Activity Mode Change:	Bus	Trace	Moderate Increase, Primarily Among Lower-Income Households
	Carpooling	Slight Increase	Some Appreciable Increase
	Trains	Trace	Trace
	Air	Slight Increase	Moderate Increase, Restricted to Higher-Income Households
	Recreation Vehicles	Decline	Further Decline
3. Activity Frequency Reduction:	Periodicity	Decrease	Further Decrease
	Duration of Activity	Slight Change	Increase
	Multi-stop Trips	Increasing	More Future Increases
4. Activity Type Change:	Rate	Increasing	More Future Increases
	Tendency	Determined by Interest	Partly Determined by Availability Nearby

Source: Corsi and Harvey, 1980: 69.

likely effects of worsening economic conditions in countries like the United States in the last decades of the twentieth century. Curtailment of living standards, frustration of aspirations towards self-betterment, loss of self-esteem, destruction of long-held values and mores, erosion of faith in 'the system' and personal stress leading to emotional and behavioural problems, are all the outcome of economic instability.

Table 9.4: Leisure in Singular and Plural Cultural Societies

	Plural Culture Society	Single Culture Society
Concept	Leisure is anything the individual chooses to do which is found pleasurable. Leisure is unlimited. An end in itself.	Leisure is a set of identifiable experiences which the individual is taught to enjoy. Leisure is limited. A means to an end.
Variation in behaviour	Range of acceptable behaviour wide.	Range of acceptable behaviour narrow.
Standards to judge behaviour	Laws set limits. No universally accepted mores by which to judge leisure behaviour.	Mores and folkways set limits of behaviour. Universal standards for leisure based upon perceived cultural necessity.
Role	Individual and sub-cultural identity linked to leisure behavior.	National identity linked to leisure behaviour.
Role Problems	Difficult to judge leisure ethically. Dispute over leisure values. Lack of meaning.	Lack of experimentation of alternatives. Persecution of that which is foreign. Easy to use leisure as a means of social control.
Government's Role	Identification of recreation needs difficult. May provide only selected kinds of services or serve certain sub-cultures or groups disproportionately.	Identification of recreation needs easy. May provide services which provide as a common denominator.
Commercial Organisation's Role	Commercial sector has more diverse opportunities. Can cater to individual or sub-culture's tastes. Easier to create needs.	Commercial sector has more limited opportunities. More difficult to create needs or cater to individual or sub-culture's tastes.
Mass Media's Role	Limited in its ability to reflect culture. Diversion and entertainment function.	Less limited in its ability to reflect culture. Transmission of culture function.

Source: Godbey, 1980: 170.

These, in turn, have serious implications for recreational patterns and opportunities.

As was noted above, any rearrangement of priorities in a time of financial stringency is likely to see recreation decline in importance. This holds equally for individuals, households and governments. Thus, vacations and pleasure travel generally become curtailed, purchases of recreation equipment are postponed and participation in recreation, in so far as it involves spending, or even the use of resources (including time) which could be income producing, is minimised. Moreover, governments and providers of recreation opportunities in the private sector also experience difficulties in meeting their commitments during periods of inflation, just when the need for recreation increases.

Maintaining the quantity and quality of recreation resources at a time when the potential customers and participants are unable or unwilling to pay very much for their production or operation is one of the greatest challenges recreation providers will ever have to face (Chubb and Chubb, 1981: 681).

In times of adversity, the availability of recreation outlets takes on renewed urgency in helping to mitigate the effects of economic hardship. Recreation, in the sense of revitalisation, can act as a compensating mechanism in allowing people to forget their worries, or at least cope better. Fresh interests can be developed and neglected, simpler pusuits rediscovered to occupy an excess of leisure time in a less cost-intensive manner. New skills and attitudes can be acquired which will enable disadvantaged sectors of the population to maintain their self-confidence, pride and hope.

At the same time there is a brighter side to inflation and recession. When governments are forced to withdraw from, or reduce their involvement in the recreation area, communities have an opportunity to query the need for continued dependence on public funding and an obligation to examine the potential of self-help, co-operation and other means of economising. Thus, hard times become a vehicle for bringing communities together, sharing the frustrations and problems, substituting voluntary effort and talent for that previously provided and in so doing, achieving a satisfying, cost-effective recreation programme at the neighbourhood or community level.

Of course, some governments and public agencies do not need the excuse of budgetary constraints to opt out of any responsibility for recreation. Even in 'normal' times, there are wide disparities, at the

Figure 9.1:
Expenditure on Parks
and Recreation, by
State, Municipal and
County Authorities,
USA

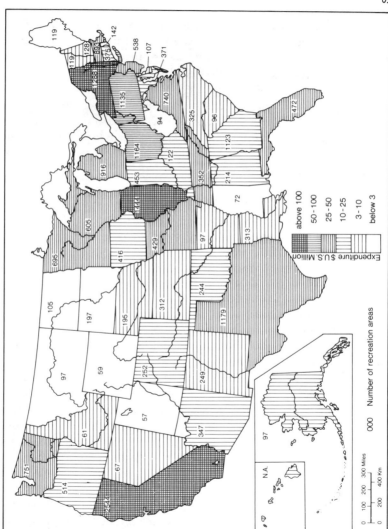

Source: Dunn, 1976: 23.

national, state and local level, in the commitment of funds and resources in this area. Figure 9.1 shows the variation between states in USA, for example, in the provision and funding of park and recreational resources. Some authorities maintain that recreation is not a legitimate field of interest for publicly-elected bodies and that private enterprise can best fill the gap (see below). Others justify reductions in funding on the grounds of past excesses and waste.the notion that public provision for leisure and recreation is somehow dispensable, or at least low in priority, can only be overcome by a well-directed campaign from those affected, the taxpaying community, to convince legislators that recreation is no longer a luxury or a privilege, but a right. In the meantime, competition for scarce public funds, overuse of available recreation resources and intensified conflicts over shrinking recreation space, can only make the relevance of planning and management of outdoor recreation opportunities even more urgent.

Outdoor Recreation Planning

Planning for outdoor recreation, as for tourism (Chapter 8), may appear paradoxical. The idea of structuring or programming people's spare time might seem an infringement upon the freedom of choice implied in the leisure concept. However, most recreation experiences do not just happen; they have to be provided for in some way. Earlier, it was noted how the availability of recreation opportunities, services and facilities influences choice in outdoor recreation. It is the expansion of choice, through a diversity of outlets for leisure to meet the many aspirations of people and society, in which planning plays an essential role. By providing a wider range of alternative recreation opportunities, the planner is contributing to the potential of leisure to stimulate and satisfy.

In short, planning for leisure environments of the future must progress beyond establishing a series of services or facilities such as parks and playgrounds. The emphasis must be on creating a physical and social environment in which individuals can satisfy their recreation interests within the economic limitations and resource constraints likely to be encountered in the world of the future.

This is the approach put forward by Burton (1974) who first proposed the term 'leisure environment' to describe systems of leisure opportunities and the complex relationships between elements within the system. In Burton's view, planning for leisure should be directed towards providing as many varied leisure opportunities as possible. The final products of the planning process — picnic areas, sporting arenas and so on — cannot stand alone but are seen primarily as components of a *system* of leisure opportunities, the urban park system in this example. The planning focus is upon the system and the interrelationships among and between different types of leisure opportunities. Burton's approach has much in common with the concept of the Recreation Opportunity Spectrum described in Chapter 2. The emphasis is on the multiplicity of individual and societal goals and the need for diversity, substitutability and choice, rather than uniformity, in meeting those goals.

In Burton's leisure activity system opportunity is seen as potential to engage in recreation and arises from the interaction of values, wants and needs with facilities, knowledge and user characteristics (Figure 9.2). Opportunity (when exercised) results in participation and this, in turn, influences future demand in a circular fasion. The planner's concern then, is with generating a sufficient array of leisure opportunities rather than with provision of specific facilities. This type of unbounded approach would seem to be well suited to the planning of future leisure environments, the dimensions of which have yet to be defined with any precision.

Public and Private Co-operation

Inevitably, it has become the function of government, at several levels, to become instrumental in the transfer of resources to recreational use (Simmons, 1975). Yet, recreation experiences frequently depend upon the use of *both* public and private resources and to ignore the contribution of the private sector is not only unrealistic but foolhardy. According to Chubb and Chubb (1981), in western nations between 80 and 90 per cent of people's recreation time is spent on activities at home (see Chapter 5) and up to ten per cent involves commercial recreation activities. These figures are not difficult to substantiate when the extent and diversity of the private recreation resource base is appreciated.

> Privately owned recreation resources range from the humblest amenities in people's homes to multimillion-dollar developments such as Disney World in Florida. Included are such diverse resources as backyard facilities, table games, restaurants, commercial theaters, private

261

, R. 75
 G. 190
 R. 39
 V. 216
nobile 80, 130, 143
ports 173
onia National Park 75, 76
oeing 130
nteraction 26
ltural factors 8, 115, 226,
; in tourism 205, 209, 216
onomic background 73
onomic factors 11, 226-9

Africa 157
Pacific 215, 216-17
Union, the 46, 188; leisure
e in 5
as a resource 43; outdoor
eation and 15
 87
9
interaction 30-1
72; individual and team 9
ld, C. 202
, G. 18, 26, 95
rks 152-3
opes 78
. 173
, J. 156
 13
tability 39-40
102-6
ja, E. 157
t 20
42, 133
 187
ng 9, 133
53, 103, 135, 142; Royal
onal Park 151, 153, 166, 169

stem 49, 55-7
C. 54
. 209
M. 136
a 157
119
gical factors 11
n 37
, O. 138
38
arks 190
ationwide Outdoor
eation Plan 128

Thomson, K. 127
Tilden, F. 96
timber getting 160
time, user's 23
Tongairo National Park 164
tourism 9, 184-220; attractions
    193-4; compared to recreation
    184; coping with 217; defined
    185-6; in developing countries
    157; earnings from 187-8; econ-
    omics of 211-16, 219, environ-
    ment and 204-11, 218-19; ethnic
    190; facilities 194; historical
    190; host communities and 206,
    209, 211-12, 216, 219-20; inter-
    national patterns of 187-8;
    landscape of 199-204, 218;
    motivation for 197-8; people and
    197-8; planning for 217-20;
    resource base for 188-91; system
    of 191-8; world 186-8
tourists 197-8; personality types
    199-200
Toyne, P. 15
traffic regulation 91
trail bikes 70, 77-8, 80, 169
transfer of development rights 123
transnational corporations 215
trapping 160
travel 30-40; cost of 126; prediction
    of 38-40; purpose of 186;
    statistics 186; time taken up by
    7; tourism and 195, 204
Trenton 101-2
trespassing 125, 131, 132
trip generation 38
Tunisia 187
Turner, L. 214
Tweedsmuir Provincial Park 152-3

US Bureau of Outdoor Recreation
    16, 46, 72
US Forest Service 53, 66, 176-7
US National Wilderness Preserv
    System 177
USA 9, 223-5, 226; coastal z
    138-40; the disabled in
    expenditure in 230; fo
    leisure time in 4-5; li
    tion forms 130; nat
    153-6; rural lands
    tourism in 188
    recreation in
    wilderness